Representations & Reflections
Studies in Anglophone Literatures and Cultures

Volume 15

Edited by
Uwe Baumann, Marion Gymnich
and Barbara Schmidt-Haberkamp

Katrin Berndt / Andrew Wells (eds)

The 'Second World' in Contemporary British Writing

With 3 figures

V&R unipress

Bonn University Press

Bibliographic information published by the Deutsche Nationalbibliothek
The Deutsche Nationalbibliothek lists this publication in the Deutsche Nationalbibliografie;
detailed bibliographic data are available online: https://dnb.de.

**Publications of Bonn University Press
are published by V&R unipress.**

Cover image: © Deutsche Fotothek / Gerd Danigel. Auf dem U-Bahnhof Schönhauser Allee, 1984.
Printed and bound by CPI books GmbH, Birkstraße 10, 25917 Leck, Germany
Printed in the EU.

Vandenhoeck & Ruprecht Verlage | www.vandenhoeck-ruprecht-verlage.com

ISSN 2198-5448
ISBN 978-3-8471-1757-5

To Peter Davison (1926–2022)

Contents

Second Glances: Retrospective Approaches to the 'Second World'

Self and Other: Becoming (in) the 'Second World'

Acknowledgements

As with all such collections, this volume is the result of the collaborative effort not only of its contributors but of a number of other individuals and institutions, whose support it is our pleasure here to acknowledge. The book is the direct result of an international conference held at Martin-Luther-University Halle-Wittenberg between 16 and 18 September 2022. Our first thanks must therefore be to all those who worked so hard to make this conference a success, particularly Aline Leuchtenberger, Maxi Kinzel, Oliver Bock, Mona Becker, and other colleagues within the Institute for British and American Studies. For financial and logistical support we are also grateful to the City of Halle (Saale), the Literaturhaus Halle, and the Gedenkstätte Roter Ochse. We would like to thank all those who presented at the conference or showed interest in the topic by submitting abstracts in response to its call for papers. We regret having been unable to invite all those who offered to present their fascinating work, but were gratified to find such a rich and varied field of interest in the 'second world' among the wider scholarly community.

As the book made its rapid way from rough concept to finished volume, we were grateful for the encouragement and cooperation from our colleagues at Halle and Kiel, from the series editors – especially Prof. Dr. Barbara Schmidt-Haberkamp – and from the team at Vandenhoeck & Ruprecht, particularly Oliver Kätsch. We owe our contributors an enormous debt for their diligence and hard work in producing and polishing their contributions in accordance with a tight schedule.

For the continued and unfailing support of friends and family, we remain extremely grateful. To these close supporters, we add our thanks to others more distant, and dedicate this book to the late Peter Davison (1926–2022) who, although unknown to us, was one of those adumbrated giants on whose shoulders we all stand. His quiet, unremunerated diligence in producing *The Complete Works of George Orwell* is a model of dedicated service to the scholarly community, one that echoes George Eliot's reflection that 'the growing good of the world is partly dependent on unhistoric acts.' Our need to listen to Orwell is as urgent as ever, and we have Davison to thank for clearing the static.

Katrin Berndt / Andrew Wells

Introduction

This collection investigates contemporary British writing whose narrative focus lies on Central and Eastern Europe of the Cold War period – the so-called 'second world.' Its motivation is twofold: to discuss British writers' engagement with settings, motifs, and characters of the 'second world' as a particular historical place and period, and to ask about the broader cultural significance of this 'second world' in British writing from the end of the Cold War to the present. The second aim in particular is connected to more recent cultural debates, which have viewed the congruence of dystopian anxieties and the disenchantment with ideas once believed to promise progress through the lens of the historical experience of the 'second world.'[1] In light of discussions on current challenges to open society and a new East-West divide, literary explorations of the 'really existing' socialist systems of the Central and Eastern European past appear both at odds with the expectation that contemporary culture should respond to present-day concerns, and oddly significant.[2]

The engagement of British writers with the 'second world' draws on established motifs of imaginative East-West encounters, which have long featured in British literature and culture. From dystopian novels on totalitarianism, such as Arthur Koestler's *Darkness at Noon* (1940) and George Orwell's *1984* (1948), which discussed 'the ideological failures of socialism'[3] and its distinctive forms of authoritarianism, to popular genres like the British thriller and the spy narrative (and their multimedia adaptations), 'literary-cultural [representations] of the

1 See, for example, John Gray. *Straw Dogs. Thoughts on Humans and Other Animals*. London: Granta, 2003. 87–102; Zygmunt Bauman. *Retrotopia*. Cambridge: Polity, 2017; Ivan Krastev. *After Europe*. Philadelphia: University of Pennsylvania Press, 2017.
2 See, for example, Anne Applebaum. 'The Enduring Appeal of the One-Party State.' *Rethinking Open Society*. Ed. Stefan Roch and Michael Ignatieff. Budapest: Central European University Press, 2018. 243–253; and Aleida Assmann. 'Go East!' *The Legacy of Division. East and West after 1989*. Ed. Ferenc Laczó and Luka Lisjak Gabrijelčič. Budapest: Central European University Press 2020. 264–274.
3 Andrew Hammond. *Cold War Stories: British Dystopian Fiction, 1945–1990*. Basingstoke: Palgrave Macmillan, 2017. 15.

"second world" provided entertainment, a foil to post-imperial Britain's national identity, and motifs to comprehend ideologies and mass phenomena in the twentieth century.[4] While there is considerable research on representations of the 'second world' in British writing during the Cold War period, and a growing body of scholarship on contemporary cultural representations of 'post-socialist' Central and Eastern Europe,[5] scholars have paid much less attention to the ways in which British writing in the three decades since the fall of the 'Iron Curtain' has continued to imaginatively engage with what had been, and arguably still is, viewed as a possible alternative to both capitalism and democracy, even for many in the West.

The persistent interest of British writers in characters, motifs, and settings of the 'second world' evidences the fact that, while the divided worlds which emerged in the aftermath of the Second World War are historical now, many of the cultural shifts they brought have continued to shape our present. In his famous essay on 'The Tragedy of Central Europe,' written in 1984, Czech writer Milan Kundera reminded the then 'First World' of the commitment of the countries behind the Iron Curtain to a shared European identity. These central European nations, he argued, represent the 'living value' and 'collective cultural memory' of what it means to be European, which 'marked the revolts of Central Europe [against totalitarianism] with an inimitable beauty that will always cast a spell over those who lived through those times.'[6] Kundera celebrated European identity as that of a 'family of equal nations, each of which – treating the others with mutual respect and secure in the protection of a strong, unified state – would also cultivate its own individuality [… within a Europe] conceived according to one rule: the greatest variety within the smallest space.'[7] Written four decades ago and five years before the Iron Curtain was torn down by the people of East-Central Europe, Kundera had argued that their recurrent revolts in the Cold War decades represented also the cultural resistance of nations he identified as 'the

---

4 Katrin Berndt. 'Writing on the Wall. The "Second World" in Contemporary British Writing.' *Memorial Volume for Christoph Houswitschka.* Ed. Susan Brähler, Kerstin-Anja Münderlein and Sebastian Kempgen. Bamberg: University of Bamberg Press, 2024. 345. For more detailed discussions on Cold War motifs in British fiction, see Richard Bradford. *The Novel Now: Contemporary British Fiction.* Malden: Blackwell, 2007; Barbara Korte, Eva U. Pirker, and Sissy Helff (eds). *Facing the East in the West: Images of Eastern Europe in British Literature, Film and Culture.* Amsterdam: Rodopi, 2010; and Joachim Frenk and Christian Krug (eds). *The Cultures of James Bond.* Trier: WVT, 2011.
5 See, for example, Kathleen Starck (ed.). *When the World Turned Upside-Down: Cultural Representations of Post-1989 Eastern Europe.* Newcastle upon Tyne: Cambridge Scholars Publishers, 2009.
6 Milan Kundera. 'The Tragedy of Central Europe.' *Re:Thinking Europe: Thoughts on Europe Past, Present and Future.* Ed. Yoeri Albrecht and Mathieu Segers. Amsterdam: Amsterdam University Press, 2016. 192, 193.
7 Kundera, 'Tragedy of Central Europe,' 194–195.

least known and the most fragile part of the West [… whose] struggle to preserve their identity' was that of civilizations 'culturally in the West and politically in the East.'[8] This struggle is a key motif of contemporary British writing on the 'second world' and has been portrayed repeatedly, in novels such as Bruce Chatwin's *Utz* (1989), Carl Tighe's *Burning Worm* (2001), and Fiona Rintoul's *The Leipzig Affair* (2014); in Tom Stoppard's play *Rock 'n' Roll* (2012); and in the memoirs of Timothy Garton Ash, *The File* (1997) and *Homelands* (2023).

In line with Kundera's characterization and the sustained interest in the 'second world,' this volume conceptualizes British writing on the subject as an 'imaginative comprehension' of 'the Cold War as a shared history' of twentieth-century ideologies and political divisions.[9] Moreover, it considers the literary representation and contemporary revisiting of historical East-Central Europe as a fertile ground for exploring a much wider array of values and concerns that are culturally shared in the present, from an awareness of digital surveillance as 'totalitarianism by consent'[10] to investment in the congruence of 'freedom and stability' as a persistent political ambition, from a shared scepticism towards state interventionism to the question of what 'is Europe' now, and 'what does it want to be' in view of both historical and more recent political developments.[11] British writers who explore these concerns within the moral geographies of the 'second world' approach it as an 'other' to integrate it into their (former) 'first world' insofar as they recognize 'difference' between these as 'not absolute but relative' and so emphasize the relational quality of both worlds as epistemologically 'constituting [one another].'[12] As several contributions to this volume show, this idea of a new, imagined community shaped by shared Cold War history becomes manifest, for example, in the work of Deborah Levy, Kazuo Ishiguro, Julian Barnes, and Patrick McGuinness: in the form of different temporal (including unspecified Central European) settings, or as historiosophic affiliation with a 'second world.'[13] Other readings foreground what Zygmunt Bauman described as a retrotopian desire to 'reconcil[e], at long last, *security* with *freedom*' that is,

---

8 Kundera, 'Tragedy of Central Europe,' 197, 192.

9 Berndt, 'Writing on the Wall,' 344.

10 Christoph Bode. 'Totalitarianism by Consent: Orwell, Huxley, and Capitalism in the Stage of Corporate Surveillance.' *Narrating Surveillance – Überwachen erzählen*. Ed. Betiel Wasihun. Baden Baden: Ergol Verlag, 2019. 34.

11 Edith Hallberg and Christoph Houswitschka. '"The silent grey foreign country which called itself Germany" in the Novels of Hugo Hamilton, Nicholas Shakespeare and Others.' *Literary Views on Post-Wall Europe*. Ed. Christoph Houswitschka, Ines Detmers, Anna-Christina Giovanopoulos et al. Trier: WVT, 2005. 96.

12 Anshuman Mondal. 'Alterity.' *The Routledge Dictionary of Literary Terms*. Ed. Peter Childs and Roger Fowler. London: Routledge, 2006. 6.

13 Metaphysical engagements with history in British writing on the 'second world' are discussed, for example, in Robert Kusek's and Ágnes Harasztos's contributions to this volume.

however, no longer projected to the future, because the idea of 'progress' now 'portends the menace of loss' and 'is associated more with social degradation than with advancement.'[14] By reviewing the 'genuine or putative' characteristics of a past that had represented both utopian potential and a violation of its promise, novels by Ian McEwan, John le Carré, and Philip Sington imaginatively engage with 'second world' settings to revisit what was 'lost' in and 'abandoned' with the past.[15]

With this collection, we hope to broaden the idea of the 'second world,' once used as a label for the countries of the Eastern bloc.[16] From approaches to these European nations as 'others' to memoirs of the Cold War experienced by British writers in East-Central Europe; from considering established motifs of political novels to more recent exchanges between realism, romance, historical writing, and popular fiction; from discussions of the utopian socialist promise to retro-topian perspectives on both its downfall and lingering presence; from past criticism of totalitarian structures and thinking to present-day responses to corporate practices, surveillance, and ideological hegemonies; from exploring the impact of Stalinism to considering courage, cowardice, complicity, and the possibility of personal responsibility; from the British writing of first- and second-generation immigrants from East-Central Europe to the telling of stories in the second person: the contributions to this collection engage with a variety of contemporary British writing on the 'second world.' They promise not only to substantiate our knowledge of the intersections of literature and politics, but also to shed light on the peculiarly British ways in which the disillusionment of disappointed utopias and the gaps that arguably resulted were manifested.

Historical Background

In many ways, exploring the 'second world' and its representations in British writing is particularly apt, for the concept of the 'second world' is arguably a British invention. Notwithstanding the etymological roots of the term, ably elucidated in Ulrich Busse's contribution to this collection, its conceptual heart

---

14 Bauman, *Retrotopia*, 8, 59.
15 Bauman, *Retrotopia*, 9, 5.
16 In the decades of the Cold War (1947–1989), 'second world' nations were 'the Soviet Union (USSR) and Eastern Europe, including, for example, Czechoslovakia, Poland, East Germany, and Hungary, [… in which] the Communist party dominated both the political and the [centrally planned] economic systems' [Anthony Giddens (with the assistance of Simon Griffiths). *Sociology*. 5th rev. ed. Cambridge: Polity, 2006. 42]. We use the 'second world' here in lower case and inverted commas in reference to the historical meaning, and to the ascriptions and perceptions that have established its epistemological significance. Depending on the focus of their discussion, other contributions in the volume proceed differently.

was present, possibly already in the interwar period but certainly no later than Winston Churchill's 'Iron Curtain' speech, delivered in Fulton, Missouri on 5 March 1946. In his address to Westminster College, Churchill warned of the rapid assumption of totalitarian control by the communist parties of eastern Europe, whose influence far outstripped the size of their membership, and drew a clear distinction between the (English-speaking) West and the 'tyranny' represented by 'all-embracing police governments' where 'there is no true democracy.'[17] In sketching out the battle lines of the Cold War – another British coinage, at least in its modern sense – Churchill underscored the fundamental dichotomy that formed the inescapable backdrop to British foreign policy until the 1990s, one that was almost inevitably characterized as a clash of enumerated 'worlds.'[18]

The roots of British fascination with the second of these worlds are broad and deep. The oldest stems from even before the Cold War, and is based on the moral authority Britain derived from its lone stand against Hitler in 1940-1941 (conveniently ignoring, of course, the major supporting role played by the Commonwealth). In a habit of thought acquired in the postwar decades, as the UK grappled with decolonization and financial retrenchment due to the crippling costs of the war, Britons *looked back* to their 'finest hour' as a source of reassurance and self-confidence. The tendency to use Britain's Second World War and its living embodiment, Churchill, as a retrospective moral touchstone has become increasingly unbridled in recent years, especially in the context of the UK's fractious relationship with the EU that culminated in the Brexit vote of 2016. But even more than the specific focus on 1940-1941 itself, this habit sought consolation for today's problems in yesterday's virtue: once acquired, this tendency to retrospection could be easily transposed and applied to the 'second world' – with all its moral certainties of East and West, socialism and capitalism – to palliate the complexities of the years after 1990.[19]

The comfort produced by this clarity was elusive during the Cold War, whose nature was another root of British interest in the 'second world.' In the postwar decades there existed an apparently clear ideological 'enemy' which posed an existential threat. The establishment of the Warsaw Pact (1955) and the help-

---

17 Randolph S. Churchill (ed.). *The Sinews of Peace: Post-War Speeches by Winston S. Churchill.* London: Cassell, 1948. 96, 101.

18 George Orwell, 'You and the Atom Bomb', *Tribune*, 19 Oct 1945. Reprinted in *The Collected Works of George Orwell: 17. I Belong to the Left.* Ed. Peter Davison. London: Secker and Warburg, 1998. 321. An earlier use of 'cold war', meaning physical conquest but by threats and intimidation rather than open warfare, appeared in *The Tribune*, 26 Mar 1938. 345.

19 Tim Shipman. *All Out War: The Full Story of Brexit.* London: William Collins, 2017. 167; Richard Overy. 'Why the cruel myth of the "blitz spirit" is no model for how to fight coronavirus.' *The Guardian.* 19 Mar 2020. <https://www.theguardian.com/commentisfree/2020/mar/19/myth-blitz-spirit-model-coronavirus> (accessed 12 Mar 2024); Mark Connelly. *We Can Take It! Britain and the Memory of the Second World War.* Abingdon: Routledge, 2014.

lessness of the West in the face of Soviet intervention, particularly in Hungary (1956), served to widen the scope of this 'enemy' from the USSR to the entire Eastern bloc (with the notable exception of Yugoslavia). Furthermore, the only way to get at this enemy, in the absence of 'hot' warfare and given Britain's relative military weakness, was through espionage.[20] Hence the boom of spy fiction in print and on film, which was the only channel by which the Western public could engage with their own spying operations, and which kept the focus squarely on the 'second world.' The espionage stories that featured in news media made depressing reading, as they were almost exclusively concerned with unmasking spies, whether gatherers of nuclear secrets like Klaus Fuchs (1950) or communist double agents such as the Cambridge Five, whose exposure was agonizingly drawn out over the period of almost the entire Cold War (1951-1990).[21]

A third source of British interest in the 'second world' is exemplified by the moral ambiguity that so often features in the work of spy fiction's late maestro John le Carré (the subject of Betiel Wasihun's contribution). Since the fall of communism in eastern Europe, there has developed a growing recognition of the moral complexity of life under totalitarian systems. Writers and readers the world over have sought to understand the violence, privations, and stark moral choices that individuals had to face under really existing socialism. This interest has a tendency to become lopsided: it would be a mistake, Timothy Garton Ash has recently written, to 'come away with the impression that life behind the Wall was all about secret police oppression and that people were somehow just waiting and yearning for the moment of liberation. It was not like that.'[22] Indeed, as Katja Hoyer's recent book *Beyond the Wall* (2023) and her interview in this volume amply demonstrate, people *could* live happy and fulfilling lives in the Eastern bloc, and the likelihood of this increased the less they had to do with the state and its security apparatus. The rub was, of course, that it was not possible to be entirely free of the state, and a life of 'inner emigration,' in which people retreat into their private lives to avoid the canker that grew from public behaviour incompatible with private beliefs – essential for survival under totalitarian systems – was not sustainable.[23]

---

20 Britain participated in no proxy wars against the USSR or China after Korea.
21 Brian Harrison. *Seeking a Role: The United Kingdom, 1951–1970*. Oxford: Oxford University Press, 2009. 87–101; Brian Harrison. *Finding a Role? The United Kingdom, 1970–1990*. Oxford: Oxford University Press, 2010. 49–55; Christopher Andrew. *Her Majesty's Secret Service: The Making of the British Intelligence Community*. New York: Viking, 1986. 43–49.
22 Timothy Garton Ash. *Homelands: A Personal History of Europe*. London: Bodley Head, 2023. 78–79.
23 See Timothy Garton Ash. *"Und willst du nicht mein Bruder sein…"*: *Die DDR heute*. Hamburg: Rowohlt, 1981. 12–13; Timothy Garton Ash. *The Uses of Adversity: Essays on the Fate of Central Europe*. New York: Random House, 1989. 11–18.

Many were aware of these difficulties before 1989, but a number of factors prevented this awareness from becoming widespread, principally access to individuals and their life stories. The fall of communism not only removed this obstacle but also made available other sorts of material, especially archival. Most dramatically, this has involved opening the secret police files in eastern Europe, a process complete by the 2010s and which has resulted in autobiographical work exploring, among other things, questions of moral ambiguity, collaboration, coercion, and resistance. The opening of regular archives has also enabled a wider reconsideration of these questions, for example in historical writing on national socialist crimes, where older canards that populations were brainwashed or individuals were coerced to murder have been thoroughly challenged.[24]

A fourth and associated root is the preoccupation with what might be termed the political-cultural mismatch of eastern Europe. Countries that are so similar to Britain – even culturally 'western,' as Kundera and others insisted before 1989 – nonetheless had a political system alien to liberal democracy and the Westminster model.[25] Since 1990, and especially since the enlargement of the EU to incorporate the nations of the 'second world' (except the former USSR, minus the Baltic states) in 2004 and 2007, these countries and their polities have become unambiguously western, meaning that the only way to explore this phenomenon is in the past. Thus the large body of journalism, cultural critique, sociology, and 'Kremlinology' that dominated discussion of the 'second world' during the Cold War has been replaced by contemporary history, memoir, and historical fiction in the years since.

Fascination with the incongruity of the culturally similar but politically alien is hardly limited to the 'second world'. It has fuelled dystopian literature and counterfactual history since the early twentieth century, resulting in such works as Koestler's *Darkness at Dawn*, Orwell's *1984*, and Alan Moore's *V for Vendetta* (1982–1989), as well as a host of allohistorical fiction and alternate history, much of which imagines Britain after a Nazi victory in the Second World War (nullifying its 'finest hour').[26] But an imagined history of totalitarian Britain lacks the plausibility of a past that actually occurred, so that the ranks of those writing on really existing socialism are swelled by authors of fiction who seek to explore the

---

24 See for example Christopher Browning. *Ordinary Men: Reserve Police Batallion 101 and the Final Solution in Poland.* Rev. edn. New York: Harper Perennial, 2017 and Robert Gellately. *Backing Hitler: Consent and Coercion in Nazi Germany.* Oxford: Oxford University Press, 2001.

25 Kundera, 'Tragedy of Central Europe.' See also Ivan Krastev and Stephen Holmes. *The Light that Failed: A Reckoning.* London: Penguin, 2020. 45–46.

26 Alan Moore and David Lloyd. *V for Vendetta.* Burbank, CA: DC Comics, 2005; Philip K. Dick. *The Man in the High Castle.* London: Penguin, 2014 [1962]; Len Deighton. *SS-GB.* London: Penguin, 2021 [1978]; Robert Harris. *Fatherland.* London: Hutchinson, 1992.

complexities of life under totalitarianism in a manner approachable by readers socialized under Western norms.

However, these norms have been shaken in recent years, and a final source of British interest in the 'second world' relates to the challenges of the early twenty-first century. These years have very recently been labelled yet another 'epoch' of East-Central European history,[27] and as representing an 'intermural' period more globally, 'a brief barricade-free interval [of three decades] between the dramatic breaching of the Berlin Wall, exciting utopian fantasies of a borderless world, and a global craze of wall-building, with cement and barbed-wire barriers embodying existential (if sometimes imaginary) fears.'[28] The journey since 1990 has indeed been rough. The West was shocked out of its complacency following the fall of communism principally by 9/11 – notwithstanding the Yugoslav tragedy – and the terrorism, war, financial collapse, and global pandemic of the ensuing two decades have left it decidedly unsteady. To these may be added Brexit and Trumpist populism, Russia's war in Ukraine, and the still-unclear long-term effects of the digital revolution, all of which have further undermined liberal democracy, the rule of law, and the stability of the Western postwar order. It is therefore hardly surprising that the Cold War era has been mobilized in different ways to provide guidance in an uncertain world. For some, the retrospectively fabricated certainties of the period are a source of comfort. For others, a closer examination of the mechanisms of totalitarianism, especially its widespread use of disinformation and surveillance, offers a beacon by which we can guard against these creeping tendencies in our own day, developments that are made even more sinister by our apparent readiness to trade freedom for security, privacy for convenience.[29]

Plan of the Book

It was in these contexts that the writing discussed in this volume was produced. The following chapters are grouped into three sections, each of which takes a fundamental characteristic of contemporary British writing on the 'second world' as its principal focus. The first, 'The Presence of the Past: Contingencies of the "Second World,"' highlights the broader politics of place and space. Ian McEwan and John le Carré, whose work is examined respectively by Richard Brown and Betiel Wasihun, used the Eastern bloc as a means to end, for the one to

---

27 Martin Aust, Andreas Heinemann-Grüder, Angelika Nußberger et al. *Osteuropa zwischen Mauerfall und Ukrainekrieg. Besichtigung einer Epoche.* Frankfurt/Main: Suhrkamp, 2022.
28 Krastev and Holmes, *Light that Failed*, 2.
29 Bode, 'Totalitarianism by Consent,' 34–36; Alwyn Turner. *All in It Together: England in the Early 21st Century.* London: Profile, 2021. 111–112.

explore the responsibility of authors to engage politically, and for the other to investigate the psychology of betrayal. Deborah Levy's recurrent emphasis on central Europe and on her belonging to this region was, as Robert Kusek argues, an aesthetic and identity-defining project. Establishing an East-Central German focus within this spatial domain, Katrin Berndt analyses the retrotopian re-imagining of the provincial 'second world' – specifically provincial cities in the GDR – in the fiction of Philip Sington and Fiona Rintoul. 'Mitropa,' the short story by Rintoul that closes this section, weaves together its threads of place, the past, and psychology in a tale set in the present day, and in a train station, from which parallel tracks lead into different directions.

The second section, 'Second Glances: Retrospective Approaches to the "Second World,"' shifts the focus to British factual writing on the 'second world,' although a recurrent theme of its chapters is on the genre-straddling that frequently occurs in such writing. Ulrich Busse's discussion of the etymology of the first, second, and third worlds is based on all possible genres of text that form the corpus on which lexicographers work, although preponderant in this case are the writings of journalists, and political and social scientists. Paul D. Morris concentrates in his contribution on one historical event, the Holodomor (the Ukrainian famine of 1932–1933) in journalism, and in written and filmic fiction derived from it, intertwining British-centred perspectives from before and after the Cold War. Andrew Wells zooms in on one individual and their exploration of memory and history, particularly on the ways in which they intertwine when faced with a diligent subject and the opportunities presented by the 'poisoned madeleine' of a secret police file. The section closes with an interview with the German-British historian Katja Hoyer, who – both here and in her recent book *Beyond the Wall: East Germany 1949–1990* (2023) – underscores the ongoing fascination with the 'second world' in Britain and America, reminding us both of the key themes and important gaps in our historical understanding of East Germany.

The book's final section, 'Self and Other: Becoming (in) the "Second World,"' contains chapters discussing texts that show how incongruent elements (freedom and control, self and other, reason and emotion) are combined in 'second world' settings in efforts to comprehend the 'self.' Several chapters here examine the Eastern bloc as an 'other,' and Ágnes Györke points to the incomplete 'otherness' of the 'second world' in contemporary British fiction: East-Central Europe is for her authors in no way the 'self,' but nor is it completely 'other,' and this gives rise to a wide range of emotional responses. One of the key emotions deriving from this region and its 'baroque' nature, according to Ágnes Harasztos, is melancholy. The baroque – and postmodernism, with which it is linked – generates melancholy because its very success precludes the meaningful communication of the self, which consigns the 'second world' to a kind of limbo in which it is always 'becoming' and never 'is.' Such also is the fate of the subaltern, and Melinda Dabis examines Kazuo Ishiguro's *The Unconsoled* (1995) in light of a postcolonial, postsocialist East-Central Europe. The split-consciousness of this 'self-coloniz-ing' region is akin to that of the individual in the Romania that features in Patrick McGuinness's *The Last Hundred Days* (2011), analysed by Therese-Marie Meyer. Her chapter explores the nuanced discussion of complicity in the novel, in which 'internal emigration' is taken to the extreme length of a moral migration from the self, where people existed in a realm apart from their actions.

This collection pursues what can be described as a cartographic interest in drawing a literary map of the 'second world' as a historical time and place and an 'imaginative [space that was] opened when the Wall came down' and that con-tinues to be imagined in British writing.[30] This seems especially important be-cause this collection was motivated by the recognition that, shifting national and ideological boundaries notwithstanding, the stories we read, and the stories we tell, are never just limited to subjective reflections on the particular and personal; they are always, also, stories about our encounters, our communities, and our shared histories. And what they tell matters just as much as that we are, and keep, telling them to one another.

References

Andrew, Christopher. *Her Majesty's Secret Service: The Making of the British Intelligence Community*. New York: Viking, 1986.

Anon. 'Hitler's Cold War.' *The Tribune*, 26 Mar 1938. 345.

Applebaum, Anne. 'The Enduring Appeal of the One-Party State.' *Rethinking Open Society*. Ed. Stefan Roch and Michael Ignatieff. Budapest: Central European University Press, 2018. 243–253.

Ash, Timothy Garton. *"Und willst du nicht mein Bruder sein…": Die DDR heute*. Hamburg: Rowohlt, 1981.

–. *The Uses of Adversity: Essays on the Fate of Central Europe*. New York: Random House, 1989.

–. *The File*. London. HarperCollins, 1997.

–. *Homelands. A Personal History of Europe*. London: The Bodley Head, 2023.

---

30 Christoph Houswitschka and Edith Hallberg. 'Introduction: Post-Wall Europe in the Liter-atures of the "Anglosphere."' *Literary Views on Post-Wall Europe*. Ed. Christoph Hous-witschka, Ines Detmers, Anna-Christina Giovanopoulos et al. Trier: WVT, 2005. 51. The authors (and the collection overall) discuss British and Irish writing 'written between the hopeful European "11/9" and the fearful American "9/11" [when] people tried to determine what the consequences and ramifications of the new post-Cold War period […] might have been' (54).

Assmann, Aleida. 'Go East!' *The Legacy of Division. East and West after 1989.* Ed. Ferenc Laczó und Luka Lisjak Gabrijelčič. Budapest: Central European University Press 2020. 264–274.

Aust, Martin, Andreas Heinemann-Grüder, Angelika Nußberger et al. *Osteuropa zwischen Mauerfall und Ukrainekrieg. Besichtigung einer Epoche.* Frankfurt/Main: Suhrkamp, 2022.

Bauman, Zygmunt. *Retrotopia.* Cambridge: Polity, 2017.

Berndt, Katrin. 'Writing on the Wall. The "Second World" in Contemporary British Writing.' *Memorial Volume for Christoph Houswitschka.* Ed. Susan Brähler, Kerstin-Anja Münderlein and Sebastian Kempgen. Bamberg: University of Bamberg Press, 2024. 344–357.

Bode, Christoph. 'Totalitarianism by Consent: Orwell, Huxley, and Capitalism in the Stage of Corporate Surveillance.' *Narrating Surveillance – Überwachen erzählen.* Ed. Betiel Wasihun. Baden Baden: Ergol Verlag, 2019. 21–42.

Bradford, Richard. *The Novel Now: Contemporary British Fiction.* Malden: Blackwell, 2007.

Browning, Christopher. *Ordinary Men: Reserve Police Batallion 101 and the Final Solution in Poland.* Rev. edn. New York: Harper Perennial, 2017.

Chatwin, Bruce. *Utz.* London: Picador, 1989.

Churchill, Randolph S. (ed.). *The Sinews of Peace: Post-War Speeches by Winston S. Churchill.* London: Cassell, 1948.

Connelly, Mark. *We Can Take It! Britain and the Memory of the Second World War.* Abingdon: Routledge, 2014.

Deighton, Len. *SS-GB.* London: Penguin, 2021 [1978].

Dick, Philip K.. *The Man in the High Castle.* London: Penguin, 2014 [1962].

Frenk, Joachim and Christian Krug (eds). *The Cultures of James Bond.* Trier: WVT, 2011.

Gellately, Robert. *Backing Hitler: Consent and Coercion in Nazi Germany.* Oxford: Oxford University Press, 2001.

Giddens, Anthony (with the assistance of Simon Griffiths). *Sociology.* 5th rev. ed. Cambridge: Polity, 2006.

Gray, John. *Straw Dogs. Thoughts on Humans and Other Animals.* London: Granta, 2003.

Hallberg, Edith and Christoph Houswitschka. '"The silent grey foreign country which called itself Germany" in the Novels of Hugo Hamilton, Nicholas Shakespeare and Others.' *Literary Views on Post-Wall Europe. Essays in Honour of Uwe Böker.* Ed. Christoph Houswitschka, Ines Detmers, Anna-Christina Giovanopoulos et al. Trier: WVT, 2005. 83–98.

Hammond, Andrew. *Cold War Stories: British Dystopian Fiction, 1945–1990.* Basingstoke: Palgrave Macmillan, 2017.

Harris, Robert. *Fatherland.* London: Hutchinson, 1992.

Harrison, Brian. *Seeking a Role: The United Kingdom, 1951–1970.* Oxford: Oxford University Press, 2009.

Harrison, Brian. *Finding a Role? The United Kingdom, 1970–1990.* Oxford: Oxford University Press, 2010.

Houswitschka, Christoph and Edith Hallberg. 'Introduction: Post-Wall Europe in the Literatures of the "Anglosphere."' *Literary Views on Post-Wall Europe. Essays in Honour of Uwe Böker.* Ed. Christoph Houswitschka, Ines Detmers, Anna-Christina Giovanopoulos et al. Trier: WVT, 2005. 51–63.

Korte, Barbara, Eva U. Pirker, and Sissy Helff (eds). *Facing the East in the West: Images of Eastern Europe in British Literature, Film and Culture.* Amsterdam: Rodopi, 2010.

Krastev, Ivan. *After Europe.* Philadelphia: University of Pennsylvania Press, 2017.

Krastev, Ivan and Stephen Holmes. *The Light that Failed: A Reckoning.* London: Penguin, 2020.

Kundera, Milan. 'The Tragedy of Central Europe.' *Re:Thinking Europe: Thoughts on Europe Past, Present and Future.* Ed. Yoeri Albrecht and Mathieu Segers. Amsterdam: Amsterdam University Press, 2016. 191–214.

Moore, Alan and David Lloyd. *V for Vendetta.* Burbank, CA: DC Comics, 2005.

Mondal, Anshuman. 'Alterity.' *The Routledge Dictionary of Literary Terms.* Ed. Peter Childs and Roger Fowler. London: Routledge, 2006. 5–6.

Orwell, George. 'You and the Atom Bomb.' *Tribune.* 19 Oct 1945. Reprinted in *The Collected Works of George Orwell: 17. I Belong to the Left.* Ed. Peter Davison. London: Secker and Warburg, 1998. 319–323.

Overy, Richard. 'Why the cruel myth of the "blitz spirit" is no model for how to fight coronavirus.' *The Guardian.* 19 Mar 2020. <https://www.theguardian.com/commentisfree/2020/mar/19/myth-blitz-spirit-model-coronavirus> (accessed 12 Mar 2024).

Rintoul, Fiona. *The Leipzig Affair.* Twickenham: Aurora Metro Books, 2014.

Shipman, Tim. *All Out War: The Full Story of Brexit.* London: William Collins, 2017.

Starck, Kathleen (ed.). *When the World Turned Upside-Down: Cultural Representations of Post-1989 Eastern Europe.* Newcastle upon Tyne: Cambridge Scholars Publishers, 2009.

Stoppard, Tom. *Rock 'n' Roll.* London: Faber and Faber, 2012.

Tighe, Carl. *The Burning Worm.* Withington: IMPress, 2001.

Turner, Alwyn. *All in It Together: England in the Early 21st Century.* London: Profile, 2021.

The Presence of the Past: Contingencies of the 'Second World'

Richard Brown

McEwan's Art of the Possible: Fiction and the Political in his 'Second World' Writing from *The Innocent* (1990) and *Black Dogs* (1992) to *Lessons* (2022)

An interest in 'second world' locations is one which McEwan has shared with a number of contemporary British writers, including such close friends as Martin Amis, Kazuo Ishiguro and Timothy Garton Ash, treated elsewhere in this volume. His engagement is one of the more vivid and yet remains elusive to critical definition. In *The Innocent* (1990) and *Black Dogs* (1992), he explored divided Berlin in different historical moments and generic modulations, as a centre of the dramatically changing circumstances of the end of the Cold War era in continental Europe, and the later novel includes an important post-holocaust scene in Majdanek, Poland.[1] More recently, in the expansive chronicle novel *Lessons* (2022) he has returned to Berlin and introduced other secondary locations, in both former East and West Germany, with the increasingly self-reflexive gaze in which the role of the writer in relation to politics and history is repeatedly explored.[2] The term 'second world' therefore draws upon but expands beyond the literal designation of former Eastern European countries. In his novels, the Cold War context and these 'second world' scenes have provided the opportunity for a self-critical articulation of the values and achievements of Western cultures in relation to their European neighbours and with much focus on the politics of personal and gender freedom, as well as the freedoms of political and economic expression that might stereotypically mark the distinction between East and West. McEwan, in many respects a quintessentially English novelist, shows in these novels a wider continental European range and ambition and, in a literary fiction which is packed with cultural references and cultural coding, acknowledges continental European, including former Eastern European influences on his work.

In this chapter I revisit such scenes of the earlier novels whilst exploring in more detail some of the workings of the former East and West German locations

1 Ian McEwan. *The Innocent*. London: Jonathan Cape, 1990 and *Black Dogs*. London: Jonathan Cape, 1992.
2 Ian McEwan. *Lessons*. London: Jonathan Cape, 2022.

and influences appearing in *Lessons*, which might reveal a latent discourse or aesthetic around political nostalgia and the 'second world.' To call this discourse latent is not to forget that McEwan's established and long-standing role as a leading English novelist of his generation has seen him frequently called upon to comment directly on topical political issues of the day, including, most recently, a prompt and unambiguous condemnation of the invasion of Ukraine in February 2022.[3] However, literary fiction has the obligation to be other than reactive political comment. This obligation is voiced in the prestigious George Orwell Foundation lecture 'Politics and the Imagination: Reflections on Orwell's 1940 "Inside the Whale," which McEwan delivered in November 2021.[4] In Orwell's famous essay he had attempted to define the relation of the writer to politics critiquing, on the one hand, the apparently disengaged 'inside the whale' quality of the high modernist writer, whilst equally strictly accusing the left-leaning, politically-engaged 1930s generation of writers of a kind of ideological blindness, even to the Stalinist atrocities in Ukraine in 1932–1933, making 'mental honesty impossible' for them.[5] McEwan's lecture traces Orwell's complex argument, no doubt finding it instructive for his own work and re-inforcing his point with a striking quotation from 'Create Dangerously,' the equally well-known essay on the writer and political engagement by Albert Camus. McEwan reads this as highlighting 'the aesthetic damage that a political conscience can inflict' quoting the memorable comment that 'it is always possible to record the social conversation that takes place on the benches of the amphitheatre while the lion is crunching the victim.'[6] My chapter title proposes that, in visiting these politically sensitive 'second world' locations in his work, we can show McEwan's as a narrative 'art of possibility,' which foregrounds a courageous, even sometimes dangerously heterodox commitment to the mental honesty of lived experience, as well as to the historical record and political engagement.

It is to the enduringly popular Berlin fictions of both Christopher Isherwood and John Le Carré, that McEwan's Berlin novel *The Innocent* (1990) is occasionally compared. On closer examination its 1950s setting (as opposed to Isherwood's 1930s) captures a historical moment in the aftermath of the Second World War but before the building of the wall in 1961 that has become a distinctive territory of his own. The mix of historic and gothic espionage elements in

3 Ian McEwan. 'We are Haunted by Ghosts – and Vladimir Putin's Sickly Dreams.' *The Guardian*. 5 March 2022. <https://www.theguardian.com/commentisfree/2022/mar/05/vladimir-putin-ukraine> (accessed 14 Feb 2024).

4 Ian McEwan. 'Politics and the Imagination: Reflections on George Orwell's "Inside the Whale." George Orwell Foundation Annual Lecture.' *Ian McEwan* 26 November 2021. 14 Feb 2024, <https://www.ianmcewan.com/resources/docs/McEwan%20_Orwell_Lecture.pdf>.

5 George Orwell. 'Inside the Whale.' *Selected Essays*. London: Penguin, 1957. 42–43.

6 McEwan, 'Politics and the Imagination.'

the novel both is and is not like le Carré. The self-interrogating, ambiguously 'innocent' protagonist Leonard Marnham in whose mind we mostly reside, the love-gender-power relations and the extended descriptive handling of the murderous outcome of the love triangle plot, are made to a recipe that is distinctively McEwan's. In the novel, English innocent Marnham is employed by American intelligence to install electronics in a surveillance tunnel built under the Russian sector to monitor Russian intelligence after the division of the city. He is also, we might say, 'enlisted' by Maria to participate in the luridly violent murder of her abusive husband Otto and the disposal of his body, before she effects a self-preserving departure to the USA by means of a marriage to Bob Glass. That the novel's characters reflect the changing power relations of their respective nations and genders, has been seen as historical allegory. The dismembering and concealment of Otto's corpse in the spy tunnels, has been taken by readers as symbolic of the post-Second World War divided and repressed condition of old Europe and its empires and of the Germany once 'unified' by another Otto, Bismarck, who, somewhat co–incidentally, defined politics as an 'art of the possible.' We might here adopt Otto's corpse as an extreme visceral symbol for Europe's 'second worlds,' at least as the 1980s imagined the echo of Second World War repressions, which are clearly still strong in the emerging Cold War configurations and their aftermaths.

McEwan described his choice of this specific retrospective historical setting in an interview:

> The attraction originally was to Berlin in the present. I was there in 1987, when I had already decided to write a novel set in the Cold War, but at that time I hadn't any clear idea of the exact period. [...] It wasn't till much later that I chose the period, the mid 1950s. [...]
> Berlin was like a fridge in a way, a deep freeze, in that the postures of the combatants in World War II were frozen in place in Berlin. So it was like history held in limbo. The period in which the novel is set was a time when the British Empire was dissolving; the war had made us virtually penniless and the Empire was coming apart for internal reasons too and the mantle was passing to the Americans who had strengthened their economy enormously through the war.[7]

The fridge or deep freeze image may be almost as resonant as that of the symbolic corpse. It points towards this double displacement of the Second World War history and the newly emerging 'second world' character of Eastern Bloc Eastern Europe in which the city was enclosed. Though the Berlin depicted were in the West, the 'fridge' approach invokes a historical stasis or defined historical space that may have something in common with the epidemic of nostalgia and the

---

7 Ian McEwan. 'Interview by Patrick McGrath.' *Bomb* 33 (1 Oct 1990). 14 Feb 2024, <https://bombmagazine.org/articles/1990/10/01/ian-mcewan/>.

generational displacement of utopia by 'retrotopia' that Zygmunt Baumann, following Svetlana Boym, identified as a condition of our contemporary culture.[8] It may then subtly anticipate such phenomena as the 'ostalgic' interest in the former Eastern Bloc countries in recent decades, especially as these became more accessible to the Western visitor and tourist.

At first sight, the two worlds of *The Innocent* are the Berlin of Leonard's traumatic adventure and the Tottenham to which he returns for Christmas. The latter is evidently Leonard's primary reality, the 'old familiar life' as opposed to the 'nightmare' of Berlin (*Innocent* 118) but Tottenham is nevertheless 'drowning in ordinariness' with 'no tension and no purpose' (*Innocent* 116) and he feels darkly drawn to the sense of adventure, mission and camaraderie of the intelligence community life in Berlin as well as to the erotic excitement of his adulterous relationship with Maria, despite the looming threat of her violent husband. Right from the start, we are told, his innocence allows him a feeling of empowerment in the place: 'It was impossible for a young Englishman to be in Germany for the first time and not think of it as a defeated nation or feel pride in the victory' (*Innocent* 4–5). Complex emotions govern his relationship to this other place and these are worked out not least in relation to the multi-dimensional and self-interrogating aspects of his innocence, which includes both sexual innocence and political naivety, and characterises his strange journey into violent killing and concealment. At the end of the novel, McEwan brings an older Leonard back to the city to retrospectively reflect on this innocence and also to experience some of the more recent changes in late 1980s Berlin, apparently thus acknowledging that it was this more recent history which had first stimulated his own imagination. Leonard's self-reflexive uncertainty is a defining aspect of his character and his English identity. This is all the more apparent in the final chapter where we see that Berlin has been the 'second world' he has constructed himself in relation to.

Whereas Leonard's story had played out in a Germany of the past, McEwan's next fiction was to explore new possibilities of that past in the context of its present day. *Black Dogs* (1992) shares some locations with *The Innocent* but has a newly dynamic approach to storytelling, offering a more topical imaginative vision of history, not least because it deals more directly with the epoch-defining event of the fall of the Wall to which *The Innocent* could only allude. Though Berlin is by no means its only location, the second-world, 'Berlin in the present' scene discussed by McEwan in the interview is more fully and distinctively drawn. Part Two has an extended description of the Berlin of November 1989, which the narrator visits with his father-in-law immediately on hearing the news of the Wall's fall. The novel has a much more episodic narrative structure, refusing

8 Zygmunt Baumann. *Retrotopia*. Cambridge: Polity Press, 2017.

explicatory linearity in favour of presenting multiple narrative worlds, jumping backwards and forwards in both place and time from England (June's nursing home in Wiltshire), to Berlin, to rural Southern France (Gorge de Vis, St Maurice de Navacelles) and, crucially for our second-world theme, to the former concentration camp Majdanek near Lublin in eastern Poland. In that way it achieves timely historical depth, contrasting the late 1980s generational perspectives of Jeremy and his wife Jenny with those of her parents Bernard and June Tremaine, whose life stories he is researching for a biographical study.

Though both are complex, McEwanish, intellectually self-conscious beings, Jeremy, the protagonist of *Black Dogs*, is a more interestingly complex character than Leonard. As a married man, he is less sexually and emotionally innocent than Leonard and he is more mobile and articulate. McEwan convincingly develops his intellectual character as a kind of doubting postmodernist, aware of historiographical alternatives, fascinated both by the gender difference and by the temperamental and ideological differences between his in–laws. Bernard is a scientist with a love of order and category, once a Communist Party member but (since 1956) reluctantly disillusioned, becoming a more typical English socialist of the post-Orwellian, arguably nostalgic or retrotopian kind. June is more intuitive, especially in relation to the natural and sometimes even supernatural world.

In *Black Dogs*, then, the second-world scenes have two or even three locations. There are the Berlin late-1980s, end-of-the-Cold War crowd scenes, full of suggestive symptomatic details, where even a cautious individual like Jeremy can be swept up in a shared euphoric moment, however complex McEwan's underlying picture of it might be (*Black Dogs* 74–100). Then there is Southern France in the present and past, where the legacy of Nazi occupation still haunts. Third is Majdanek, offering a brief but intense narrative and psychic pivot in the novel. It is the place where Jeremy has met and fallen in love with his wife Jenny and here McEwan is able to find a possible way to describe the deeply impossible scene of the concentration camp (*Black Dogs* 105–113). This, we might say, is impossible first in the sense of it having been practically repressed and invisible to the Western gaze in Poland through the early Cold War period and then in the sense that (for Adorno) poetry after the holocaust is impossible, a situation which all post-Second World War writers face whether as direct witnesses, historical researchers or writers of imaginative fiction. Jeremy's experience as a cultural visitor is deftly poised as an act of rediscovery of that repressed holocaust history by a younger generation of the time, for whom this rediscovery is still itself a vitally traumatic cultural event, and it brings him and Jenny together in a climactic moment that opens their lives to each other, to history and to the work of the novel which, for McEwan as well as for Jeremy, is to reveal truths beneath repressions. After the visit, 'reticent' Jeremy, 'liberated from the usual constraints of selfhood,' spontaneously kisses Jenny and they spend the next three days making love in their hotel (*Black Dogs* 112). Another well-known quotation from Orwell's essay 'The Prevention of Literature' comes to mind: 'Unless spontaneity enters at some point or another literary creation is impossible.'[9]

Neither the Berlin nor the Majdanek scenes in *Black Dogs* are retrotopic in the way the Berlin location of *The Innocent* may be thought to be, but they form the contexts in which Jeremy's retrospective curiosity is framed, including his curiosity about Bernard's retrotopian politics. Whilst they are considering possible political re-unification futures, Jeremy 'obligingly argued that the East Germans might retain attachments to some features of their system,' and Bernard suggests that 'the enormous popular momentum against the East German state had reached a stage where lingering attachments would only be too late, in the form of nostalgia' (*Black Dogs* 73). That Bernard is self-conscious about such a form of political nostalgia indicates that the novel itself is not limited by a nostalgic aesthetic. It pushes beyond it to something more up-to-date, differently self-conscious, more historically layered, psychologically complex and uncertain. The Berlin scenes are characterised by the exciting and urgent attempt to understand a changing history, and even the scenes in Southern France carry something of the 'second world' in the totalitarian ghosts of its Nazi occupied past. The traumatic holocaust-memorial landscape of Majdanek is paradoxically charged with a moment of intense bonding intimacy that has built a future.[10]

One text that may sit behind McEwan as well as other British writers of the 1980s generation is Hungarian author Stephen Vizinczey's widely popular work *In Praise of Older Women*, subtitled *The Amorous Recollections of Andras Vajda* and originally published in 1965. One of a number of cultural exiles at the time of the Hungarian uprising in 1956, Vizinczey's literary career in the UK represents a Cold War, eastern European influence on contemporary British writing.[11] In the 1960s and 1970s, the novel captured a libertarian mood that was expressed in different ways in the Eastern Bloc and the West. It seems to have enjoyed something of a reputation for acceptable sexual explicitness along with such works as Lawrence's *Lady Chatterley* and Cleland's *Fanny Hill* as the censorship of literary work was collapsing. When it was reprinted in Penguin Classics in 2010, the edition included a chorus of critical admiration for its honesty, humour and importance as a historical record. The tenor of several comments is that

9 George Orwell. 'The Prevention of Literature.' *The Collected Essays, Journalism and Letters of George Orwell*. Vol. IV. New York: Harcourt, Brace and World, 1968. 71.

10 Richard Brown. '"A Wilderness of Mirrors": The Mediated Berlin Backgrounds for Ian McEwan's *The Innocent*.' *Anglistik* 21.2 (2010): 49–56; Richard Brown. 'Cold War Fictions.' *The Cambridge Companion to Ian McEwan*. Ed. Dominic Head. Cambridge: Cambridge University Press, 2019. 75–90.

11 Stephen Vizinczey. *In Praise of Older Women*. London: Penguin Classics, 2010.

Vizinczey forged a contemporary language in which a Casanova-like memoir could capture the changing times. Vajda's preference for more mature partners seems to assist his growing articulacy and self-understanding as well as developing a sense of the cultural agency and emotional experience of those partners themselves. The title alone became a catch phrase as can be seen in Martin Amis's 1973 debut novel *The Rachel Papers* whose adolescent hero Charles Highway has the ambition on the eve of his twentieth birthday (and implicitly of the twenty-first century) to 'sleep with an Older Woman [*sic*],' Rachel being slightly older than he.[12]

It is notable then that McEwan's Maria too is a version of the 'older woman' for the innocent Leonard. Vizinczey's cool handling of sexual encounters embodied a zeitgeist that feeds much of the early McEwan. It seems highly relevant to *Black Dogs* that the novel's importance as a record of the growing freedoms in private life in 1950s Hungary speaks to the political as well as to the personal. This is especially evident in the character Bobby in the novel, a 34-year-old divorcee who Andras meets at the Lukacs baths. She is described as 'a second-row violinist with the Budapest Symphony Orchestra, a sensuous but independent-minded woman who made short work of men if they didn't behave to her liking.'[13] She tells her history of 'one hundred and twenty-seven days and four hours' in Auschwitz where her parents, like his, were murdered, an experience that seems to have brought her to her personal joyful version of 'Einstein's Law' that 'Pleasure turns into energy.'[14] The narrative tone emphatically reinforces its power of witnessing and the juxtaposition of their frankly sexual love affair with the profound trauma of the concentration camp. There seems a strong link between this and McEwan's representation of Jeremy's experience of spontaneous energisation during the visit to Majdanek in *Black Dogs*.

So it is with some well-established and highly nuanced structures of feeling and patterns of narrativity that we come to *Lessons* in 2022, a memorially-driven, lifetime chronicle of its hero Roland Baines. He is a school drop-out, born in 1948, a greetings card poet, performer of hotel restaurant 'munch music' on the piano (*Lessons* 269), part-time tennis coach and one-parent father, whose marginality in relation to the political and economic history he observes and is shaped by makes him all the more resonant as an authentic bit-part player in the history of the everyday. In his Orwell lecture, McEwan praised Italo Calvino's *The Watcher,* whose protagonist's political role in the democratic world is to observe provincial local elections and whose very marginality constitutes his representative significance. *Lessons* is an ambitious fictional autobiography and self-

---

12 Martin Amis. *The Rachel Papers.* London: Jonathan Cape, 1973.
13 Vizinczey, *In Praise of Older Women,* 108.
14 Vizinczey, *In Praise of Older Women,* 113.

consciously contemporary (if not exactly postmodernist) historical novel, revealing a McEwan now working in the years after the Jonathan Coe of *Middle
England* and John Lanchester of *Capital*, English state-of-the-nation novels that
emerged from the 2008 financial crisis, the 2012 London Olympics and the run up
to Brexit.[15] It revisits several symbolic and pivotal moments from the last century
and takes its characters to several specific geographical locations in England
including Suffolk (where Roland goes to school) and the village of Erwarton
(where his piano teacher lives), Eskdale in the English Lake District (where his
second wife Daphne gives Roland 'a lesson in dying,' *Lessons* 412), Balham (where
Roland later locates his former piano teacher and lover) and the environs of
Aldershot, Farnborough and Ash in Hampshire. This is the location of the
military wartime and immediate post-war experiences of Roland's father and
mother, from which a complicated family back story emerges.

The structures of feeling also draw deeply on both first and 'second world'
German locations. Roland's parents are absent, stationed in post-war West
Germany whilst he is sent to boarding school. Having dropped out, he takes
German lessons at the Goethe Institute in Kensington and, on a trip to Berlin in
1980 with his French girlfriend Mireille Lavaud, he meets up with a couple from
East Berlin: Florian and Ruth Heise and their two daughters. Roland braves the
border guards and the rumours of Stasi torture prison to bring them such forbidden Western luxuries as the eponymous 1969 vinyl LP *The Velvet Underground*, which is the only one of the band's records missing from Florian's
collection (*Lessons* 170–171). This gives Roland an Orwellian political voice in
left-wing circles and then a campaigning role attempting to track another loss as
the Heise family do indeed suffer for their culturally subversive activity. Florian is
imprisoned and the couple separated from their children Hanna and Charlotte,
albeit briefly, before being banished to Schwedt near the Polish border, as Roland
later learns through Mireille's diplomat father. At a Bob Dylan concert in Earls
Court in 1981 (which he attends as a nostalgic 'act of solidarity' with them,
Lessons 179), he meets his German tutor Alissa Eberhardt again. That meeting
leads them to develop a relationship and an ill-fated marriage whose aftermath,
involving her disappearance to Germany, (initially apparently to Munich), becomes one of the novel's primary concerns. 'How did Berlin and the renowned
Alissa Eberhardt come into his life?' is the Nabokovian question that opens
Chapter 5 (*Lessons* 157).

The return to something like the *Black Dogs* 1989 scenes at the Wall at the end
of Chapter 6 show a Roland who is more knowing and experienced than the
recently arrived journalistic crowd, thrilled by the optimism of the moment but

---

15 Jonathan Coe. *Middle England.* London: Penguin, 2018; John Lanchester. *Capital.* London:
   Faber, 2012.

still obsessed with his personal losses of the Heise family and Alissa, who he does in fact meet again just as her first novel *The Journey* is appearing in print (*Lessons* 221–243). It is the power of her novel, itself compared to Nabokov, that ultimately captures his attention. She may at moments seem an imagined re-incarnation of the empowered Grete who intervenes against violence on behalf of Bernard in Berlin in *Black Dogs* (*Black Dogs* 78–79) but far outgrows that mould in the plot and in terms of her literary significance. Her novels only just miss out on the Nobel Prize.

There are significant former West German locations for the action. These include Liebenau, near the confluence of the Weser and the Grosse Aue, where Alissa's parents live, where Roland visits with her and where their son Lawrence Heinrich is conceived (*Lessons* 74). Their wartime story links to that of his own parents (and recasts Jeremy's interest in his in–laws in *Black Dogs*). Her father is the veteran of a Munich-based anti-Nazi resistance group, the 'White Rose,' about which her English mother had been commissioned by *Horizon* magazine to write. Alissa abandons them all (including baby Lawrence at seven months old) to pursue her literary ambitions, which eventually transform her into the author of major contemporary feminist revisionist German historical novels that boldly exploit her mother's story and shamelessly accuse her of political cowardice. Both Roland and Lawrence revisit Liebenau and Berlin in their attempts to track Alissa down. Another port of call in the novel is Duisburg at the confluence of the Rhine and Ruhr, which boasts Europe's largest inland port, and to which Ruth and Florian move when travel to the West is finally permitted for them, though Florian, somewhat nostalgically, finds it little more to his taste than East Berlin (*Lessons* 398).

These scenes provide a return with a difference to the scenes of the former novels, subtly re-orienting the reader, who sees them here filtered through nostalgic affect when they are later recalled across the novel's time scheme through Roland's increasingly nostalgic structures of feeling. McEwan can now chart the changing story of Germany and of Anglo-German relations since the polar hostilities and repressions of the Second World War which had deprived Roland of his parents, through generations for whom Berlin became a prime location for the division between East and West and then part of the accessible everyday landscape of European communication and exchange once again in the years of the EU, the German economic miracle, language study, study abroad and gap year travels and the developing community of East and West. The Chernobyl disaster appears in the novel as one historical marker that implicitly underscores the communality of experience between the West and former East. Chernobyl might have seemed to be a 'faraway place' in 1986 but now we know better. 'A cloud of self-deception was general across Europe' as Roland's free-indirect style memoir puts it in an environmentalist turn (*Lessons* 67).

Meanwhile, the German language regularly punctuates the text. Roland's attempts to recall the syntactic structures of the language make him think at one point: 'German, like Alissa, belonged in an abandoned past' (*Lessons* 214). By the 2020s, his son Lawrence Heinrich has moved to a job in Potsdam. His grandchildren speak German and call him 'Opa' (*Lessons* 480–483).

There is an obvious relevance of *In Praise of Older Women* to one of the most prominent personal-political plot lines in *Lessons:* Roland's seduction by his childhood piano teacher Miriam Cornell and its ramifications in the story of his later life. McEwan's handling of this topical plot thread shows the deft slippage from the innocent everyday to the uncanny, the gothic and the political which can be found throughout his work. Told from Roland's point of view, the earlier scenes have the character of adolescent sexual initiation and awakening more than of child exploitation. However, a detective, Charles Moffat, has followed up on a colleague's earlier investigation into a phrase in Roland's notebook, which he wrongly suspected might reveal some criminal element in Alissa's disappearance. In what seems like another age, Moffat finds in Roland's previous explanation of the notebook actual evidence of his 'historic sexual abuse' by his teacher. Chillingly, he has prosecution 'targets' of historic abuse to meet, including the rarer cases perpetrated by women (*Lessons* 334–338). Both detectives are portrayed to draw a parallel with the Heises' experience with the Stasi in the former East Berlin. The suggestion in the novel that Moffat's politically correct investigation into historical child sexual abuse is blunt and repressive is reinforced by a mode of narration which had allowed it to be initially presented as somewhat idealized.

Nostalgia for a more sexually liberal world is meanwhile placed against the novel's suggestion that Miriam's actions have caused Roland an enduring psychic wound. The incident at once propels and stunts Roland's self-development, causing him to fail all his school exams and at times justifying the accusation that he is a 'fantasist' who 'can't achieve anything' which Alissa has made to her mother as her excuse for leaving him and their child (*Lessons* 219).

In the scene in Balham where Roland finally confronts Miriam as an adult, he is subject to the 'tipping falling tumult of these contrary notions' (*Lessons* 346–358). McEwan's narrative handling of the topic across time, generates emotional and ethical ambivalence. It is balanced to allow the novel to chronicle the sea change in public attitudes and media concerns across the 60–70 years it covers, from the libertarian aspirations of the late 1950s and early 1960s. He records the schoolboys' reaction to the Suez crisis – 'What if you died before you'd had it[?]' (*Lessons* 112) – as well as the anxieties around 'historic sexual abuse,' exploitation and paedophilia that have marked the media in recent years. The 'brilliant idea' that love is 'a *Ding an sich*, a thing itself,' articulated in spontaneous Kantian German, by which Roland had extracted himself from the increasingly oppressive

relationship with his piano teacher earlier in the novel (*Lessons* 263), retains a
liberatory truth, but the later chapters are dominated by his surviving need to
hear Miriam's side of the story and to see her acknowledge her responsibility,
even if he refrains from bringing a criminal charge. One quasi-Kantian gloss
might say that there is no such '*Ding an sich*' beyond the perception of it by the
senses and emotions, which these later chapters explore.

Had McEwan acknowledged Vizinczey in relation to this plot line in *Lessons*,
he might have found further opportunities to explore such ethical ambivalences
across time and in a 'second world' context. At any rate both the hyperliterate
McEwan and his conscientious autodidact vehicle Roland had many profoundly
resonant subtexts to allude to and enlist to help convey the affective texture of the
situation.

One example is, appropriately enough, a continental European literary classic
which charts an ironic affective modernity of an earlier age: Gustave Flaubert's
Sentimental Education (1867).[16] McEwan allows the suggestive word 'sentiment'
to resonate through the book in Roland's greetings cards (*Lessons* 101) and the
music he performs (*Lessons* 277). He pointedly has Roland himself read a section
of the novel, noting self-reflexively the information supposedly in the introduction to his paperback that 'Flaubert himself had fallen in love at the age of
fourteen with a twenty-six-year-old woman, also married' (*Lessons* 315–316) and,
somewhat sentimentally, feeling that the 'carnal impatience' of the 1960s was as
'many steps behind' as it was in advance of that of the 1860s. Later, Roland
comments ironically on his own 'erotic and sentimental education' in the 'py-
jama week' (*Lessons* 437) with Miriam.

Both sentiment and irony are Flaubert's territory as much as they are McE-
wan's in this novel. Flaubert's intention to write what he called '*l'histoire morale
des hommes de ma génération; "sentimentale" serait plus vrai. C'est un livre
d'amour, de passion; mais de passion telle qu'elle peut exister maintenant*' [the
moral history of the men of my generation, 'sentimental' would be closer to it. It's
a book of love, of passion, but of such passion as can exist in these times][17] is
echoed in McEwan's novel, as it was in James Joyce's stated intention to write a
'moral history' in his *Dubliners*.[18] Joyce too is quoted or recalled at times in the
text: a phrase from the end of his story 'The Dead' in the 'general across Europe'
phrase quoted above. *Lessons* has an intriguing epigraph from *Finnegans Wake*:

---

16 Gustave Flaubert. *A Sentimental Education: The Story of a Young Man*. Ed. Douglas Parmee.
   Oxford: Oxford University Press World's Classics, 2008.
17 Gustave Flaubert. 'Letter to Mademoiselle Leroyer de Chantepie 6 October 1864.' *Correspondance*. Vol. 3 (Janvier 1859 – Décembre 1868). Ed. Jean Bruneau. Paris: Gallimard, 1991.
   409 [emphasis added; transl. by the author].
18 James Joyce. 'Letter to Grant Richards. 20 May 1906.' *Letters of James Joyce* Vol. 1. Ed. Stuart
   Gilbert. London: Faber, 1957. 64.

'First we feel. Then we fall' (vii). In context this has a sentimental flavour. In another sense the first 'feel' will recirculate throughout the novel, which opens with a plausibly *Wakean* sentence: 'This was an insomniac memory, not a dream' (*Lessons* 3). The pyjamas from D. H. Lawrence's 'Snake' as well as Lawrence's poem 'Piano' and his Anglo-German marriage, resonate as does Roland and Alissa's choice of the name Lawrence for their son. McEwan apparently uses such allusions to remind his readers of the modernist writers defended by Orwell in 'Inside the Whale' and even (in placing Roland's school by the River Orwell) of Orwell's essay itself and its approach to the politics of fiction.

These modernist novels are not in themselves texts of the socialist world but, in the 'second world' contexts of McEwan's *Lessons*, they seem to map the cultural and affective freedoms on which the West prides itself and to which citizens of the 'second world' may aspire. Roland, as he explores the 'other world' of his East Berlin friends, contrasts the 'repressive tolerance' of the West, with a society where for Florian and Ruth 'the system was an active enemy' (*Lessons* 173).

Roland is a writer and, significantly, a musician, who for all his self-taught literacy, is a drop-out from formal education, so it seems particularly appropriate that one of the most nostalgic 'second world' scenes has its affective power coded through a work of popular music and one that articulates shared cultural and political aspirations. The importance of popular music in the counter cultures of East and West in the 1960s, and to the 1989 Prague Velvet Revolution, was central to Tom Stoppard's important play *Rock 'n' Roll,* which had been performed in London in 2006 and 2007, and the approach to the political aspects of popular music in the 'second world' context in *Lessons* has some interests in common with and in contrast to Stoppard's play.[19] The Velvet Underground LP Roland has brought Florian and Ruth on his last visit, to which they have listened 'many times at fearless full volume' (*Lessons* 168), has one song especially highlighted:

> 'Finally, with everyone drunk, they sang along to 'Pale Blue Eyes' – *If I could make the world as pure* … They knew the words by now. Arms round each other's shoulders, they rose lustfully to the refrain, *linger on … your pale blue eyes,* and turned it into an ode to joy.' (*Lessons* 171–172).

The lyrics are made to allude to various story elements. The 'pale blue eyes' are partly those of Daphne, Roland's second wife, whose death from cancer just after their wedding (*Lessons* 211) overtakes the emotional losses of both the Miriam and Alissa relationships, perhaps also repeating them. The continuation of the quoted line 'If I could make the world as pure/ and strange as what I see/ I'd put you in the mirror/ I put in front of me' connects to the reflective observation of Roland's sensibility and that of the novel which defamiliarizes the everyday,

---

19 Tom Stoppard, *Rock 'n' Roll.* London: Faber, 2024.

seeing the strange in the familiar. The following couplet 'Skip a life completely/ stuff it in a cup' suggests the summary overview of Roland's whole life and his recurrently dismissive self-evaluations.

In terms of a 'second world' aesthetic, the black and white album cover photograph feels like the Heises' flat. In 1973 The Velvet Underground also recorded the song and album *Berlin*, with its long piano-playing title song exuding the nostalgia of *film noir* piano-bar music.

'Pale Blue Eyes' is reprised later when Roland has decided to marry Daphne and is playing through his sentimental lunchtime piano repertoire imagining Daphne in the audience, when, noticing four others, he decides to include a version of it for the first time with its 'tender' guitar-specific accompaniment rendered on the piano. When he looks up the woman of the family group, who is Ruth Heise, is crying and the four, re-united in what is by now the era of Friends Reunited, make an 'affectionate scrum of an embrace.' They slip into German, '"*Jetzt weinst du auch*"' [Now you're crying too!]. The language returns from its 'abandoned past' to heighten the affect (*Lessons* 395).

The song, beautifully simple, brief, elegiac and, sung together in this way, forms an expression of local and global community perhaps more so than the tendency towards isolatedness which Baumann diagnoses as a dangerous tendency of nostalgic politics. Florian confesses 'I was happier when I was longing for things' and Ruth explains their reaction to the song as being 'very sad [...] for the old times that we never want to see again. Anywhere!' (*Lessons* 398–399).

Later still, Roland has begun to evaluate his 1989 experience as a 'peak' of democratic optimism, 'a portal, a wide opening to the future, with everyone streaming through,' especially contrasted with the 'shame' for democracy of the disaffected Trumpist storming of the American Capitol in January 2021 after the Biden presidential victory (*Lessons* 474). The reader, who, like Florian, may have committed the words of the song to memory, may recall that the word 'peak' also occurs in it.

We could then think of the nostalgia of the reprise as having a retrotopic politico-affective dimension, heavily loaded with 1940s *Casablanca*, *film noir*, piano-bar affect. If so, it marks a retrotopia which conjures up the lost aspirations of the political left, both communitarian and democratic, as well as the traumatic separations of Europe in the two World Wars and the Cold War, the damage to domestic affect that may be inflicted by politicising gender or literary ambition, or the crisis for humanity represented by the concentration camps and the global nuclear and environmental threat.

At any rate the 'second world' locations of *Lessons* appear to have developed substantially from those of the earlier novels most of all in their articulation of the complex and ambivalent character of affect across time. Much is possible in this whole-life-writing kind of fiction, as it was for McEwan in the equally successful 2005 single-day novel *Saturday* with which it contrasts, in these terms if not necessarily in all aspects of its narrativity. The affective turn and its displacement to various German 'second world' settings is certainly recognisable in Baumann's analysis of the contemporary when he writes that 'Nostalgia is but one member of the rather extended family of affectionate relationship[s] with an "elsewhere."'[20] Through such nostalgia, we may well conclude that there are more ways than one of reading the rich and textured structures of feeling in McEwan's *Lessons*, including the functioning of the 'second world' elements that energise its imaginative journeyings. It may be difficult or impossible to fully reconcile the commitment to representing lived experience with all forms of political engagement, though this remains a compelling obligation for the post-Orwellian writer and one that McEwan's practiced narrative 'art of the possible' pursues, often by embracing contradiction and increasingly by exploring nostalgia as retrotopic political affect.

Fortunately for McEwan's protagonist Roland Baines, his mixed career path, unlike Alissa's or that of McEwan himself, partly excuses him from this daunting task. In the final scene both he and his granddaughter Stephanie have been reading *Flix*, a 1990s illustrated children's book about a dog living in a world of cats by the prolific Tomi Ungerer who died in 2019 and whose output also included much alternative, politically flavoured work for adult readers.[21] After her account of it Roland asks 'Do you think the story is trying to tell us something about people.' She replies: 'Don't be silly, Opa. It's about cats and dogs.' (*Lessons* 481). Compared to his explanation of an imaginary book 'a hundred years long' that he pretends to her he has been reading, which perhaps resembles *Lessons* in some ways (and which he immediately regrets mentioning), her younger-generation perspective offers a refreshing, imaginative note on which to end.

References

Amis, Martin. *The Rachel Papers*. London: Jonathan Cape. 1973.
Baumann, Zygmunt. *Retrotopia*. Cambridge: Polity Press, 2017.
Brown, Richard. '"A Wilderness of Mirrors": The Mediated Berlin Backgrounds for Ian McEwan's *The Innocent*.' *Anglistik* 21.2 (2010): 49–56.
–. 'Cold War Fictions.' *The Cambridge Companion to Ian McEwan*. Ed. Dominic Head. Cambridge: Cambridge University Press, 2019. 75–90.
Coe, Jonathan. *Middle England*. London: Penguin, 2018.
Flaubert, Gustave. *Correspondance*. Vol. 3 (Janvier 1859 – Décembre 1868). Ed. Jean Bruneau. Paris: Gallimard, 1991.

---

20 Baumann, *Retrotopia*, 3.
21 Tomi Ungerer. *Flix*. Transl. Anna von Cramer-Klatt. Zürich: Diogenes, 1997.

–. *A Sentimental Education: The Story of a Young Man*. Ed. Douglas Parmee. Oxford: Oxford University Press World's Classics, 2008.

Joyce, James. *Letters of James Joyce* Vol. 1. Ed. Stuart Gilbert. London: Faber, 1957.

Lanchester, John. *Capital*. London: Faber, 2012.

McEwan, Ian. 'Interview by Patrick McGrath.' *Bomb* 33 (1 Oct 1990). 14 Feb 2024, <https://bombmagazine.org/articles/1990/10/01/ian-mcewan/>.

–. *The Innocent*. London: Jonathan Cape, 1990.

–. *Black Dogs*. London: Jonathan Cape, 1992.

–. 'Politics and the Imagination: Reflections on George Orwell's "Inside the Whale." George Orwell Foundation Annual Lecture.' *Ian McEwan* 26 November 2021. 14 Feb 2024, <https://www.ianmcewan.com/resources/docs/McEwan%20_Orwell_Lecture.pdf>.

–. 'We are Haunted by Ghosts – and Vladimir Putin's Sickly Dreams.' *The Guardian*. 5 March 2022. <https://www.theguardian.com/commentisfree/2022/mar/05/vladimir-p utin-ukraine> (accessed 14 Feb 2024).

–. *Lessons*. London: Jonathan Cape, 2022.

Orwell, George. [1940] 'Inside the Whale.' *Selected Essays*. London: Penguin, 1960. 42–43.

–. [1946] 'The Prevention of Literature.' *The Collected Essays, Journalism and Letters of George Orwell*. Vol. IV. New York Harcourt, Brace and World, 1968. 59–72.

Stoppard, Tom. *Rock 'n' Roll*. London: Faber, 2024.

Ungerer, Tomi. *Flix*. Transl. Anna von Cramer-Klatt. Zürich: Diogenes, 1997.

Velvet Underground, The. *The Velvet Underground*. MGM Records. 1969.

Vizinczey, Stephen. *In Praise of Older Women*. London: Penguin Classics, 2010.

Betiel Wasihun

Retrotopian Settings for Traitors: John le Carré's Spy Fiction

The Moral Legitimacy of Betrayal

John le Carré, alias David Cornwall, literarily portrayed the 'second world' as a historical phase marked by treachery, doubleness, falsity, and paranoia. He was invested in exploring the complex intrigues during the Cold War, an era which seemed to have nourished an atmosphere of betrayal as the journalist Margret Boveri stated in her historical account of the Cold War period, *Treason in the Twentieth Century*.[1] More recently, Eva Horn has examined fictional representations of treason and espionage in a wide-ranging meditation on the 'recursion of fiction into reality and reality into fiction' in what is now being called the long twentieth century.[2] In *Intrigue: Espionage and Culture*, Allan Hepburn observes that '[d]uring the twentieth century, a period of formalized and unprecedented spying, cultural fantasies and deformations of history created a representational legacy of treachery, doubleness, and paranoia.'[3] The twentieth century had been portrayed as *A Century of Spies* already in its final decade by Jeffrey T. Richelson in his eponymous study.[4] Tellingly, the first chapter of this historical analysis of espionage reads 'A Shady Profession,' positing ambiguity as a key feature of real spies which resonates with le Carré's fictional representations that 'capture the mood of the Cold-War world'[5] and its opaque system of various intelligence agencies in which most of le Carré's characters find themselves.

Le Carré's interest in the multifaceted phenomenon of betrayal stemmed not least from his biography. After being a spy proper, he became the author of

1 Margret Boveri. *Der Verrat im 20. Jahrhundert*. 4 vols. Hamburg: Rowohlt, 1956–60.
2 Eva Horn. *The Secret War: Treason, Espionage, and Modern Fiction*. Evanston, Illinois: Northwestern University Press, 2013. 353.
3 Allan Hepburn. *Intrigue: Espionage and Culture*. New Haven, CT: Yale University Press, 2005. xiii.
4 Jeffrey T. Richelson. *A Century of Spies. Intelligence in the Twentieth Century*. Oxford: Oxford University Press, 1995.
5 Toby Manning. *John le Carré and the Cold War*. London: Bloomsbury, 2018. 2.

world-famous spy novels. For his fictional worlds, he drew directly from the world of agents in the 1950s and 1960s, from a time when he himself worked for the Security Service (MI5) as well as the Secret Intelligence Service (MI6). Moreover, as Tom Maddox states, le Carré's ongoing engagement with betrayal went beyond his professional experience as a spy and is to be sought in his upbringing. Abandoned by his mother at the age of five, his father played a crucial role in his life:

> His rogue father, Ronnie Cornwell – a con man with vast social ambitions and few, if any, scruples – taught him the intricacies of deception and impersonation, and in the process gave him the terrible gift of being a permanent outsider. Experiencing public schools – both as pupil and master – revealed to Cornwall the intimate ways of the English upper (or aspiring) classes in all their baroque eccentricity and almost insane snobbery.[6]

At the centre of John le Carré's spy fiction are questions dealing with the ambivalence of the traitor, a topic that has become particularly prominent in contemporary discourses since the scandal of Edward Snowden's revelation of NSA surveillance in 2013. Heated debates about whether whistle-blowers are traitors or heroes continue to feature heavily in public discussion. This question, however, is not new. There is a 'millennia old dialectic' of Jesus and Judas in which hero and traitor are dependent on each other.[7] According to Horn, 'Jesus and Judas, betrayed and betrayer, are a pair: they refer to each other; the hero needs the traitor, a vicarious agent and historical counterfigure, as his negative reflection.'[8]

The concept of betrayal becomes elusive because of its multifarious manifestations. Indeed, betrayal has many faces; traitors can appear as agents, double-agents, defectors, moles, sleepers, partisans, renegades, saboteurs or conspirators. It has therefore proven difficult to establish a single definition of betrayal, although there are certain features generally associated with it.[9] On the one hand, betrayal was and is commonly understood as a serious offence – for Dante it was one of the worst crimes of all; he famously placed traitors in the lowest circle of hell.[10] On the other hand, betrayal is essentially double-dealing, that is, ambivalent, for traitors are arguably caught up in a double-bind of

---

6   Tom Maddox. 'Spy Stories: The Life and Fiction of John Le Carré.' *The Wilson Quarterly* 10.4 (1986): 161.
7   Horn, *The Secret War*, 35.
8   Horn, *The Secret War*, 35.
9   See Betiel Wasihun and Kristina Mendicino (eds). *Playing False – Representations of Betrayal.* Oxford: Peter Lang, 2013.
10 See Dante Alighieri. *The Divine Comedy of Dante Alighieri: Inferno, Purgatory, Paradise.* Transl. Henry Wadsworth Longfellow. New York: The Union Library Association, 1935. 1265–1321 (Inferno, Canto XXXIV, lines 22–45, verses 1–24).

honesty and hypocrisy. As highlighted above, the figure of Judas incarnates the ambivalence of the betrayal that characterizes him. The resulting moral questions have been le Carré's main concern. He insisted on the distinction between 'bad' and 'good' traitors. In all his books, le Carré grapples with the moral legitimacy of betrayal – at least when it is committed by the 'good guys.' For example, his novel *Our Kind of Traitor* (2010) encapsulates his ethical premises: traitors like us are 'the good guys' readers are encouraged to sympathise and identify with.

The traditional spy novel, however, usually follows a simple 'good vs. bad' convention in describing a struggle between hero and antagonist. It is due to the genre that there is nothing in between. In that respect, le Carré has gone down in history as the grand master of the spy novel who has revolutionised the genre's basic structure. His ideal spy is a hero who reveals secrets out of a morally understandable conviction. He is similar to the whistleblower – the discloser or revealer – who creates transparency for the benefit of liberal democracy, thereby defending the individual rights of each person. The notion of a 'positive traitor'[11] evokes an ambiguity that challenges the Manichaeism of the spy narrative. Believing in the existence of 'positive traitors,' and writing against the backdrop of political uncertainty after World War II, le Carré made the moral legitimation of betrayal his main task. Le Carré was still working for MI6 when he began writing. His breakthrough came with his third book, *The Spy Who Came in from the Cold* (1963), after which he turned his back on the (real) world of espionage for good. With this successful novel, le Carré's epitome of a positive traitor also became famous: his legendary spy George Smiley has a brief but important appearance – the character had already premiered as protagonist in le Carré's first novel *Call for the Dead* (1961).

In this chapter, I argue that the 'second world' is le Carré's preferred 'place' – *topos* – for exploring the psychology of the traitor through the spying eyes of his most famous 'secret companion,' George Smiley. In comparing one of his first novels, *The Spy Who Came in from the Cold* (1963), with his post-1990 novel *A Legacy of Spies* (2017), I will shed light on how le Carré's 'retrotopian'[12] settings provide the basis for his ethical account of traitors, whilst also conveying dystopian warnings. In connection with his nostalgic 'return to'[13] an imagined past of the Cold War era, le Carré recreates the period as a laboratory space for his explorations of the ambiguities of traitors and their moral legitimation against the backdrop of intrigue and deception within the covert sphere of intelligence.

---

11 In 2012, I had a personal encounter with John le Carré at an event at Lincoln College at the University of Oxford. When I told him that I was researching the phenomenon of betrayal, the tall John le Carré, alias David Cornwell, bent over me and whispered into my ear in an almost conspiratorial manner that there were 'positive traitors,' too.

12 See Zygmunt Bauman. *Retrotopia*. Cambridge: Polity Press, 2017.

13 Bauman, *Retrotopia*, 10.

The Spy Who Came in from the Cold (1963)

It is a challenge to provide a synopsis of le Carré's breakthrough novel *The Spy Who Came in from the Cold* due to its complexity, subtexts and the double and triple bluffs which keep the readers on their toes. *The Spy Who Came in from the Cold* is the story of a complicated deadly triple bluff perpetrated by British intelligence against its enemies in the German Democratic Republic. The text sets off at an American checkpoint on the Berlin Wall, soon after its construction in 1961. The protagonist Alec Leamas, a British secret agent, is dispatched to the GDR pretending to have defected from MI6, but who is actually ordered to disseminate misleading information about an important East German intelligence officer. He becomes a double agent to bring down the head of the Communist intelligence agency in East Germany. Leamas had worked from West Berlin but was recalled to England after the head of counterintelligence in the Ministry of State Security (MfS, more commonly referred to as the Stasi), Hans-Dieter Mundt, destroyed Leamas's network of agents in the GDR. To make his defection seem plausible to the East German secret service, Leamas's social decline was feigned, and it was while this was underway that he met and fell in love with Liz Gold, a British communist. At the end it is revealed that Mundt was actually a British spy.

The following depiction is noteworthy insofar as it captures the tone and ambience of this historical period in ways that permeate the entire narrative:

> It was cold that morning; the light mist was damp and grey, pricking the skin. The airport reminded Leamas of the war [...] Everywhere that air of conspiracy which generates among people who have been up since dawn – of superiority almost, derived from the common experience of having seen the night disappear and the morning come.[14]

The notion of chill and indifference evokes an opposition between the *outside* (external spaces) and the *inside* (inner spaces) that structures the entire narrative. The title *The Spy Who Came in from the Cold* functions as a leitmotif, foreshadowing the development of the spy from a marionette of false plays to a morally conscious human being. The title reference to 'coming in' means 'coming home,' in other words 'becoming human.' This view is further underscored by 'Control,' the character who is head of the Secret Service (the 'Circus'[15]), who briefs Leamas for a mission:

> 'We have to live without sympathy,' Control muses. Then adds: 'That's impossible, of course. We act it to one another, all this hardness; but we aren't like that really. I mean ...

---

14 John le Carré. *The Spy Who Came in from the Cold*. London: Penguin Books, 2011. 71.
15 The unofficial name of MI6 headquarters in the 1960s due to its location at Cambridge Circus.

one can't be out in the cold all the time; one has to come in from the cold ... d'you see what I mean?' (*Spy* 17)

The end of the novel, however, evokes a contradiction, reinforcing the importance of Leamas's choice not 'to come in from the cold' as a spy (he refuses the option to survive offered by his colleagues) but as a person, as an empathic and responsible human being. Both Leamas and Liz had trusted Smiley, unaware that she was under observation by the Stasi and had become pivotal to MI6's covert operation, which included Smiley's visit to Liz and the settlement of her flat lease. When Leamas finally realises that Smiley had never intended to save Liz but that by double-checking on her whereabouts he had only wanted to make sure that she was dead, all the betrayals he had suffered culminate in this very final betrayal.[16] Leamas was left with no other ethically sound option but to commit suicide by climbing back down to the wall to the East, ignoring the 'voice in English from the Western side of the Wall [saying] "Jump, Alec! Jump, man!"' (*Spy* 253), whereupon he is shot just like Liz. This act of loyalty towards the woman he loves demonstrates what the final chapter's title 'In From the Cold' promises – namely a process of humanisation, a homecoming of the human – which is ultimately possible only through death. Here, destruction and humanisation coincide. Written in the tradition of classical British spy thrillers such as Joseph Conrad's *Under Western Eyes* (1911), which also explores betrayal and love as intertwined motifs, le Carré's spies find themselves undermining popular and morally unambiguous spy fiction such as Ian Fleming's novels.[17] Their protagonist James Bond, or so le Carré argued in a 1966 interview with Malcolm Muggeridge, does not represent the moral challenges of the period which he came to symbolize:

I'm not sure that Bond is a spy. Nor for that matter is he a mystic. I think it's a great mistake if one is talking about espionage literature to include Bond in this category at all. It seems to me he's more some kind of international gangster with, as they said, a license to kill. He's a man with unlimited movement, but he's a man entirely out of the political context...It's the consumer goods ethic, really. That everything around you, all the dull things of life, are suddenly animated by this wonderful cache of espionage.[18]

---

16 Cf. William Boyd. 'Rereading: *The Spy Who Came in from the Cold* by John le Carré.' *The Guardian.* 24 June 2010. <https://www.theguardian.com/books/2010/jul/24/carre-spy-came-cold-boyd> (accessed 20 Jan 2024).

17 See Jeremy Hawthorn. *Studying the Novel.* Eighth Edition. London: Bloomsbury Academic, 2023. 104–105.

18 Dyer Murphy. 'John le Carré and the most interesting author interview you will ever see.' *CrimeReads.* 10 Dec 2020. <https://crimereads.com/john-le-carre-and-the-most-interesting-author-interview-you-will-ever-see/> (accessed 20 Jan 2024).

The world of the Cold War, as portrayed by le Carré, offers an ambience of divisions, intrigues, suspicion, and mistrust, all of which reflect the morally compromised frame of mind of traitors and spies.

Furthermore, it is noteworthy – as William Boyd observes – that there is an omniscient narrative point of view which is a rather unusual perspective in spy narratives, a genre that arguably prefers limited narrative perspectives. Boyd states that le Carré's is

> a dangerous choice, because with authorial omniscience you cannot have your cake and eat it. If you are saying to the reader that you can enter the thoughts of any character and can comment on the action or events in your own voice, then any deliberate withholding of information counts as a black mark. The narrative house-of-cards begins to collapse; the reader's trust in the author's control dissipates immediately.[19]

Boyd's reflections are important because narrative perspectives establish the epistemological parameters of the respective fictional worlds created. Indeed, there is a danger here since the authorial – or omniscient – narrator is 'reminiscent of surveillance practices [...] in the broadest understanding of the term.'[20] As a result, the authorial narrator (not the author: Boyd is imprecise here) becomes suspicious for the reader – unreliable and thus not trustworthy.

And yet, there is a quest for reliability and trustworthiness in *The Spy Who Came in from the Cold* which presents a world that is marked by instabilities, lack of loyalties and moralities. Against this backdrop, Leamas's outburst towards the end of the novel, summarising the resentments he has against the deeds committed in the name of his country, is significant:

> 'What do you think spies are: priests, saints and martyrs? They're a squalid procession of vain fools, traitors too, yes; pansies, sadists and drunkards, people who play cowboys and Indians to brighten their rotten lives. Do you think they sit like monks in London, balancing the rights and wrongs?' (*Spy* 243)

Leamas – taking on a double identity as a defector – is lamenting the lack of ethical consciousness in spies and describes them as pathetic human beings.

---

19 Boyd, 'Rereading: *The Spy Who Came in from the Cold* by John le Carré.'
20 Betiel Wasihun. 'Resisting Authority: Surveillance in Contemporary American and German Fiction.' *Narrating Surveillance – Überwachung erzählen.* Ed. Betiel Wasihun. Baden-Baden: Ergon, 2019. 172. Even considering the legitimate controversy in narrative theory regarding the equation between authorial narrators and surveilling entities (see Dorrit Cohn. 'Optics and Power in the Novel.' *New Literary History* 26 (1995): 3–20; John Bender. *Imagining the Penitentiary: Fiction and the Architecture of Mind in Eighteenth-Century England.* Chicago: University of Chicago Press, 1987; Mark Seltzer. *Henry James and the Art of Power.* Ithaca, NY: Cornell UP, 1984), analogies between surveillance strategies and narrative techniques can be made on a symbolic level (see Wasihun, 'Resisting Authority,' 170–175; and also Monika Fludernik. *Towards a 'Natural' Narratology.* London: Routledge, 1996. 368–369).

However, he himself proves to be quite the opposite. As the end of the novel suggests, he turns out to be a spy with moral principles.

Retrotopia for Traitors: *A Legacy of Spies* (2017)

Fifty-four years after the publication of *The Spy Who came in from the Cold*, le Carré published *A Legacy of Spies* which is a case in point for how the East-West encounters during the Cold War have become le Carré's *retrotopia* in Zygmunt Bauman's understanding of the term. According to Bauman, 'retrotopia' emerges from a significant shift in common perception 'from investing public hopes of improvement in the uncertain and ever-too-obviously untrustworthy future, to re-investing them in the vaguely remembered past, valued for its assumed stability and so trustworthiness.'[21] Similar to the past remembered nostalgically, the significance of the retrotopian past is not historical accuracy but that it provides a *topos* for hopes that can be 'located in the lost/stolen/abandoned but undead past.'[22] In other words, (the belief in) progress is not solely dependent on the past. Instead of gesturing towards a (linear) development of a somehow better future, it is projected as an intrinsic quality onto the past. Moreover, Bauman's concept of the 'retrotopia derives its stimulus from the hope of reconciling, at long last, *security* with *freedom*.'[23] In this way, le Carré's fiction can be understood as retrotopian because it is not merely a 'romance with the past'[24] but is more invested in the potential of an imagined past[25] as a reference point for reflection on the present.

Although published in 2017, the focus of *A Legacy of Spies* lies on the Cold War period, following up on the central narrative strands in *The Spy Who Came in from the Cold*. *A Legacy of Spies* is in fact both prequel and sequel to le Carré's third novel and works as a commentary on the latter, helping to understand his most famous and arguably most complex spy thriller. The notion of 'retro,' that is 'backward,' in 'retrotopia' is thus performed on various levels, since *A Legacy of Spies* revisits and illuminates *The Spy Who came in from the Cold* and its 'second world' setting. In the 2017 pre/sequel, British secret agent Peter Guillam, who recounts the story from a first-person perspective, has retired to a remote farm in Brittany when he receives a letter from London summoning him to MI6 headquarters. The secret intelligence service's legal adviser, A. Butterfield, known as

---

21 Bauman, *Retrotopia*, 6.
22 Bauman, *Retrotopia*, 5.
23 Bauman, *Retrotopia*, 8.
24 Bauman, *Retrotopia*, 9.
25 '[N]ot the past […] "as it genuinely was,"' as Bauman writes with reference to Leopold von Ranke (*Retrotopia*, 10).

'Bunny,' and a historian whose first name is Laura question Guillam about past operations, for which the Circus's files have disappeared.

The interrogation soon focuses on two operations – namely 'Mayflower' and 'Windfall' – from the late 1950s and early 1960s, respectively, at the peak of the Cold War marked by dangerous confrontations like the Cuban missile crisis in 1962. 'Mayflower' was the code name for East German doctor Karl Riemeck, who became a British spy. He established contact with 'Tulip' (Doris Gamp), leading to Guillam's involvement. When 'Tulip's' cover was at risk, the British exfiltrated her from East Germany. However, she later died, manipulated by East German spy Hans-Dieter Mundt. Control initiated an operation to support Mundt against Stasi rival Josef Fiedler. Alec Leamas was sent to establish Mundt's loyalty, but his tragic fate, along with his girlfriend Liz Gold, implicated Smiley and Guillam. This event also weakened their division 'Covert' against the rival 'Joint' division led by the traitor Bill Haydon, later exposed as the Soviet mole.

Now the former spies of British Intelligence are sued by the children of the victims – Christoph Leamas, Karen Gold and Gustav Quinz – who blame them for ruthless Cold War spy operations long after Guillam and Smiley have retired. Gustav – Tulip's son – blames Peter Guillam because he had incited Doris Gamp to commit acts that she could not reconcile with her conscience. Only after hiring his own lawyer does Guillam realise that the key to his defence lies in the disclosure of all the documents about the failed operations that have been set aside on Smiley's behalf. He manages to track down George Smiley, who now lives in Freiburg and grants Guillam release of the documents. At the end of the novel, well after these events, Guillam returns to his tranquil life in Brittany, though he continues to anticipate letters from England.

As stated above, *A Legacy of Spies* offers a retrospective of the espionage missions depicted in *The Spy Who Came in from the Cold*. The protagonist of the 2017 novel is forced to account for his actions during 'Operation Windfall' – and he is full of 'outrage at having [his] past dug up and thrown in (his) face,' as he admits at the beginning of chapter 7.[26] The story alternates between Guillam's recollections of the events that led up to Leamas's downfall, the attempts at justification in Guillam's present and the revelation of the many files that had been hidden and through which he is now plodding.

The novel's opening paragraphs introduce the protagonist, Guillam, as coming to terms with his treacherous acts of the past that are now catching up with him. The opening passage reveals many important details, explaining main incidents of le Carré's third novel:

---

26 John le Carré. *A Legacy of Spies*. London: Penguin Books, 2017. 139.

> What follows is a *truthful account*, as best I am able to provide it, of my role in the British *deception operation*, codenamed Windfall, that was mounted against the East German Intelligence Service (Stasi) in the late nineteen fifties and early sixties, and resulted in the death of the best British secret agent I ever worked with, and of the innocent woman for whom he gave his life. (*Legacy* 1; emphases added)

With the very first sentence the first-person narrator distances himself from what is believed to be the spy's main task, namely: discovering secret information incognito. The homodiegetic narrator demonstrates a desire to assume responsibility for his actions and to disclose the truth about his past complicity in keeping secrets. Fifty years later, *uncovering* secrets has become the main duty of the former secret agent. Both the story and narrative perspective aim at rehabilitating the spy as a complex human being struggling with the ethical ambivalence of his work. *A Legacy of Spies* begins where *The Spy Who Came in from the Cold* ends. The fact that we are now encountering a first-person narrator must be read along these lines. The quest for moral truth is at the heart of *A Legacy of Spies*. At the end of the novel, George Smiley notably reflects that 'an old spy in his dotage seeks the truth of ages' (*Legacy* 345–346).

In Defence of 'Positive Traitors'

Interestingly, in both of the novels discussed here, George Smiley hardly appears in person but his central importance is made clear nevertheless as he impresses with his *absent presence*. In one of the opening passages of *A Legacy of Spies*, Peter Guillam casts off any guilt and responsibility for his acts and reproaches Smiley and Control:

> If you're looking for scalps, I told them, go to those grand masters of deception George Smiley and his master, Control. It was their refined cunning, I insisted, their devious scholarly intellects, not mine, that delivered the triumph and the anguish that was Windfall. (*Legacy* 1–2)

Guillam is consistent in shifting blame; at the end of the narrative, he reiterates his reproaches towards George Smiley for the acts of betrayal he ended up committing:

> Who was to blame for my lifetime of dutiful dissembling, if not George Smiley? Was it *I* who had suggested I should befriend Liz Gold? Was it *my* idea to lie to Alec, our tethered goat, as Tabitha had called him – then watch him walk into the trap George had set for Mundt? (*Legacy* 344)

George Smiley is the prime example of le Carré's understanding of a 'positive traitor.' The author created a character who was diametrically opposed to Ian Fleming's popular James Bond figure, which he thought was a misinterpretation of real espionage life. Smiley lacks the glamorous, suave qualities that have made Fleming's agent popular: he is described as overweight, short, bald, and wearing glasses. Moreover, Smiley is modest and polite, which conceals and belies his genius as a spy.

> Smiley is an idealist wrapped in an enigma. Half the time he puts up with life as a reclusive scholarly figure, regularly cuckolded by his aristocrat wife and disobliged by ambitious, purblind colleagues. When yoked into action he embodies the best one would expect of the Western democratic conscience.[27]

It is this characterization that forms the foundation of his career as one of the most powerful British spies. Remarkably, *The Guardian* has referred to George Smiley as 'the sort of spy this country believes it ought to have: a bit shabby, academic, basically loyal, and sceptical of the enthusiasms of his political masters.'[28] Maddox argues that the contrast between Smiley's remarkable abilities and his ordinary appearance

> embodies a humanity that is consistently at odds with his profession. The secret service wishes to dispense with that humanity, the consensus on high being that humane virtues have outlasted whatever limited usefulness they might have had.[29]

The potential ethical conflict between the morals of the individual agent and the political agenda of the institution for which he works has been recognized as a distinctive feature of the 'new realist school' of British spy thrillers by le Carré and Len Deighton, among others:

> The combination of unknowability and alienation made the spy novel one of the key Cold War genres, […] which exchanged the sensationalism of earlier espionage writers for gritty accounts of subterfuge, betrayal and death. With its focus on the unchecked power of institutions, and particularly on the solitary agent 'out in the cold,' spy fiction was not without dystopian qualities, evoking a 'worst of all possible worlds' composed of political violence and existential despair. As a result, criticism was soon arguing that the spy narrative is 'a major expressive phenomenon of modern culture' and that '[t]he soul of the spy is somehow the model of our own.'[30]

In his writing after the end of the Cold War, le Carré's retrospective look back on and relationship with the 'second world' as *retrotopia* is twofold. On the one hand, the 'second world' is depicted as an ideal setting for exploring the ambiguities of the traitor. The moral distance, the ruthless ambition and pursuit of political interests, and the inhumanity shaping this historical period still justify

---

27 Richard Bradford. *The Novel Now: Contemporary British Fiction.* New York: Wiley, 2009. 110.
28 'In the Praise of George Smiley.' Editorial. The Guardian. 6 Sept 2011. <https://www.thegua rdian.com/commentisfree/2011/sep/06/in-praise-of-george-smiley> (accessed 15 Feb 24).
29 Maddox, 'Spy Stories,' 166.
30 Andrew Hammond. *Cold War Stories: British Dystopian Fiction, 1945–1990.* Basingstoke: Palgrave Macmillan, 2017. 43.

and possibly vindicate deceptive operations, false plays, and betrayals. And even if the treacheries of cold war espionage do not resonate as much as they used to, le Carré seems to be suggesting that the divisiveness of the period still impacts upon present times. In other words, his re-creation of the bygone second world bears dystopian warnings. He seems to be conveying that the heritage of the Cold War represents a latent threat with potentially disastrous outcomes. According to Synder, the 'artistry of *Legacy* consists in its oblique reappraisal of the Cold War past as both a diametrical contrast to and formative matrix of the present era.'[31]

As is well known, le Carré was very critical of contemporary political developments and expressed his discontent openly. He was worried about the geopolitical location of the West in the light of a present which was lacking in orientation, in any sense of direction. In an interview shortly before the publication of *A Legacy of Spies* he was asked why he had actually decided to revisit the Cold War in this novel, and le Carré replied that he felt a discomfort about 'this vacuum in which we live at the moment' when 'everything [...] is up for grabs.'[32] In another interview with the National Public Radio, he made this point even more explicit, when he was asked why he wrote 'about a spy forced to face his responsibility for two deaths decades ago':

> I think because, back then, we had a clear philosophy which we thought we were protecting. And it was a notion of the West. It was a notion of individual freedom, of inclusiveness, of tolerance – all of that we called anti-communism. That was really a broad brush because there were many decent people who lived in communist territories who weren't as bad as one might suppose. But now, today, this present time in which these matters are being reconsidered in my novel, we seem to have no direction.
> We seem to be joined by nothing very much except fear and bewilderment about what the future holds. We have no coherent ideology in the West, and we used to believe in the great American example. I think that's recently been profoundly undermined for us. We're alone.[33]

In that very same interview, le Carré also expressed how dismissive he was of the 'appalling' support for Brexit in the United Kingdom and the rise of Trumpocracy in the United States:

> I think I feel most strongly about the timing of Brexit, which is appalling. At the very moment when Europe needs to be a coherent single bloc able to protect itself morally, politically, and if necessary, militarily, we've left it. And we're stuck in the Atlantic and, as George Smiley remarks, himself, citizens of nowhere at the moment.[34]

---

31 R.L. Synder. 'Secret Cold Warriors.' *Orbis Litterarum* (75) 2020: 15–23.
32 Stuart Lyall. 'Spies like us.' *New York Times Book Review* (27 Aug 2017): 15–17.
33 Terry Gross. 'Novelist John Le Carré Reflects On His Own "Legacy" Of Spying.' *Fresh Air*. National Public Radio 5 September 2017. Transcript. <https://www.npr.org/transcripts/54863 2065> (accessed 21 Jan 2024).
34 Gross, 'Novelist John Le Carré Reflects.'

Moreover, on the same occasion le Carré articulates that with writing *A Legacy of Spies* he wanted 'to make a case for Europe which has now become an endangered species' – especially in the wake of Brexit and its pivotal actors like Theresa May, to whose criticism of elite cosmopolitanism in 2016 he refers: 'If you believe you're a citizen of the world, you're a citizen of nowhere. You don't understand what the very word 'citizenship' means.'[35] What is at the heart of Bauman's concept of 'retrotopia' resonates with le Carré's line of thought: 'The road to future turns looks uncannily [like] a trail of corruption and degeneration. Perhaps the road back, to the past, won't miss the chance of turning into a trail of cleansing from the damages committed by futures, whenever they turned into a present?'[36] Towards the end of the novel, when Guillam finally encounters Smiley, there is an important dialogue substantiating the author's intention. Guillam is shifting guilt and responsibility again but this time from Smiley to Control and Mundt in an attempt to comfort Smiley: '"But George," I protest. "Windfall was Control's operation. You just went along with it." / "Which is by far the greater sin, I fear. [...]"' (*Legacy* 348). As opposed to Guillam – whom Smiley calls a 'loyal foot soldier' whose job was not to ask 'why the sun rose every morning' (*Legacy* 350), thereby relieving Guillam's guilt – Smiley stands by his guilt and is quite conscious about his moral wrongdoings: 'We were not pitiless, Peter. We were *never* pitiless. We had the larger pity. Arguably it was misplaced. Certainly it was futile. We know that now. We did not know it then' (*Legacy* 349).

The George Smiley in *A Legacy of Spies* is drawn as a character who is morally conscious and at peace with himself. Building on his characterization as embodying the conscience of liberal democracy, he remains 'a sceptic, distrusting of all abstract systems of ideology, but [with ...] an instinctive, empowering recognition of the basic distinctions between right and wrong.'[37] At the end of chapter 13, Smiley gives an account of his actions, that is, of his many acts of betrayal:

> 'So was it all for *England,* then?' he resumed. 'There was a time, of course there was. But *whose* England? Which England? England all alone, a citizen of nowhere? I'm a European, Peter. If I had a mission – if I was ever aware of one beyond our business with the enemy, it was to Europe. If I was heartless, I was heartless for Europe. If I had an unattainable ideal, it was of leading Europe out of her darkness towards a new age of reason. I have it still.' (*Legacy* 350–351)

35 Theresa May. 'Speech at the 2018 Conservative *Party* Conference in Birmingham.' *The Spectator.* 5 October 2016. <https://www.spectator.co.uk/article/full-text-theresa-may-s-con ference-speech/> (accessed 31 Jan 2024).
36 Bauman, *Retrotopia*, 6.
37 Bradford, *The Novel Now*, 110.

Smiley explains that the incentive for his intelligence work was motivated by the hope to contribute to stabilising peace. He states that he has acted for the 'greater good' which resonates with the author's own voice. Asked in a radio interview whether he had 'to suppress [his] humanity [...] to be a good spy,' le Carré admits:

> Yes, I did. In the greater cause, I felt I had to suppress my humanity. I – where I was, asking people to do things, I tried to persuade them that they were doing it for the greater good. And I was doing it for the greater good. Where I had to deceive people, I felt I was doing that for the greater good, too. But then you get – you get alongside the borderline of how much of this stuff can we do and remain a society that is worth protecting?[38]

John le Carré invented George Smiley as the embodiment of the 'positive traitor' whose deceptions and lies were justified by his ambition to contribute to higher, and morally unambiguous, goals. The author's motivation clearly was to defend the existence of 'positive traitors' outside his fictional worlds of spies as well. Ultimately, however, 'positive traitors' never get rid of their moral ambiguity – be it in the fictional or real world. This is why, as Peter Guillam observes, George Smiley *freezes* right after his moral account of his deeds which he justified through his utilitarian view on the world:

> A silence, deeper, longer than any I remembered, even from the worst times. The fluid contours of the face frozen, the brow tipped forward, shadowy eyelids lowered. A forefinger rises absently to the bridge of his spectacles, checking that they are still in place. Until, with a shake of the head as if to rid it of a bad dream, he smiled. (*Legacy* 351)

The retrotopian settings of the Cold War era in the novels discussed have both inspired the author's imagination and provided an ideal scenario for psychological explorations of various kinds of traitors as its complex and opaque ambience of treachery, deception, and double standards mirrors the intricate inner states of traitors. Le Carré kept revisiting this 'elsewhere'[39] fictionally to gain a better understanding of the present and future after the end of the Cold War. His core belief in acting for the 'greater good' helped to justify the moral dilemma traitors are by definition caught up in.[40] Spies, whistleblowers, and secret agents are as ambivalent as they are perceived. They are heroes to some, traitors to others. Not surprisingly, the ambivalence of the traitor is also at the heart of the posthumously published novel *Silverview* (2021). The question of the moral legitimacy of betrayal has survived le Carré.

---

38 Gross, 'Novelist John Le Carré Reflects.'
39 Bauman, *Retrotopia*, 3.
40 See also Myron J. Aronoff. *The Spy Novels of John Le Carré, Balancing Ethics and Politics*. New York: Palgrave Macmillan, 1999. [Online]. Available: https://doi.org/10.1057/9780312299453. Accessed: 13 Jan 2024; especially the last chapter on 'Learning to Live with Ambiguity: Balancing Ethical and Political Imperatives,' 201–214.

References

Alighieri, Dante. *The Divine Comedy of Dante Alighieri: Inferno, Purgatory, Paradise*. Transl. Henry Wadsworth Longfellow. New York: The Union Library Association, 1935.

Aronoff, Myron J. *The Spy Novels of John Le Carré. Balancing Ethics and Politics*. New York: Palgrave Macmillan, 1999. [Online]. Available: https://doi.org/10.1057/9780312299453. Accessed: 13 Jan 2024.

Bauman, Zygmunt. *Retrotopia*. Cambridge: Polity Press, 2017.

Bender, John. *Imagining the Penitentiary: Fiction and the Architecture of Mind in Eighteenth-Century England*. Chicago: University of Chicago Press, 1987.

Boveri, Margret. *Der Verrat im 20. Jahrhundert*, 4 vols. Hamburg: Rowohlt, 1956–1960.

Boyd, William. 'Rereading: *The Spy Who Came in from the Cold* by John le Carré.' *The Guardian*. 24 June 2010. <https://www.theguardian.com/books/2010/jul/24/carre-spy-came-cold-boyd> (accessed 20 Jan 2024).

Bradford, Richard. *The Novel Now: Contemporary British Fiction*. New York: Wiley, 2009.

Cohn, Dorrit. 'Optics and Power in the Novel.' *New Literary History* 26 (1995): 3–20.

Fludernik, Monika. *Towards a 'Natural' Narratology*. London: Routledge, 1996.

Gross, Terry. 'Novelist John Le Carré Reflects On His Own "Legacy" Of Spying.' *Fresh Air*. National Public Radio 5 September 2017. Transcript. <https://www.npr.org/transcripts/548632065> (accessed 21 Jan 2024).

Hammond, Andrew. *Cold War Stories: British Dystopian Fiction, 1945–1990*. Basingstoke: Palgrave Macmillan, 2017.

Hepburn, Allan. *Intrigue: Espionage and Culture*. New Haven, CT: Yale University Press, 2005.

Hawthorn, Jeremy. *Studying the Novel*. Eighth Edition. London: Bloomsbury Academic, 2023.

Horn, Eva. *The Secret War: Treason, Espionage, and Modern Fiction*. Evanston, Illinois: Northwestern University Press, 2013.

'In the Praise of George Smiley.' Editorial. *The Guardian*. 6 Sept 2011. <https://www.theguardian.com/commentisfree/2011/sep/06/in-praise-of-george-smiley> (accessed 15 Feb 24).

le Carré, John. *The Spy Who Came in from the Cold*. London: Penguin Books, 2011.

–. *A Legacy of Spies*. London: Penguin Books, 2017.

Lyall, Stuart. 'Spies like us.' *New York Times Book Review* (27 Aug 2017): 15–17.

Maddox, Tom. 'Spy Stories: The Life and Fiction of John Le Carré.' *The Wilson Quarterly* 10.4 (1986): 158–170. [Online]. Available: http://www.jstor.org/stable/40257078. Accessed: 18 Jan 2024.

Manning, Toby. *John le Carré and the Cold War*. London: Bloomsbury, 2018.

May, Theresa. 'Speech at the 2018 Conservative *Party* Conference in Birmingham.' *The Spectator*. 5 October 2016. <https://www.spectator.co.uk/article/full-text-theresa-may-s-conference-speech/> (accessed 31 Jan 2024).

Murphy, Dyer. 'John le Carré and the most interesting author interview you will ever see.' *CrimeReads*. 10 Dec 2020. <https://crimereads.com/john-le-carre-and-the-most-interesting-author-interview-you-will-ever-see/> (accessed 20 Jan 2024).

Richelson, Jeffrey T. *A Century of Spies. Intelligence in the Twentieth Century*. Oxford: Oxford University Press, 1995.

Seltzer, Mark. *Henry James and the Art of Power*. Ithaca, NY: Cornell University Press, 1984.

Synder, R.L. 'Secret Cold Warriors.' *Orbis Litterarum* (75) 2020: 15–23.

Wasihun, Betiel and Kristina Mendicino (eds). *Playing False – Representations of Betrayal*. Oxford: Peter Lang, 2013.

Wasihun, Betiel. 'Resisting Authority: Surveillance in Contemporary American and German Fiction.' *Narrating Surveillance – Überwachung erzählen*. Ed. Betiel Wasihun. Baden-Baden: Ergon, 2019. 169–191.

Robert Kusek

'Like a spectre lurking inside [her]': The 'Second World' in Deborah Levy's Writing[1]

Deborah Levy: A Central European writer?

On 26 October 2019, the acclaimed Polish novelist Olga Tokarczuk, who only two weeks before had been named the winner of the 2018 Nobel Prize in Literature, took part in the Conrad Festival, a major literary event held annually in the city of Kraków, where she conversed with the distinguished literary critic and academic Michał Paweł Markowski. At one point, Markowski asked the new Nobel Prize laureate about her relationship with fellow writers, as well as her 'elective affinity [/-ies]' in the 'world republic of letters.'[2] In her response, Tokarczuk put special emphasis on a sense of 'kinship' that characterises her relations with other Central European writers, the Bulgarian novelist Georgi Gospodinov in partic-ular, as well as their shared feeling of belonging to the Central European 'im-agined mother/fatherland.'[3] However, she soon hastened to explain that the before-mentioned feeling of belonging neither follows the laws of geography nor succumbs to the regimes of national identities. To prove her point, she listed one example of this transnational kinship, namely the South Africa-born British writer Deborah Levy. 'Oh, this simply means that she *is* from Central Europe,'[4] Markowski immediately retorted.

Although Markowski's somewhat jocular and essentially rhetorical remark had no ambition to build any serious argument with regard to Levy's identity or aesthetic position, it strikes one with its unintentional incisiveness and accuracy;

---

1 This research was funded in whole by the National Science Centre, Poland, grant no. 2020/39/ B/HS2/02083. For the purpose of Open Access, the author has applied a CC-BY public copy-right licence to any Author Accepted Manuscript (AAM) version arising from this submission.
2 Pascale Casanova. *The World Republic of Letters*. Transl. M.B. DeBevoise. Cambridge and London: Harvard University Press, 2004. 338.
3 Olga Tokarczuk and Michał Paweł Markowski. 'Postacie na wolności.' *Tygodnik Powszechny* 45 (2019). 12 Sept 2023, <https://www.tygodnikpowszechny.pl/postacie-na-wolnosci-160985>.
4 Olga Tokarczuk and Michał Paweł Markowski. 'Spotkanie z Olgą Tokarczuk na Conrad Fes-tiwal.' *Facebook.com*. 26 Oct 2019. <https://www.facebook.com/130216013661699/videos/540 125593229241> (accessed 12 Sept 2023). [emphasis added].

as does Tokarczuk's claim about a special kind of 'kinship' or affinity that exists between Levy and Central European literary and cultural (especially visual) tradition. The very assertion that Levy, who was born in Johannesburg in 1959 into the family of Jewish immigrants from Lithuania, might belong more to the Central European 'hinternational'[5] (grand-)motherland[6] than to South Africa (where she was born and grew up), Britain (where she attended schools, raised a family with the playwright David Gale, and lived), or France (where she now resides), finds substantial anchoring in Levy's diverse body of works, starting with her 1985 play *Pax*. The Keeper, one of the play's four characters and, simultaneously, an archetype of Europe and its past, will repeatedly voice her (and, one assumes, her creator's) desire for the 'other' Europe which, in the aftermath of WWII, remains inaccessible to her. She will chant the following lines again and again: 'I want to go back to Prague'; 'I want to go back to Yugoslavia'; 'I want to go back to Romania'; 'I want to go back to Slavia […].'[7] Over the next two decades, the pages of Levy's consecutive works of fiction will be – in a truly unprecedented manner – populated by a plethora of Central European characters who 'by a strange set of circumstances' (*Pax* 46) have found themselves in Western Europe and for whom the experience of dislocation and the loss of home have induced in them a 'set of intellectual, psychological, and aesthetic displacements'[8]: the likes of Lapinski from her debut novel *Beautiful Mutants* of 1989, Monika from *The Unloved* (1994), Magret's Polish lover from 'Vienna' (2007), Józef Nowogrodzki from *Swimming Home* (2011), or Pavel from 'Pillow Talk' (2013), to name but a few. Those Central European 'wanderers, bums, émigrés, refugees, deportees, ramblers'[9] will be described by Levy as the continent's 'eerie child[ren]' who are 'disoriented, […] walk[ing] in zigzags, […] displaced and dizzy' (*Geography* 153, 173, 148) In their nostalgic search for their potentially 'redemptive' homeland

---

5 After Claudio Magris, I understand 'hinternationalism' as an instrument to acknowledge a mutual embeddedness of discontinuous hinterland topographies, identities, and histories, as well as a means to annul the restrictive homogeneity of the imperial gaze and cartography. Claudio Magris. *Danube: A Sentimental Journey from the Source to the Black Sea*. Trans. Patrick Creagh. New York: Farrar, Straus and Giroux, 2008, 24.

6 Deborah's paternal grandparents came to South Africa from Krekenava in Lithuania. In an interview that Deborah Levy gave to Robert Kusek and Wojciech Szymański, she talks about the formative role played by her paternal grandmother in introducing the idea of Central Europe to her. Deborah Levy. 'Two Silver Herrings.' Interview by Robert Kusek and Wojciech Szymański. 23 Jan 2023. Unpublished.

7 Deborah Levy. *Pax*. Deborah Levy. *Plays: I*. London: Methuen Drama, 2000. 8, 14, 19. What should be noted is that the Keeper desires a wide array of spaces/places that constitute the 'other' Europe: its capitals (Prague), real states (Romania), or imaginative ethnospaces (Slavia).

8 André Aciman. *Alibis: Essays on Elsewhere*. New York: Farrar, Straus and Giroux, 2011. 197.

9 Deborah Levy. *Swallowing Geography*. Deborah Levy. *Early Levy*. London: Penguin Books, 2014. 173, 148.

(*Geography* 153), they will be joined by other characters who, despite no obvious links to the 'second world,' will be overtaken by their often inexplicable Central European nostomania-cum-nostophobia, namely the commixture of obsession with and fear of Central Europe. While travelling (both physically and imaginatively) to Czechia ('Shining a Light'), (East) Germany (*Swallowing Geography*), or Poland ('Black Vodka'), Levy's characters do not follow the existing maps but, instead, create their own – the kinds that can 'swallow geography,' as the metaphorical title of Levy's 1993 novel suggests. The process of unlearning geography is supplemented by the act of unlearning one's own inheritance and electing a new homeland. If 'to name someone is to give them a country,' as the narrator of *Swallowing Geography* argues (183), the Kafkaesque initials 'J.K.' selected by the protagonist of the book unambiguously point to the choice that she has made: her (imagined) homeland is Central Europe. It is also, one may argue, an elected home of Deborah Levy.

Levy's election of Central Europe as her intellectual and aesthetic *(grand-) matrimoine* should be traced to the period when Levy studied at the Dartington College of Arts, where she was first exposed to theatrical practices from Central Europe – especially the work of the experimental theatrical company Akademia Ruchu [Academy of Movement/Behaviour] and one of its founders Andrzej Maria Borkowski. Borkowski, who in the 1980s escaped state-socialist Poland and settled in Britain, not only performed in the original 1985 production of *Clam* (in which he played Lenin) but also designed the cover for Levy's first short story collection *Ophelia and the Great Idea* (1989), as well as created the cover and provided illustrations for the first edition of her poetic piece *An Amorous Discourse in the Suburbs of Hell* (1990). It was also in the early 1980s that Levy discovered the work of the Polish visual artist and playwright Tadeusz Kantor and performer Zofia Kalińska. The former, whose plays Levy saw when they were staged at the Riverside Studios in 1980 and 1982,[10] should certainly be recognised as one of her major influences – particularly Kantor's exploration of the theme of repression and forgetfulness, the role of objects and images in the process of excavating one's painful history and confronting one's traumas, or his playing with time.[11] The latter provided an impetus for Levy's seminal 1988 journey to communist Poland where she documented the workshop held by Kalińska for an international group of actors and performers.

Levy's Central European affinities did not disappear with the collapse of the Iron Curtain. In 2016, she published *Stardust Nation*, a graphic novel which was

---

10 Katarzyna Murawska-Muthesius and Natalia Zarzycka (eds). *Kantor Was Here*. London: Black Dog Publishing, 2011. 182.

11 See Levy, 'Two Silver Herrings' and Jacques Testard. 'Interview with Deborah Levy.' *The White Review* (August 2013). 10 Sept 2023, <https://www.thewhitereview.org/feature/interview-deborah-levy/>.

the result of an artistic collaboration with the Polish artist Andrzej Klimowski, her colleague from the Royal College of Art. Among her recent sources of inspiration, one should also find the Czech film-maker Věra Chytilová, the Prague-based visual artist Tereza Stehlíková, or the surrealist artist Eva Švankmajerová who is referenced in *The Man Who Saw Everything* (2019). In an interview that she gave in January 2023, while speaking of her life-long relationship with Central European artists, she unambiguously acknowledged her intendedness to them: 'I am the sum of all those influences, I have nothing but gratitude to the [Central European] artists who lit up my imagination, who had skills, incredible skills and strategies with which to speak, even if it was silence. [...] [M]y influences are from Central Europe. They are.'[12]

Traces of those influences are to be found throughout Levy's writing. One of their most explicit articulations is in her 2013 collection of short stories entitled *Black Vodka* in which she explores a variety of Central European motifs, tropes, and topographies. A piece that appears to be particularly relevant in the context of the present discussion is the titular short story 'Black Vodka' which focuses on the main character/narrator – a copywriter who works on a promotional campaign for a new brand of vodka – and his potential romance with a woman named Lisa whom he invites for a dinner at the Polish Club in London. However, instead of a conventional love story, the readers of 'Black Vodka' are exposed to a surrealist narrative about Central European heritage and its fate. Although the book's diegesis understood as 'l'univers où advient cette histoire [the universe where the story takes place]'[13] is unmistakably British, it is Central Europe that becomes a permanent point of reference for the main character and a lens through which he perceives the reality. 'Instructed in the art of Not Belonging,' he reads his life, the life of a 'lost property' through the prism of Central European traumatic history (e. g. when he is bullied at school, he interprets it as a 'sort of ethnic cleansing').[14] Wartime and post-WWII Poland in particular becomes a site of 'mental excavation'; it turns into his 'ersatz home,' a place where he escapes even in his dreams (or nightmares) ('Black Vodka' 16). The uncanny simultaneity of England and Poland, of here and there, of the present and the past, is best illustrated by the surrealist scene of the dinner at the Polish Club. Even while approaching the venue, the narrator notes that under the twenty-first-century pavement of South Kensington there is another reality: one that is closer or more intimate to him. But only when he sits down to dinner, will he cross the border between here and there, now and then. When he bends down to pick a silver fork

---

12 Levy, 'Two Silver Herrings.'
13 Gérard Genette. *Palimpsestes. La littérature au second degré*. Paris: Éditions du Seuil, 1982. 419.
14 Deborah Levy. 'Black Vodka.' Deborah Levy. *Black Vodka: Ten Stories*. Sheffield and London and New York: And Other Stories, 2013. 4, 10, 3.

that he has dropped, underneath the carpet he discovers a dark Polish forest 'covered in new snow in the murderous twentieth century' ('Black Vodka' 15). In Levy's vision, one space-time overlaps over another: in the former, in the first decade of the twenty-first century, the customers of the West London-based Polish club eat herring with sour cream; in the latter, a grey wolf 'prowls' through the Polish forest and 'dig[s] up an unnamed grave that has just been filled in soil' ('Black Vodka' 15, 16). This gesture mirrors the larger practice of Levy in which Kraków, Berlin, or Prague are superimposed over Johannesburg or London. Still, the most powerful evidence of the narrator's (and, by extension, Levy's) Central European heritage – where 'heritage,' after Sharon Macdonald, is defined as one's 'meaningful past'[15] – is the fact that the narrator of 'Black Vodka' has a 'little hump on [his] back, a mound between [his] shoulder blades' ('Black Vodka' 3). His kyphosis is by no means accidental since it allows one to recognise in him another version of Walter Benjamin's 'hunchback'[16] who, in Arendt's seminal interpretation, is the figure of fate.[17] Levy's own *'bucklicht männlein'* is thus an acknowledgement of her character's Central European genealogy (and, simultaneously, teleology), a testament to his Central European traumatic fate.

It could be argued that the best illustration of the idea that Central Europe has been haunting the characters of Levy's books (as well as their author) is her 2011 Booker-shortlisted novel *Swimming Home* which opens with its main character, Joe Jacobs, discovering the body of a teenage girl in the swimming pool of his French summer house. There are several reasons why Kitty Finch – whose body, alive not dead, is found by Jacobs – should be read as a metaphor of Central Europe. For one, she has evolved from another character created by Levy, namely Magret who features in the short story 'Vienna'[18] and who is unambiguously defined as 'Central Europe': 'She is middle Europe. [...] She is strudel dusted with white icing sugar. [...] She is made from the horn of deer found deep in the pine forests of middle Europe.'[19] Kitty Finch appears in the life of Jacobs a few weeks before his planned visit to Kraków where this 'famous poet, the British poet, [...]

---

15 Sharon Macdonald. *Difficult Heritage: Negotiating the Nazi Past in Nuremberg and Beyond.* London: Routledge, 2009. 1.

16 Walter Benjamin. *Berlin Childhood around 1900.* Transl. Howard Eiland. Cambridge and London: The Belknap Press, 2006. 119–121.

17 Hannah Arendt. 'Walter Benjamin 1892–1940.' *Walter Benjamin. Illuminations: Essays and Reflections.* Ed. Hannah Arendt. Transl. Harry Zohn. New York: Schocken Books, 2007. 1–58.

18 When 'Vienna' was first published in *Ambit*, it was fleshed out with an illustration by Charles Shearer which showed naked Magret lying motionless on the bottom of the pool. Thus, the closing scene of 'Vienna' in which Magret is swimming in the pool below her apartment is, simultaneously, the opening scene of *Swimming Home*. What is more, if Magret is a version of Kitty Finch and Magret is Central Europe, then the equation 'Kitty Finch = Central Europe' is true. Cf. Deborah Levy. 'Vienna.' *Ambit* 187 (2007): 56–60.

19 Deborah Levy. 'Vienna.' Deborah Levy. *Black Vodka: Ten Stories.* Sheffield and London and New York: And Other Stories, 2013. 36.

the Jewish poet, the atheist poet, the modernist poet, the post-Holocaust poet'[20] is about to give a talk. His trip to Poland is also a way of travelling back to the titular 'home' – the home country of Joe/Józef Nowogrodzki who was born in Łódź in 1937 and who in 1942 was transported to Britain and in this way was spared the fate of his parents and sisters killed in the Kulmhof (Chełmno) concentration camp. His Polish homecoming is not something he has been looking forward to. On the contrary, Joe/Józef's past is a taboo subject: not only is it well hidden and avoided but also forgotten. When Mitchell, one of his fellow vacationers, will ask Joe about the place of his birth, he will respond: 'I don't remember' (*Swimming Home* 41). It is no coincidence that Joe's best-known and widely translated poem is the piece about forgetting one's own history.

But Central Europe and its traumatic past will not consent to be entirely forgotten. Its latest apparition is the enigmatic, spectral, and tricksterish figure of Kitty Finch. Incessantly lying about her own life, emaciated, and suffering from affective disorders, Kitty is the only character in the novel who knows about the poet's true past. It is Kitty who writes the poem 'Swimming Home' in whose speaker Joe recognises himself. It is Kitty who appears in the poet's life on the exact day Joe's late sister would celebrate her birthday. It is Kitty who visits Nina's (i. e. Joe's daughter) dreams and speaks to her in Yiddish. If, as Magdalena Waligórska would argue, traumatic surrealism is a mode of writing which, by reversing the logical order of things, allows the Poles to come to terms with the 'difficult knowledge' about their role in the Holocaust,[21] then *Swimming Home* should be recognised as a work of traumatic surrealism *à rebours* – one in which the Jewish ghosts which haunt the non-Jewish population of Central Europe are replaced by Central Europe (and its many apparitions) which haunts its former (Jewish) inhabitants.

Kitty's main task, however, is to prepare Joe for his suicidal death. Being a messenger from the past, the ghost of Joe's sister, the spectre of Central Europe, Kitty makes Joe realize that homecoming is not possible; that his visit to Poland cannot take place; that his dream about Kraków's trams, hiking in the Tatra mountains, tasting jams and cheeses in Kraków's food market cannot come true. In *Swimming Home*, Central Europe – a site of traumatic events and a source of traumatic memories – becomes a home to which one cannot return. While driving 'home' (i. e. Joe's vacation house) from the dinner in Nice, Kitty reveals the reason for showing up in Joe's life: 'Life is only worth living because we hope it will get better and we'll all get home safely. But you tried and did not get home

---

20 Deborah Levy. *Swimming Home*. Sheffield and London and New Haven: And Other Stories, 2017. 152.
21 Magdalena Waligórska. 'Healing by Haunting: Jewish Ghosts in Contemporary Polish Literature.' *Prooftexts* 34.2 (2014): 226–227.

safely. You did not get home at all. That is why I am here, Jozef' (*Swimming Home* 146). Ultimately, Kitty appears in Joe's life to remind him of the promise he gave to his father in 1942: 'His father had tried to melt him into a Polish forest when he was five years old. He knew he must leave no trace or trail of his existence because he must never find his way home. That was what his father had told him. You cannot come home' (*Swimming Home* 143). Joe will not get back home – next day, his body will be found in the swimming pool in the French villa, exactly where just a few days earlier the body of Kitty Finch was discovered.

In the 'Second World'

Among Levy's Central European narratives, a distinct position is occupied by a group of texts which allude to or closely address the 'second world' before or immediately after the end of the Cold War. The very claim that the period of communism or state-socialism in the countries of Central Europe has always been of major interest to Levy finds support in the two early plays (*Pax* and *Clam*) that emerged in the aftermath of Levy's commission to write 'anti-nuclear' plays and which, when published in a collection of her drama, were grouped under a telling sub-heading, namely '1980s, Cold Wars' (*Pax* 2–4). In both, one can identify a longing for the 'other Europe,' which, as already noted, is most explicitly voiced by the character of the Keeper (*Pax*). Not only does she express a desire to return to the countries which lie behind the Iron Curtain (and which she was forced to leave) but deliberately misleads the fellow characters – the archetypes of the past, the present, and the future – by providing them with the (wrong) maps of Central and Eastern Europe. In *Clam*, Levy conjures up a surrealist scene in which the triple character of Alice/Nadia Krupskaya/Patient[22] finds the whole of Central Europe shipwrecked on an English beach. The image of thousands of people (children playing in the sand, sunbathing adults, ice-cream sellers, etc.) running to the beach to help the marooned state-socialist countries and show affection to them ('[some] turned Romania on its side and began to feel it … […] a woman in a bikini put Poland on her belly … placed her lover's hand there too …. an old man buried his head in Lithuania and wept'[23]) can be interpreted as an expression of belief in a sense of comradeship across the West-East divide and hope for the future unification of both Europes. In this extra-

---

22 In the play, the female characters merge into each other which brings to one's mind Levy's strategy of one space-time overlapping the other. However, the names of the characters also allude to them being manifestations of different aspects of the self (or archetypes given Levy's interest in archetypal theatre): the domestic or fantastical (Alice), the historical or political (Lenin's wife Nadia Krupskaya), the subconscious or the infirm (Patient).

23 Deborah Levy. *Clam*. Deborah Levy. *Plays: I*. London: Methuen Drama, 2000. 73.

ordinary image, the shipwrecked Central Europe is not only in a state of catastrophe but also in the process of 'surfacing out of history,' as Hans Blumenberg
would note in his study of the shipwreck metaphor.[24] The theme of a divided
Europe (East vs. West, communist vs. democratic, opulent vs. impoverished) will
also appear in Levy's *Swallowing Geography*. In the book's concluding chapters,
J.K. arrives in a recently unified Berlin where she observes the legacy of the city's
divided past. Set in one of the city's supermarkets, the scene shows two groups of
Berliners: the West Berliners who, with their arms full of groceries, are irritated by
a delay in the queue caused by a woman from East Berlin; and the East Berliners,
who either queue for shopping trolleys ('because a sign tells them to') or push
empty trolleys across the shop with little money to pay for anything (*Geography*
167). The cry of the woman ('I queued for food for twenty years, you can queue
for twenty minutes') and the insults that follow in its wake (she is called a 'White
Turk' by West Berliners) show that Levy's optimism about bringing together the
'first' and 'second' worlds expressed five years earlier in *Clam* might have not
been well-founded (*Geography* 168).

Clearly, the most irrefutable proof of the impact of the Cold War onto Levy's
creative practice is to be found in the first volume of Levy's 'living autobiography.' *Things I Don't Want to Know* (2013) does not open with a memory of her
childhood in Johannesburg – as one would expect given the autobiographical
nature of this literary project – but with a recollection of her visit to Poland in
1988. Crossing the Iron Curtain to take part in a series of workshops held by the
actress and director Zofia Kalińska in five Polish cities is presented as a central
and defining event for Levy's creative development. Levy notices that the
guidelines offered by Kalińska to her actors (ones that Levy diligently put down
in her notebook and kept returning to throughout her life) have served her as a
kind of toolbox and major points of reference for her own writing. For example,
Kalińska's understanding of hesitation as both 'an attempt to defeat the wish' and
an action that should not be concealed but shown[25] is echoed by the following line
in *The Man Who Saw Everything*: 'He did not speak spontaneously, certainly not
the first thoughts that came to mind. Perhaps he said the third thought that came
to mind. It was not a matter of finding a flow but finding a way to stop the flow.'[26]
But Levy's account of her visit to communist Poland and its subsequent pri-
oritisation does not only testify to Levy's unique genealogy which seeks its roots

---

24 Hans Blumenberg. *Shipwreck with Spectator: Paradigm of a Metaphor for Existence.* Transl.
    Steven Rendall. Cambridge and London: The MIT Press, 1997. 21. Blumenberg also pays
    attention to another aspect of the shipwreck spectator that can be identified in Levy's play,
    namely the 'suspicion of [their] reflective self-enjoyment' which is based on them standing on
    firm ground. Blumenberg, *Shipwreck*, 38–39.
25 Deborah Levy. *Things I Don't Want to Know.* London: Penguin, 2013. 15.
26 Levy, Deborah. *The Man Who Saw Everything.* London: Penguin, 2019. 77.

not in English-language modernism or South African realism but the experimental and avant-garde artistic practices from the European core. It also
reveals that a number of scenes, characters, and events that feature in Levy's
writing have their origin in this very trip. Suffice it to mention the image of a
young soldier kissing his mother, sister, and girlfriend on a train in Warsaw
which has re-emerged in 'Black Vodka'; or the Polish menus that Levy collected
during her visit to Poland and which are later sent to Józef Nowogrodzki by the
people who have been organising his reading in Poland (*Swimming Home*); or the
LOT Polish Airlines stewardesses that morph into nurses in *Stardust Nation*. In a
recent interview, Levy has re-affirmed the centrality of this experience to her life
and work: 'The trip had a huge influence on me. [...] I felt a great affinity with the
people I met. I felt *at home* with them.'[27] In the same interview, she has also talked
about her memories of the 'second world': 'I have this memory of going on trams
and the trams being completely silent. No one was speaking. It was just before the
fall of the Iron Curtain so it was a very stressful time.'[28]

Levy's memories of 1988 and the state-socialist reality 'in the middle of a
political catastrophe' (strikes, demonstrations, shortage of food) (*Things* 13)
have received their most elaborate articulation in her 2019 novel *The Man Who
Saw Everything*. The novel, whose title alludes to Isaac Babel's auto/biographical
short story 'You Must Know Everything' published in English in 1966,[29] is –
similarly to Babel's piece – vitally concerned with the weight of memories. It is the
burden of remembering (and forgetting) that appears to crush the book's main
protagonist: Saul Adler, a historian who specialises in the communist past of
Central and Eastern Europe and who, in the first part of the book set in 1988,
travels to East Berlin; and, in the second part of the novel set in 2016, becomes a
prisoner of the events that happened almost three decades earlier.

It can be argued that *The Man Who Saw Everything* is populated by more
spectres and ghosts than any other work by Levy. The name and surname of the
main protagonist is the 'spectre haunting Mrs Stechler,' a Kraków-born Holocaust survivor (*The Man* 26); Karl Marx is a 'spectre haunting Europe' (*The Man*
11).[30] The work of Jennifer, who in 1988 was Saul's girlfriend and who in 2016 is a
world-famous visual artist, is profoundly concerned with images within images,
with photography and spectrality. Adler himself lives almost exclusively in the
world of ghosts and apparitions – those of his mother who was brought to Britain
on the Kindertransport, of his German lover Walter, of Walter's sister Luna, of
his dead son Isaac, as well as of Rainer, a Stasi officer. The sense of being haunted

---

27 Levy, 'Two Silver Herrings' [emphasis added].
28 Levy, 'Two Silver Herrings.'
29 Isaac Babel. 'You Must Know Everything.' Transl. Max Hayward. *The New Yorker* (April
    1966): 36–37.
30 The phrase is, of course, the opening line of *The Communist Manifesto* of 1848.

by the figures from the past grows larger in the second part of the book when Saul, having been hit by a car, remains in one of London hospitals.

However, I should like to argue that the most important characteristic (and theme) of the novel is the mutual overlapping between different topographies, temporalities, and identities – the very feature which I recognise as Levy's distinctive method of writing and reading history, geography, and the self, and which can be traced to Levy's reading of Antoine Artaud[31] and watching the plays by Tadeusz Kantor.[32] In the world according to Levy, time and space 'overcome' (*The Man* 96) Saul Adler. In 1988, he is haunted by the foresights of the future: in the receiver of Mrs Stechler's phone he will hear the voice of his son Isaac who is to be born months after the incident; his weekend with Walter at a lake in East Germany will be full of flashes from the future, from a different time and space, from a different lake in which Saul will be swimming with Jennifer one day; he will terrify his GDR hosts with the detailed knowledge of the fall of the Berlin Wall in two years' time. What is more, he will be uttering sentences whose content does not belong to 1988 but to the 21st century. This topsy-turvy reality will become even more pronounced in 2016. While in a hospital bed, Saul will insist on speaking German. He will also be deeply convinced that he still lives in the GDR, Europe remains divided by the Iron Curtain, nurses and doctors are Stasi officers and informers, while the man who visits him in the hospital and whose car hit him on a zebra crossing is Wolfgang – the rector of the university where he carried out his research in 1988. Finally, he will continue to be haunted by the visions of Walter, Luna, and, most importantly, his mother and her relatives who were murdered by the Nazis.

Levy's poetics described herein should not, by any means, be limited to a process of dismantling and commixing the existing orders/realities with an aim to create a reversed (*à rebours*) diegetic universe and demonstrate the writer's avant-garde provenance.[33] Nor should her book be read exclusively as a means of attesting to the very longevity and vitality of Central European difficult heritage – particularly the region's traumatic history and its impact on the lives of those who have been forced to abandon their Central European homelands. I shall argue that the vision offered by Levy in *The Man Who Saw Everything* is es-

---

31 Antoine Artaud. 'Van Gogh, the Man Suicided by Society.' Antoine Artaud. *Selected Writings*. Ed. Susan Sontag. Berkeley and Los Angeles: University of California Press, 1976. 483–514. What Levy found particularly attractive in Artaud's writing, was his distorted vision of time symbolised by the idea of Van Gogh having a bullet in his belly well before he actually shot himself. See Artaud, 'Van Gogh,' 490; cf. Levy, 'Two Silver Herrings.'

32 Particularly *Wielopole, Wielopole* and *The Dead Class* with their co-existence of the past and the present. Cf. Tadeusz Kantor. *Wielopole, Wielopole*. Kraków: Wydawnictwo Literackie, 1984.

33 This characteristic is best exemplified by Jennifer's art piece entitled 'A Man in Pieces' – a Baconesque triptych which features mingled and re-sized fragments of Saul's body.

sentially historiosophic. Saul is not only an academic historian of communist Europe. He is history itself, its 'angel,' which, as Hannah Arendt observes, 'does not dialectically move forward into the future, but has his face "turned toward the past."'[34] The signs that Saul, this 'man who saw everything,' might, in fact, be Benjamin's 'angel of history,'[35] are scattered all over the book: they are to be found in Saul's androgynous look, his white suit, or the pearls that he has inherited from his mother and wears all the time. When Walter meets Saul for the first time, he immediately recognises him as an angel: 'When I first saw you, Saul, at the station in Friedrichstraße,[36] you were like an angel, full lips, high cheekbones, blue eyes, a classical body like a statue, but then I discovered your wings were wounded. I had to carry your bag and you became human' (*The Man* 59). Later, Saul will declare of himself: 'I was no longer officially a minor historian. Perhaps I was history itself, flailing around [Saul's arms? Or, more likely, his wings? – author's note] in a number of directions, sometimes all of them at the same time' (*The Man* 178). But in order to be 'now, then, there, here' (*The Man* 92), Saul needs to first arrive in East Berlin and on the façade of the House of Travelling situated in Alexanderplatz see a gigantic copper relief sculpture by Walter Womacka titled 'Man Overcomes Time and Space.' In this sense, the (difficult) knowledge of Central Europe and its past, which the angel of history does not see as a 'chain of events' but as a 'catastrophe which keeps piling wreckage upon wreckage and hurls it in front of his feet,'[37] becomes – in Levy's philosophy of history – a *sine qua non* condition for the proper understanding of the present. It becomes indispensable as it allows Saul to identify another (or the same) catastrophe once he wakes up out of coma. Because Saul wakes up on 24 June 2016, a day after the Brexit referendum.

---

34 Arendt, 'Introduction,' 12.
35 Walter Benjamin. 'Theses on the Philosophy of History.' *Walter Benjamin. Illuminations: Essays and Reflections.* Ed. Hannah Arendt. Transl. Harry Zohn. New York: Schocken Books, 2007. 257.
36 In the Cold War period, the station was the major rail crossing point between East and West Berlin. Though located entirely in East Berlin, it had access to the West Berlin underground, S-Bahn, and long-distance trains from the countries west of the Iron Curtain. Its threshold position thus corresponds to the liminal status of Saul (as well as angels). I am grateful to Katrin Berndt and Andrew Wells for directing my attention to the link between Berlin Friedrichstraße station and Saul's subject position.
37 Benjamin, 'Theses on the Philosophy of History,' 257.

Conclusion: At home

The aim of this chapter was to show Central Europeanness and/or 'Second-Worldness' of Levy's writing. This feature, however, should not be restricted to the simple thematization of the region and its history (particularly pre-1989/1990 history) by the writer; nor to selecting Berlin, Kraków or Prague for the setting of her novels and short stories. What is more, the ultimate evidence of Levy's Central Europeanness is not to be sought in her frequent decisions to make inhabitants (or migrants from) Central Europe the principal characters of her works. Additionally, Levy does not consider Central Europe a reservoir of tropes and symbols only and, as such, its role goes beyond being merely a source of creative inspiration. Also, Levy's writing does not favour or promote just one reading and interpretation of Central Europe – as, for example, the object of nostographic longing or site of traumatic memory. Finally, Central Europe is much more than just a tool to showcase the writer's avant-garde or surrealist genealogy. I shall claim that Levy's Central Europeanness/'Second-Worldness' is to be acknowledged as a distinctive instrument which allows her not only to position herself in the world but also to create, to write; it is both an aesthetic and identity-defining project. If one agrees with André Aciman that home is 'out-of-home,'[38] then Levy's Central Europe with its "uncanniness"[39] (*Unheimlichkeit*) and existential modus of 'not-being-at-home'[40] (*das Nichtzuhause-sein*) is not the place which one escapes. The 'mysterious voice'[41] that calls from the European core is, in fact, the very voice which summons one back home. For Levy, writing about Central Europe is – I am bound to conclude – an act of going back home.

References

Aciman, André. *Alibis: Essays on Elsewhere*. New York: Farrar, Straus and Giroux, 2011.
Arendt, Hannah. 'Walter Benjamin 1892–1940.' *Walter Benjamin. Illuminations: Essays and Reflections*. Ed. Hannah Arendt. Transl. Harry Zohn. New York: Schocken Books, 2007. 1–58.
Artaud, Antoine. 'Van Gogh, the Man Suicided by Society.' *Antoine Artaud. Selected Writings*. Ed. Susan Sontag. Berkeley, Los Angeles: University of California Press, 1976. 483–514.

---

38 Aciman, *Alibis*, 197.
39 Martin Heidegger. *Being and Time*. Transl. John Macquarrie, Edward Robinson. Oxford and Cambridge: Blackwell, 2001. 189.
40 Heidegger, *Being and Time*, 189.
41 Heidegger, *Being and Time*, 318.

Babel, Isaac. 'You Must Know Everything.' Transl. Max Hayward. *The New Yorker* (April 1966): 36–37.

Benjamin, Walter. *Berlin Childhood around 1900.* Transl. Howard Eiland. Cambridge and London: The Belknap Press, 2006.

–. 'Theses on the Philosophy of History.' *Walter Benjamin. Illuminations: Essays and Reflections.* Ed. Hannah Arendt. Transl. Harry Zohn. New York: Schocken Books, 2007. 253–264.

Blumenberg, Hans. *Shipwreck with Spectator: Paradigm of a Metaphor for Existence.* Transl. Steven Rendall. Cambridge and London: The MIT Press, 1997.

Casanova, Pascale. *The World Republic of Letters.* Transl. M.B. DeBevoise. Cambridge and London: Harvard University Press, 2004.

Genette, Gérard. *Palimpsestes. La littérature au second degré.* Paris: Éditions du Seuil, 1982.

Heidegger, Martin. *Being and Time.* Transl. John Macquarrie, Edward Robinson. Oxford and Cambridge: Blackwell, 2001.

Kantor, Tadeusz. *Wielopole, Wielopole.* Kraków: Wydawnictwo Literackie, 1984.

Levy, Deborah. *Pax.* Deborah Levy. *Plays: I.* London: Methuen Drama, 2000. 5–60.

–. *Clam.* Deborah Levy. *Plays: I.* London: Methuen Drama, 2000. 61–78.

–. 'Vienna.' *Ambit* 187 (2007): 56–60.

–. 'Black Vodka.' Deborah Levy. *Black Vodka: Ten Stories.* Sheffield and London and New York: And Other Stories, 2013. 1–17.

–. 'Vienna.' Deborah Levy. *Black Vodka: Ten Stories.* Sheffield and London and New York: And Other Stories, 2013. 31–39.

–. *Things I Don't Want to Know.* London: Penguin, 2013.

–. *Swallowing Geography.* Deborah Levy. *Early Levy.* London: Penguin Books, 2014: 105–189.

–. *Swimming Home.* Sheffield and London and New Haven: And Other Stories, 2017.

–. *The Man Who Saw Everything.* London: Penguin, 2019.

–. 'Two Silver Herrings.' Interview by Robert Kusek and Wojciech Szymański. 23 Jan 2023. Unpublished.

Macdonald, Sharon. *Difficult Heritage: Negotiating the Nazi Past in Nuremberg and Beyond.* London: Routledge, 2009.

Magris, Claudio. *Danube: A Sentimental Journey from the Source to the Black Sea.* Transl. Patrick Creagh. New York: Farrar, Straus and Giroux, 2008.

Murawska-Muthesius, Katarzyna and Natalia Zarzycka (eds). *Kantor Was Here.* London: Black Dog Publishing, 2011.

Testard, Jacques. 'Interview with Deborah Levy.' *The White Review* (August 2013). 10 Sept 2023, <https://www.thewhitereview.org/feature/interview-deborah-levy/>.

Tokarczuk, Olga and Michał Paweł Markowski. 'Postacie na wolności.' *Tygodnik Powszechny* 45 (2019). 12 Sept 2023, <https://www.tygodnikpowszechny.pl/postacie-na-wolnosci-160985>.

–. 'Spotkanie z Olgą Tokarczuk na Conrad Festiwal.' *Facebook.com.* 26 Oct 2019. <https://www.facebook.com/130216013661699/videos/540125593229241> (accessed 12 Sept 2023).

Waligórska, Magdalena. 'Healing by Haunting: Jewish Ghosts in Contemporary Polish Literature.' *Prooftexts* 34.2 (2014): 207–231.

Katrin Berndt

In the Middle of Elsewhere: Retrotopian Projections in Philip Sington's *The Valley of Unknowing* (2012) and Fiona Rintoul's *The Leipzig Affair* (2014)

Introduction

Since the beginning of the twenty-first century, British novels on the 'second world' have imaginatively revisited an increasing variety of East-Central German settings, characters, and motifs. While Berlin has remained the most popular German location for British writers portraying an(y) aspect of the Cold War decades, several more recent works depict other cities, such as Leipzig and Dresden, but also smaller towns, the border regions, and rural areas.[1] This deviates from British writers' otherwise persistent fascination with Berlin, whose rich diversity of historic sites has been meaningful not only for German, but also for British audiences. During the Cold War, the significance of Berlin as a setting symbolizing the period's divisions and the popularity of espionage fiction mutually enhanced one another. This correlation has remained so far unperturbed by the dissolution of the Eastern Bloc, and few contemporary British authors who reimagine twentieth-century Germany have resisted the temptation to pay the city at least a fleeting visit in their writing.[2]

Given the dominance of Berlin as setting before and after 1989, the budding interest of contemporary British writers in exploring other parts of East-Central Germany invites critical attention.[3] Major cities like Dresden and Leipzig, which

---

1 Novels that include less prominent East German settings and characters are Nicholas Shakespeare's *Snowleg* (2004), Jo McMillan's *Motherland* (2015), and Ian McEwan's *Lessons* (2022), which feature Leipzig, Potsdam, and Schwedt, respectively. The first novel in the crime fiction series by David Young, *Stasi Child* (2015), is set predominantly in Berlin, but subsequent novels introduce a variety of East German urban centres and rural areas to the British reader, including Eisenhüttenstadt, Gardelegen, and the Baltic Coast.
2 This includes the novels chosen for this analysis which also feature scenes in, or references to Berlin. Among the more recent British novels predominantly set in Berlin are Max Hertzberg, *Stealing the Future* (2015), Jack Grimwood, *Nightfall Berlin* (2018), Alex Gerlis, *The Berlin Spies* (2019), and Emma Harding, *The Berliners* (2022) – to name but a few.
3 East-Central Germany is the region usually referred to as 'Mitteldeutschland' in present-day Germany. It roughly covers the federal states Thuringia, Saxony, and Saxony-Anhalt, which

are portrayed in Philip Sington's *The Valley of Unknowing* (2012) and Fiona Rintoul's *The Leipzig Affair* (2014), respectively, claim historical significance in their own right. They had vied for the distinction of being the GDR's second city, and have (re)gained broader cultural and economic significance since German reunification. These characteristics have undoubtedly contributed to their fictional recognition in British writing, but the same cannot easily be said for smaller cities like Halle (Saale) or rural areas such as the Harz Mountains, which also feature in more recent fiction.[4] Another quality these novels share is that they all seem motivated by an interest not in the adventures of British spies and other Western agents, but in the common lives of more ordinary people in East Germany, who are (the) main characters and depicted in various encounters with the state apparatus. Motifs such as surveillance, the Stasi, and a general suspicion towards the Communist regime loom large in their stories, but the novels are not conventional spy thrillers – and only some also feature British characters.[5] Rintoul's and Sington's are novels of contemporary history, whose temporal settings contemplate historical and more recent concerns of restrictions of agency, political disillusionment, and personal responsibility, all of which are explored in, but also transcend their Cold War setting.[6]

Their present-day concerns in particular have motivated this discussion, which argues that contemporary British fiction set in East Germany's larger provincial cities and rural areas encourage a *retrotopian* reading of the Cold War past that critically engages with the utopian promise the socialist project once represented. Proposed by Zygmunt Bauman, the concept of the *retrotopia* is a

---

had been in the territory of the GDR until 1990. The term also has broader historical and cultural connotations (see Martyn Rady. *The Middle Kingdoms. A New History of Central Europe.* London: Allen Lane, 2023). As such, it is employed by present-day German media, religious, and business organisations (e.g. *Mitteldeutscher Rundfunk, Mitteldeutscher Verlag, Evangelische Kirche in Mitteldeutschland, Metropolregion Mitteldeutschland*). For the historical discussion, see also Györke (176–177 and fn 22) in this volume.

4   Leipzig and Dresden are well-known to a British audience, for historical (the POW camp for Allied officers in Colditz Castle; WWII aerial bombing) and more contemporary reasons (reconstruction of the Dresden Frauenkirche 1994–2005; the RB Leipzig football club). Less well known, Halle (Saale) is most likely to be connected with the eighteenth-century composer George Frederick Handel and the German Enlightenment, whereas the Harz Mountains are marketed as 'fantastically Teutonic' tourist destination that includes not the Berlin, but 'the Devil's Wall' and was 'the last refuge of the Saxon Pagans' [Daniel Hardaker. 'A trip to Germany's enchanted, fairy-tale heartland.' *The Telegraph.* 10 Oct 2023. <https://www.teleg raph.co.uk/travel/destinations/europe/germany/a-trip-to-harz-germanys-enchanted-fairy-tale-heartland/> (accessed 26 Feb 2024)].

5   The crime fiction series of David Young falls more readily into the category of popular suspense fiction, but Young's scrupulous incorporation of further historical, cultural, and social details easily exceeds genre conventions.

6   A considerable number of post-Cold War British novels, like Sington's and Rintoul's, include different temporal settings – in times before and after the fall of the Berlin Wall.

political-philosophical approach to comprehend the contemporary want of utopian idea(l)s in light of the unfulfilled promises of the socialist regimes of the past. These investments differ from what Svetlana Boym defined as nostalgia: 'a longing for a home that no longer exists or has never existed' and that is driven by 'a sentiment of loss and displacement, […] a romance with one's own fantasy' which 'tempt[s] us to relinquish critical thinking for emotional bonding.'[7] In contrast, Bauman describes neither a nostalgic longing for a totalitarian past, nor an ambition to (re)create socialism in the future, but a desire to reimagine 'genuine or putative aspects of the past'[8] in view of the utopian prospect that it had once represented. Adopting this concept, this chapter will focus on Sington's *The Valley of Unknowing* and Rintoul's *The Leipzig Affair* to discuss their 'second world' fictions as retrotopian: their spatial, emotional, and ethical vocabulary will be considered as meaningful for exploring both the failure of the utopian promise of socialism in its historical actuality, and the congruence of dystopian anxieties and disenchantment with liberal democracy in the present.[9]

Through the lens of the retrotopia, these struggles become meaningful with regard to understanding the Cold War as a shared history of liberal democracies and socialist regimes, including Britain and Germany.[10] What is more, they also help to comprehend longings for 'self-assurance and certainty' in the present 'age of disruptions and discrepancies,' which is informed by a division of 'power and politics' insofar as 'politics is haunted by an interminable shortage of power' that has resulted in 'institutionalized incapacity and instrumental indolence.'[11] What Bauman conceptualized as the retrotopian perspective 'derives its stimulus from the hope of reconciling, at long last, *security* with *freedom*' – a hope that, since the end of the Cold War, is no longer projected to the future, but becomes imaginatively 'located in [an] abandoned but undead past.'[12] According to Bauman,

> The great historical accomplishment of the socialist idea was [that it not only laid] bare the social ills endemic in the status quo […] but also encouraged] remedial action. Without such a utopia[n] presence, those ills would grow and proliferate uncontrollably

---

7　Svetlana Boym. *The Future of Nostalgia*. New York: Basic Books, 2001. xiii, xvi.

8　Zygmunt Bauman. *Retrotopia*. Cambridge: Polity, 2017. 9.

9　See, for example, Ivan Krastev and Stephen Holmes. *The Light that Failed: A Reckoning*. London: Penguin, 2020.

10　Bauman's concept is taken up in several contributions to this volume. Betiel Wasihun invites retrotopian reconsiderations of the traitor character and the motif of betrayal overall in John le Carré's spy thrillers, whereas Richard Brown argues that Ian McEwan's 'second world' writing intertwines nostalgia with retrotopian affect.

11　Bauman, *Retrotopia*, 153, 154.

12　Bauman, *Retrotopia*, 8, 5.

with the moral standards of society together with quality of life bound to become the first, and perhaps the most regrettable, collateral victim of that growth.[13]

This double function – to be a 'presence,' that is, to exist *elsewhere* in order to expose the ills of, and to inspire action in, locations where, by definition, it was decidedly *not* dwelling – this he considered the 'major, indeed paramount role' of socialism for Western liberal democracies.[14]

The collapse of the totalitarian regimes of 'actually existing socialism' meant that they could no longer provide a utopian presence 'elsewhere' – ironically coming full circle to the original meaning of utopia, which had always implied the actual non-existence of this particular 'good place.'[15] After the end of the Cold War in the late twentieth century, Bauman argues, the 'prospects of human happiness' became transformed into an 'individualized, privatized and person-alized' responsibility.[16] Promoted as the promise of individual self-fulfilment, these prospects, he claims, have turned out to be frightening rather than liberating:

> [B]reaking free from the stern demands of subordination and discipline [came] at the cost of social services and state protection. [...] Annoyances of constraints were re-placed with no less demeaning, frightening and aggravating risks [... such as the] agonizing horror of inadequacy. As the old fears drifted gradually into oblivion and the new ones gained in volume and intensity, promotion and degradation, progress and retrogression changed places.[17]

The post-Cold War decades have seen the transformation of once-progressive ideas into uncanny spectres of their erstwhile potential, a consequence of the 'deepening gap between [...] the ability to have things done and the capability of deciding what things need to be done.'[18] The longing for a(nother) unifying social project persists, but, according to Bauman, it is now a projection onto the past that knows about the failure of previous designs.

The retrotopian perspective on the 'second world' is both employed here and identified in the novels selected for analysis. As my readings aim to demonstrate,

---

13 Efrain Kristal and Arne De Boever. 'Disconnecting Acts. An Interview with Zygmunt Bau-man.' *Los Angeles Review of Books.* 11 Nov 2014. <https://lareviewofbooks.org/article/di sconnecting-acts-interview-zygmunt-bauman-part/> (accessed 10 Jan 2017).

14 Kristal and De Boever, 'Disconnecting Acts'.

15 Sir Thomas More adopted the term *utopia* for his philosophical treatise (1516) from the Ancient Greek: the word combines '*ou*, "not" + *topos*, "place" [but also includes ...] a pun on *eutopia*, "[the] place (where all is) well" [... a play with words that foregrounds the] im-possibility of utopia (and the many failures to create it)' (J.A. Cuddon. 'Utopia.' *The Penguin Dictionary of Literary Terms and Literary Theory.* Fourth Edition. London: Penguin, 1999. 957, 959).

16 Bauman, *Retrotopia*, 4.

17 Bauman, *Retrotopia*, 5, 6.

18 Bauman, *Retrotopia*, 12.

they neither nostalgically long for nor mourn the loss of an actual or imagined past. Instead, they fictionally recreate the past to discuss the concurrence of the hopes with which it had been invested and the forms of oppression that had shaped it. I will focus on two novels set 'elsewhere' – that is, in provincial German places rather than the metropolitan hotspot of espionage – and on the common characters who inhabit them, to investigate the contingency of past hopes, and whether they are concurrent with new or resurgent forms of oppression.[19]

Past Present and Future Allegory: Philip Sington's *The Valley of Unknowing*

The title of Philip Sington's *The Valley of Unknowing* (2012) refers to what was well-known in the GDR as the 'Tal der Ahnungslosen,' which translates literally into the somewhat less elevated 'valley of the clueless.'[20] An example of the wry humour that was subversively mocking the claim of the GDR system to both moral supremacy and the truth, the phrase was used by East Germans for regions such as eastern Saxony including Dresden, in which West German TV and radio broadcasts could not be received.[21] Sington's novel is set in Dresden, and engages with several meanings of 'unknowing' – from actual ignorance to deliberate denial and conniving in harmful actions. More generally, the novel exemplifies many of the characteristics of contemporary British fiction set in Cold War East-Central Europe: it features main characters from both the 'first' and the 'second' world; several time levels, here realized as a frame and an embedded story; an East-West romance interwoven with a love triangle; references to communist ideology and the presence of the domestic secret service; and, connected with the latter but more broadly developed, the motif of deception.

The protagonist is the fictional East German author Bruno Krug who, at the beginning of the embedded story, is awarded with the honorary title 'People's Champion of Art and Culture.'[22] His renown rests on his greatest success, a both

---

19 Fukuyama's phrase has enjoyed popularity partly because it was misunderstood as proposing that historical changes and transformations had come to an end (rather than the dominance of liberal democracy after 1990 he had in mind); the phrase has also been adopted in 'second world' British writing, for example in the subtitle of Lea Ypi's memoir (Francis Fukuyama. *The End of History and the Last Man*. New York: Free Press, 1992; Lea Ypi. *Free: Coming of Age at the End of History*. London: Allen Lane, 2021).

20 The phrase was also used by the Nigerian-Welsh-German director Branwen Okpako for her film, *Tal der Ahnungslosen* (2003), which tells the fictional story of a black German police officer who is confronted with the GDR past of her parents.

21 In addition to the area around Dresden, the eastern part of Western Pomerania – the region around the city of Greifswald – also could not receive West German TV and radio broadcasts.

22 Philip Sington. [2012] *The Valley of Unknowing*. London: Vintage, 2013. 22.

popular and politically well-regarded novel, *The Orphans of Neustadt*, published twenty years previously. The toponym refers to Dresden's Neustadt quarter, but holds also a more generic meaning as reference to urban areas more recently built,[23] and a metonymic significance of 'neu' ('new'), since the novel portrays the first years of the GDR as informed by the youthful idealism of those who built it. Several decades later, in the present-time of the story, Krug has reached middle age and no longer writes; he appears to have lost his own idealism altogether. His love affair with Theresa Aden, a much younger Austrian exchange student, emotionally revives him, as does a manuscript he reviews for his publisher, and which appears to have been intended as a sequel to his most famous novel. For years, Krug had avoided producing one, claiming that the open ending of *Orphans of Neustadt* represented his creative vision because it was 'more true to life [...] an open ending is destroyed by a sequel. The ambiguities are cleared up, the possibilities reduced to one. To every question there is now an answer, definitive and inescapable' (*Valley* 12).

Unlike Krug's lauded classic, which was written in realist style and set in 'actually existing socialism,' the supposed sequel, named 'The Valley of Unknowing,' belongs to the genre of science fiction. To Krug, it reads like an allegory of their present, and not only because of the title:

> 'The Valley of Unknowing' [...] referred specifically (often sneeringly) to the place we inhabited, a place where, for topographical reasons, it was impossible to receive Western television transmissions. Why did that matter? Because it made the whole book metaphorical, contemporary, relevant. It might appear to be about an imaginary time and place, but it was really about the here and now, about our society, our system, our state. (*Valley* 37)

Unknown to Krug's lover, the author of the manuscript is Theresa's previous boyfriend, Wolfgang Richter, a promising young GDR writer who dies under mysterious circumstances shortly after Krug casually comments on the novel's subversive significance to his contact at the Stasi. When Theresa mistakenly believes Krug to be the author, he claims the novel as his, but convinces her to have it published in West Germany and under her name – a double deception that sets in motion a string of dramatic events which eventually coincide with the Peaceful Revolution in 1989.

---

23 'Neustadt' is both the individual name for several towns and villages in Germany, such as Neustadt (Rennsteig), and a generic name given to parts of a given town that were added after their historic market centre was built. As such, it can also be read as synonym for 'everyplace,' although in the East-Central German region, two 'Neustadts' are known to differ considerably: In Dresden, the district Neustadt is well known for its impressive baroque architecture; in Halle (Saale), the district Neustadt is well known for its post-WWII multi-storey concrete building blocks.

In Sington's novel, both the Dresden location and the protagonist bear the marks of once-pursued utopian hopes. Interestingly, they are drawn as not so much failed as abandoned in indifference and exhaustion. The setting of the novel is a Bakhtinian chronotope – 'time and space are together conceived and represented'[24] – which conjures up the past vision of a future that had not emerged. Historically, a better tomorrow was promised to those who worked towards realizing a communist state, a promise often incorporated in the propaganda of the system: in the slogan, for example, 'Our work today will define how we live tomorrow.'[25] Banners showing it were usually stored in people's workplaces or kept by the local party official, and were taken out whenever an official demonstration was scheduled; inevitably, they began to look time-worn after a few years. In *The Valley of Unknowing*, the rhetoric of a better future is shown to have become threadbare as well. Krug's present time, the late 1980s, is not the future he and others had once hoped for, but a see-through fabric(ation) of past prospects. His voice and observations – rendered in autodiegetic narration – draw his environment through spaces, objects, and colours that communicate this sentiment:

> The publishing company operated from the fourth floor of a concrete office block overlooking Ferdinandsplatz, a windswept semicircle of asphalt and puddles bounded to the east by tramlines. The area, like many in the city, was one of perpetual reconstruction. Every second lot was piled high with earth, mixers and diggers and generators standing idly about, like children's toys in a sandpit. Occasionally a gang of workers carrying shovels and pickaxes would jump down from the back of a lorry and march off to one site or another – only to disappear again for weeks or months, leaving behind no discernible evidence of their stay. Meanwhile the pale yellow trams, dirty and sparking, moaned back and forth, adding to the air a smell of burning and a din of grinding steel. (*Valley* 6)

The material-spatial construction of the setting becomes alive through sensual impressions, sounds and smells that reflect the labour of the working class. The atmosphere is characterized by a juxtaposition of progression and inertia, the latter seemingly caused by the simple indifference of those – the working class – in whose interest the pursuit of a better future supposedly was undertaken. The

---

24 Simon Dentith. *Bakhtinian Thought: An Introductory Reader*. London: Routledge, 1995. 52.

25 This statement ('So wie wir heute arbeiten, werden wir morgen leben') was supposedly made by Frieda Hockauf in 1954. Hockauf was a weaver, an activist and Hero of Labour, who served as a role model both for the planned socialist economy and for the emancipation of women, who were encouraged to turn away from bourgeois gender and family conventions, and to join the labour force in order to participate in the success of the socialist project. Gerd Dietrich. *Kulturgeschichte der DDR. Band II: Kultur in der Bildungsgesellschaft 1958–1976*. Bonn: Bundeszentrale für politische Bildung, 2019. 859, 1367.

demand for conformity has bred a lack of enthusiasm, both of which are reflected in the monotonous and nondescript colours of the living environment:

> Aesthetic shocks, it could be said, were eschewed generally in the Workers' and Peasants' State [...] Contrast was contained, partly by accident (if soot can be called accidental), partly by design. Colours stood in fraternal relation [...], none enjoying more than its fair share of attention. I have only to close my eyes and there they are, the distinctive hues of Actually Existing Socialism: grey, brown, grey-brown, caramel brown, rust brown, brown ochre, burnt sienna, coffee, beige. These were the colours of the apartment blocks and factories, offices and shops, of construction and decay and all points in between. (*Valley* 48)

The colour symbolism has socialism appear cowed, withdrawing into a variety of grey-brown shades; its utopian promise – equality, the ideal of all men becoming brothers – has transmogrified into a uniform apathy and irreverence. Other contrasts are the state's grandiose rhetoric and the resigned tiredness of its common citizens, who are shown to be more concerned with avoiding brushes with the system than with progress of any kind. Bruno Krug's narration is interspersed with phrases like 'a fiction was called for [...] honesty served no useful purpose' (*Valley* 49), drawing attention to his various attempts to keep things secret and to avoid risks. When he reads the science fiction manuscript that appears to be a sequel to his own realist novel, he recognizes it as allegorically exposing the sham security he lives in: 'The non-political setting concealed a deeply political intention and the title gave that intention away. [The] story was not a vision of a war-torn future; it was a vision of the war-torn past and of the present – a present in which peace and order were maintained only by violence and the threat of violence' (*Valley* 37). What the sequel to Krug's greatest success foregrounds is, in an ironic twist of the title, the awareness – the *knowing* – of socialism's failure, metafictionally communicated also in the science fiction genre of the story which locates the future of this idea in an otherworldly 'elsewhere.'

Sington's reimagining of the final years of the socialist project provides a retrotopian perspective insofar as a 'desire to retrieve' utopian ideas is evident in the attempt to comprehend the GDR's failure to live up to their promise. The socialism it came to represent, or so the story's time, space, voice, and aesthetic configurations appear to suggest, ceased to serve as a foil to the 'endemic ills' of the West, because it provided neither 'security' nor 'freedom.' In fact, Krug's reluctance to engage with others, his recurrent attempts to avoid confrontation, and the self-silencing of his creative voice – he prefers working as a plumber to writing – bespeak the absence of both: his anxious uneasiness as well as the circumscribed living conditions in late socialism overall. In the case of Richter, as Krug finds out, silence becomes an act of courage, and resistance: the young author died after being interrogated and without betraying others, 'his silence more eloquent than a lifetime of literature' (*Valley* 247). The embedded story in Sington's novel concludes with the Peaceful Revolution in 1989; subsequent events are referred to briefly in the frame narrative. Krug's decision to write again, years after the Wall had come down, is eventually made 'not to justify myself […], but in part-fulfilment of a debt. This is the story Wolfgang Richter wanted me to write' (*Valley* 291). Afraid his own complicity will be made known, and conscious of the fact that he has never left the 'valley' and that his 'mind was [still] elsewhere,' Krug intends his account to be a story only about 'the past[;] to be precise, on what could have been and never was. The future was no longer of any great concern' (*Valley* 294, 293). The utopian hopes once invested in it, or so Sington's novel suggests, will not be salvaged.

Other Selves, Second Lives: Fiona Rintoul's *The Leipzig Affair*

The Leipzig Affair (2014) deals with the present contingency of (past) hopes and ills in greater detail, for Fiona Rintoul portrays the novel's two time periods, the mid-1980s and the early twenty-first century, with comparable attention. In fact, the figure and notion of 'two' shapes several forms and themes in a novel that engages past and present in an ongoing dialogue. In addition to the two temporal settings, which are predominantly represented in Parts One and Two, the novel features two autodiegetic narrative perspectives: the first-person narration of Robert, a Scottish PhD student who comes to Leipzig in the 1980s to conduct research on the German Romantic writer Heinrich Heine; and the second-person narration of Magda, an East German student of translation committed to the ideals, but no longer to the reality of socialism, who becomes his lover. Their voices are given equal consideration, and complement, mirror, and/or challenge one another. The overall sequence of events is chronological, with Robert's perspective on the past framed as present-time recollection. The spatial settings offer two more pairings, overlapping with the temporal: whereas in the time period before 1989, the geographical affiliations (of the main characters) are St Andrews and Leipzig, the narrative present relocates them to their capital cities, London and Berlin.

The motif of duality reflects the historical context of the two 'worlds' or rival blocs of the Cold War. And the narrative perspectives that epitomize them, the East German and the British, describe various aspects of everyday life in the mid-1980s and the socialist appeal in a wider sense – on both sides of the Iron Curtain. While Magda and Robert's voices draw on their different backgrounds and experiences, both characters represent normative British values: decency, a commitment to fairness, and disdain for opportunism and vanity. What distinguishes them most is Robert's initial ignorance of life in an authoritarian system, which leaves him unprepared for the brutal treatment he receives from the state apparatus. He comes to study in Leipzig only because his professor at St Andrews had mistakenly forgotten to forward his application to Düsseldorf; another lecturer, 'a card-carrying member of the [British] Communist party' who 'walked about town with a copy of *Marxism Today* tucked under his arm' and whose 'pose' includes a 'fake streets-of-London accent' suggests applying to Leipzig instead (*Leipzig* 54). Robert dislikes the antics of the bohemian, upper-class socialist, but he accepts the offer for want of alternatives and in spite of having 'only the vaguest of notions as to what lay behind the Iron Curtain' (*Leipzig* 53–54).

In Part One, Robert's chapters are told retrospectively, using the simple past as dramatic, narrative present, and so framing his experiences in the GDR as backstory to his current struggle with depression and alcoholism. His first encounter with East Germany takes place at a border crossing near Oebisfelde, a small town in Saxony-Anhalt, to him the proverbial middle of nowhere. Looking back on it, he wonders how much his memory has been re-coloured in light of subsequent developments – be they personal or political: '[W]hen I think of it now, I see it in black and white – a monochrome blur of concrete, metal tracks and glaring searchlights. Or perhaps the many black and white photographs I've seen since have distorted my recollection' (*Leipzig* 63). As Hallberg and Houswitschka point out, in the early 1990s, East-Central Europe is often explored 'in the form of maps and photographies. [... This focus] is typical of a British perspective on post-wall Europe which is determined less by an original interest in Europe but rather as the "other" that helps to define one's own identity.'[26] *The Leipzig Affair* acknowledges the existence of such pre-conceived, imaginary notions in moments of reminiscing, but otherwise offers a British perspective that is committed to, and curious about the 'elsewheres' of East-Central Europe, which is manifested in the choice of settings and the main characters' elaborate engagements with them.[27] Robert's first impressions are labelled as those of a foreigner, who lists details to make sense of the unfamiliar environment: 'The landscape was alien. The huge fields of the collective farms. The tiny Toy Town cars with their dim headlights. The poster on a siding that read: 1ST MAY – THE

---

26 Edith Hallberg and Christoph Houswitschka. '"The silent grey foreign country which called itself Germany" in the Novels of Hugo Hamilton, Nicholas Shakespeare and Others.' *Literary Views on Post-Wall Europe. Essays in Honour of Uwe Böker.* Ed. Christoph Houswitschka, Ines Detmers, Anna-Christina Giovanopoulos et al. Trier: WVT, 2005. 90.

27 In addition to Leipzig and the inner German border region, Prague is another setting covered in the novel, where Magda talks in Czech with a local woman (*Leipzig* 119–122). The scene gestures towards the linguistic and ethnic diversity of historical East-Central Europe (see also Rady, *Middle Kingdoms*, 7–8).

FIGHTING HOLIDAY OF THE WORKING CLASS! It was another world' (*Leipzig* 67). However, his observations are also ironically knowledgeable when he contrasts the grandiose claim, rendered in capitals, of the propaganda slogan with the unimposing cars he sees on the streets.

Historical information on Saxony and Leipzig extends the motif of duality into a broader dimension of the continental past: 'Leipzig train station was built [...] by the Saxon and Prussian rail companies. It has twenty-six tracks, thirteen for the Prussians and thirteen for the Saxons. It was forbidden to bring Prussian trains into the Saxon part of the station and vice versa, *Everything was duplicated: two reception halls, two staircases, two waiting rooms*' (*Leipzig* 73; emphasis added). Such details foreshadow the strict regulations and the duplicity Robert will encounter in the GDR, and which constitute his own eventual betrayal of his friends' escape plans that, or so he believes, resulted in one of them being killed. Symbolized here in spatial and material manifestations, they also draw the so-cialist regime as a continuation of pre-existing divisions and antagonisms.

Interestingly, these details are not recalled, but added in hindsight, when Robert relates his experiences during therapy in the present-time of the narrative. He makes a point of looking them up to impress his therapist, a young woman who finds it 'fascinating' (*Leipzig* 25) that he had spent time behind the Iron Curtain, but who had

> never been to Germany and knew nothing about it. [...] She was shocked when I told her about crossing the border. [...] People who've grown up with central heating, easy credit and aubergines in every supermarket don't understand that there was once a time when there were power cuts across Britain, plane tickets were beyond most people's reach and Prague wasn't a stag party destination. (*Leipzig* 73, 74)

To his therapist, the Cold War past appears to be more alien than East Germany was for Robert when he went behind the Iron Curtain. Her obliviousness stretches to more recent British history such as the economic and technological advances of the New Labour years, and the ensuing changes in culture and consumption. The twenty-first-century commodity that Prague has become for British tourists is drawn as a glaring, almost crude, contrast to the Prague Magda and Robert visit in the 1980s, where they are confronted with still lingering resentment to Germans. To Robert, the indifference to such correlations repre-sents an additional burden: to come to terms with his emotional scars, it is not enough to recount personal experiences. He has to render meaningful the con-gruence of oppression and promise socialism once represented, and how the latter was meant to legitimize the former. His explanations are met with disbelief, and his disdain for contemporary consumerism is also not understood. The decision to return to Leipzig and to find Magda again is motivated in part then by his longing to reconnect with a place imbued with the historical complexities that have shaped his own disillusionments, one where he would not have to translate them.

Magda struggles with feelings of disenchantment already when she first meets Robert. Her second-person narration is always related in the present tense, which gives her perspective an immediate and intimate quality. That includes the portrayal of the Leipzig setting, complete with local details, activities, factually correct or imaginatively revised names of streets and public places, and walks taken from one to the other.[28] The description of houses entered through back courts, of secret hideaways and illegal bars is a subtle homage to British espionage fiction. With these undescribed landmarks, the novel draws an original map of ordinary East German life, where people aim to preserve, and take pleasure, in freedom where they find it – including that which is to be found in a 'crumbling and forgotten attic department, still registered to Kerstin's grandmother,' where Magda illegally cohabits with her friend and fellow student, and which she considers her 'only home' (*Leipzig* 60–61).[29] Together, they look after an elderly neighbour, who had fought against the Nazis and survived imprisonment in Buchenwald concentration camp, a detail that corroborates the retrotopian interest in failed utopian promises: like Magda, Frau Dannewitz has become disillusioned with the major and minor injustices of East German society. Unlike Magda, who pretends to be complicit with it, the older woman takes the liberty to reject favours from the state – in her case, a modern flat with a private, indoor toilet.

Magda's conflicted insider perception of somebody once loyal to, and now at odds but still going along with the authoritarian system, represents her country in this historical period.[30] She repeatedly confronts her own thoughts, and struggles with her values and conscience. The second-person narration has her approaching her experiences as if they were those of another that require explanation, a psychological conflict that remains unresolved, and merges with her anger and pain about the disappointment this socialism turned out to be. When she introduces Robert to the city of Leipzig, she realizes that

---

28 Several names of streets and localities, such as Grimmaische and Shakespeare Street, or Moritzbastei, are toponyms; other references are ironic: *The Sharp Corner*, a venue frequented by Magda and her friends, was the name of the local Stasi headquarters in historical Leipzig, not an underground club. See also Fiona Rintoul. 'On the trail of Leipzig's communist past.' *VoiceMap*. Last updated 29 Feb 2024. <https://voicemap.me/tour/leipzig/on-the-trail-of-leipzig-s-communist-past> (accessed 1 March 2024).

29 The character of Kerstin takes centre-stage in a sequel to *The Leipzig Affair*, the short story 'Mitropa' in this volume.

30 Cf. Roxana Oltean. 'Romance and Belligerence Behind the Iron Curtain: Cold War Gender Identities in Anglo-American Perspective.' *Synergy* 15.1 (2019): 14.

[d]espite it all, you want him to like it here, to be a little bit impressed. You know what westerners are like. How they laugh at the World Clock on the Alexanderplatz in Berlin that spins round showing the time in all the places of the world that GDR citizens cannot visit. How they mock the so-called workers' palaces built in the 1950s on the great boulevards [...] It pains you, because you know how much effort and commitment went into clearing the rubble after the war to make room for those homes. Your father gave over one hundred hours to the National Rebuilding Campaign and has a pin and gold certificate to prove it. The workers' palaces may be stuffed full of apparatchiks now but they were built with hope. (*Leipzig* 80–81)

The alienation from her environment renders Magda a tragic character not only because as an individual, she is 'more sinned against than sinning,' but because she struggles to understand what error of judgment had led to the corruption of the utopian prospect to which her society had once aspired.[31] The internal focalization illustrates how the totalitarian regime alienated those it was supposed to serve; it denounced as enemies idealists like Magda, who had supported the progress it claimed to represent, but who turned away from its moral corruption and political oppression.[32] Magda uses socialist terminology because she is still emotionally invested in the erstwhile motivation of the socialist agenda, whereas Robert observes from an ironic distance its slogans and material achievements. From his perspective, the latter can be dismissed as insignificant. Magda's disappointment is not related to economic aspects however: it is caused by the unfulfilled promise of equality and civil participation, and by her own complicity. She is ashamed that she is 'playing [her] part' like so many others who, she feels, 'allow themselves to be terrorised' (*Leipzig* 83, 82).

In the present time of the narrative, the early twenty-first century, the tables appear to have turned. Now Robert is disillusioned with his life's decisions, and ashamed of his compliance not with a political system, but a branch of the economy he feels is in conflict with his left-leaning values: he works in asset management. The job pays extraordinarily well, but the company's uninhibited materialism depresses him:

It was in tune with the Zeitgeist. Thatcher had crushed the unions. Mining and ship-building were the past; tinkering cleverly with money was the future. [...] We were hiring and building a new European headquarters at Cheapside. It was a glitzy tower with a vast

---

31 Giovanni Boccaccio (1313–1375) understood the tragic hero as a character who 'does not act but is acted upon by outside forces, and is [... in Shakespeare's King Lear's words] "more sinned against than sinning"' (Grace Ioppolo. 'Introduction.' *A Routledge Literary Sourcebook on William Shakespeare's* King Lear. Ed. Grace Ioppolo. London: Routledge, 2003. 4).
32 I discuss the novel's second-person narration in greater detail in 'Writing on the Wall. The "Second World" in Contemporary British Writing.' *Memorial Volume for Christoph Houswitschka.* Ed. Susan Brähler, Kerstin-Anja Münderlein and Sebastian Kempgen. Bamberg: University of Bamberg Press, 2024. 354–355.

glass atrium: empty space that told the world how little we needed to worry about money. (*Leipzig* 189)

Robert has dived into this life to stop thinking about the events in Leipzig, and drinks to keep performing in ebullient spirits – and because he does not manage to forget the past. He suffers from nightmares, and wakes to 'the dreadful real-isation that I'd screwed up [...] My courage had failed when it really mattered' (*Leipzig* 191). Eventually, his drinking excesses cost him his job, and almost his life.

In the meantime, Magda serves a prison sentence for attempted flight from the GDR, and later takes part in the demonstrations that bring about the Peaceful Revolution in 1989. Subsequently, she establishes herself as a photographer: her profession gives her a modest income, and a creative outlet. She is no longer complicit with an overall structure she holds in contempt – but also views with dissatisfaction the inequalities and conformities in the new, reunified Germany. Like Robert, she suppresses her memories and keeps her anxieties to herself. She tries to take refuge in her private world, and avoids whatever might open old wounds.

It is this reluctance to confront that lends itself to another retrotopian reading, for it makes evident the lasting psychological impact of totalitarian means of oppression, including the suspicion towards others that still informs social in-teractions. The repercussions of the period are shown to influence the characters in their present-day lives, which are determined by coming to terms with not only the disillusions of previously existing socialism, but with their own behaviour at the time. Robert and Magda cannot forgive themselves for their involvement and consent. In spite of the different lives they have built, which awards them either financial security or creative independence, both exhibit a pattern of behaviour that has been described as the 'double life' withdrawal in totalitarian structures. According to Timothy Garton Ash, this includes establishing one's life in '[...] niches. The split between the public and the private self, official and unofficial language, outward conformity and inward dissent – in short, the double life – is a phenomenon common to all Soviet-bloc countries [... and] naturally implies double standards: I applaud conduct [... in public] that I would never endorse in private life.'[33] To both characters, this 'double life' is a remnant from the past – but also a mechanism with which to locate existing ills and disruptions in an 'abandoned but undead past' because that is where they can be comprehended.[34]

The East German setting provides the location, vocabulary, and sensitivities to consider also the present-day gap between public approval and private resent-

---

33 Timothy Garton Ash. *The Uses of Adversity. Essays on the Fate of Central Europe.* New York: Random House, 1989. 10.

34 Bauman, *Retrotopia*, 5.

ment, the crisis of power and participation; it takes up the motif of disillusion-ment to critically reflect on concerns of present-day society, such as emotional isolation, drug abuse, and the problematic equation of social and individual fulfilment with economic success – related to what Bauman had termed the 'agonizing horror of inadequacy.'[35] Rintoul neither sensationalizes nor senti-mentalizes the concurrence of political crises, but the novel does offer its char-acters a possibility of reconnecting – with one another, and their societies. It concludes with Magda's decision to confront her own 'demons' and to 'do something' that will take her 'outside of the private sphere' again (*Leipzig* 230, 248):

> 'My idea is to cover as much territory as possible,' […]
> 'I want to show two worlds – or two ways of seeing the same world. I want to use my images to show one side, and the Stasi's images to show the other. I suppose part of what I want to do is show what we've lost as well as what we've gained.' (*Leipzig* 258)

Significantly, the two 'worlds' she envisages become creatively translated into a triptych composition that opens up to the third dimension of reflection. The epilogue adds a third narrative perspective as well, assumed by the friend whose gallery now provides the space for Magda's artwork. With these gestures, the novel moves on to new and uncharted territory, inviting the reader along the way to also revisit unfulfilled longings of the past.

To conclude, Sington's and Rintoul's novels share an engagement with past and present notions of utopian promises, which are located in East-Central German settings of the Cold War period that provide the space and the vo-cabulary to meaningfully comprehend systemic moral corruption, complicity, and the possibility of individual responsibility. In this regard, their 'second world' settings represent moral geographies that transcend their *topos* and time: they are retrotopian locations that exemplify both the disillusionment of dis-appointed utopias and the gaps the latter have left, and whose main function – to allegorically exhibit present-day ills in a way that would re-energize human aspiration and spur political engagement – becomes tentatively resurrected.

References

Ash, Timothy Garton. *The Uses of Adversity. Essays on the Fate of Central Europe.* New York: Random House, 1989.

Bauman, Zygmunt. *Retrotopia.* Cambridge: Polity, 2017.

Berndt, Katrin. 'Writing on the Wall. The "Second World" in Contemporary British Writing.' *Memorial Volume for. Christoph Houswitschka.* Ed. Susan Brähler, Kerstin-

---

35 Bauman, *Retrotopia*, 6.

Anja Münderlein and Sebastian Kempgen. Bamberg: University of Bamberg Press, 2024. 344–357.

Boym, Svetlana. *The Future of Nostalgia*. New York: Basic Books, 2001.

Cuddon, J.A.. 'Utopia.' *The Penguin Dictionary of Literary Terms and Literary Theory*. Fourth Edition. London: Penguin, 1999. 957–960.

Dentith, Simon. *Bakhtinian Thought: An Introductory Reader*. London: Routledge, 1995.

Dietrich, Gerd. *Kulturgeschichte der DDR. Band II: Kultur in der Bildungsgesellschaft 1958–1976*. Bonn: Bundeszentrale für politische Bildung, 2019.

Fukuyama, Francis. *The End of History and the Last Man*. New York: Free Press, 1992.

Gerlis, Alex. *The Berlin Spies*. Oxford: Canelo, 2019.

Grimwood, Jack. *Nightfall Berlin*. London: Penguin, 2018.

Hallberg, Edith and Christoph Houswitschka. '"The silent grey foreign country which called itself Germany" in the Novels of Hugo Hamilton, Nicholas Shakespeare and Others.' *Literary Views on Post-Wall Europe. Essays in Honour of Uwe Böker*. Ed. Christoph Houswitschka, Ines Detmers, Anna-Christina Giovanopoulos et al. Trier: WVT, 2005. 83–98.

Hardaker, Daniel. 'A trip to Germany's enchanted, fairy-tale heartland.' *The Telegraph*. 10 Oct 2023. <https://www.telegraph.co.uk/travel/destinations/europe/germany/a-trip-to-harz-germanys-enchanted-fairy-tale-heartland/> (accessed 26 Feb 2024).

Harding, Emma. *The Berliners*. London: John Murray, 2022.

Hertzberg, Max. *Stealing the Future*. Leeds: Wolf Press, 2015.

Ioppolo, Grace. 'Introduction.' *A Routledge Literary Sourcebook on William Shakespeare's King Lear*. Ed. Grace Ioppolo. London: Routledge, 2003. 1–8.

Krastev, Ivan and Stephen Holmes. *The Light that Failed: A Reckoning*. London: Penguin, 2020.

Kristal, Efrain and Arne De Boever. 'Disconnecting Acts. An Interview with Zygmunt Bauman.' *Los Angeles Review of Books*. 11 Nov 2014. <https://lareviewofbooks.org/article/disconnecting-acts-interview-zygmunt-bauman-part/> (accessed 10 Jan 2017).

McEwan, Ian. *Lessons*. London: Jonathan Cape, 2022.

McMillan, Jo. *Motherland*. London: John Murray, 2015.

Oltean, Roxana. 'Romance and Belligerence Behind the Iron Curtain: Cold War Gender Identities in Anglo-American Perspective.' *Synergy* 15.1 (2019): 7–24.

Rady, Martyn. *The Middle Kingdoms. A New History of Central Europe*. London: Allen Lane, 2023.

Rintoul, Fiona. *The Leipzig Affair*. Twickenham: Aurora Metro Books, 2014.

–. 'On the trail of Leipzig's communist past.' *VoiceMap*. Last updated 29 Feb 2024. <https://voicemap.me/tour/leipzig/on-the-trail-of-leipzig-s-communist-past> (accessed 1 March 2024).

Shakespeare, Nicholas. [2004] *Snowleg*. New York: Vintage Books, 2005.

Sington, Philip. [2012] *The Valley of Unknowing*. London: Vintage, 2013.

Tal der Ahnungslosen. Dir. Branwen Okpako. Perf. Nisma Cherrat, Angelica Domröse, Kirsten Block. Berlin: TeamWorx Television & Film GmbH, 2003.

Ypi, Lea. *Free: Coming of Age at the End of History*. London: Allen Lane, 2021.

Fiona Rintoul

Mitropa

It's all different now. It's gone, in fact. The place you knew.

You see that at once when you climb down from the train on to the platform, using your stick to steady yourself. The train station is as vast as ever, light streaming through the glass ceiling, but beyond that it is unrecognisable.

How could it be otherwise? The country you grew up in is gone.

For a moment, you consider turning around and going straight back to Berlin. Why are you here? You stay away from the East. You live in West Berlin as if it were still an island set in a Communist sea, and there's a reason for that. But no. You decide to carry on. This is your native city. You want to see it again. It's time. And no one will recognise you now. For goodness me, you've changed.

Your hip is killing you. Your doctor says it'll be better once you've had your hip replacement. You'll be able to throw away your stick. Get fit again. You grimace as you limp down the platform. Across the concourse is a pizza place with tables and chairs arranged outside automatic sliding glass doors. That must be where the Mitropa was.

You limp towards it, though it's obvious that it will disappoint. Hovering in the doorway, you poke your nose inside. The place smells of dough and disinfectant. Servers in red T-shirts and black baseball caps are asking customers complex questions about toppings before shovelling pizzas into cardboard boxes. Choice. That's the essence of capitalism. Bamboozle them with too much choice.

'Are you going to stand there all day?' A harsh male voice. You flinch and step aside. A burly middle-aged man in a beige Jack Wolfskin fleece brushes past, glaring at you.

'And?' you snap, making a face at him.

'Fat cow,' he mutters under his breath.

You smile to yourself and look down. It still comes as shock when people say that. And people do it say it. Don't anyone be fooled. There are so many things you can't say these days. Bad as the old days. Bad as actually existing socialism. So much for freedom of speech. But you can still tell a middle-aged woman she's a fat cow. That's fine. That's okay. Always has been. Always will be.

How long have you been big? This big, maybe five years. But you've been overweight for much longer than that. It's funny, you can't put your finger on exactly when it started. When did you stop being the voluptuous, dark-haired girl with Kohl-rimmed eyes who was almost as beautiful as her gorgeous friend and start piling on the kilogrammes? No idea.

Or perhaps you do know. Perhaps you just don't want to put your finger on it. Perhaps it started when you stopped coming here. When you felt you couldn't anymore. An ending and a beginning all in one.

'You've got it all,' she said to you when she found out what you'd done. 'And my life is shattered.' It was true. You had everything. A well-off husband. Two lovely children. A good job. A four-bedroom apartment in Charlottenburg with a roof terrace.

'Come on.' You smiled encouragement. 'Your life isn't shattered. You have your son. You have your work. You have that lovely apartment in Prenzlauer Berg.'

She looked you straight in the eye. Those penetrating grey-green eyes of hers. Unchanged. 'I imagine Charlottenburg gets kind of boring. I know it's better where I Iive. But don't tell me that my life isn't shattered, Kerstin. Because it is.'

You could have said that it wasn't your fault. Well, it wasn't, was it? There was a whole complex of reasons why things turned out the way they did. But you didn't want to antagonise her. People like to blame others when their lives don't turn out how they'd hoped. You decided to let her have that. It was the least you could do. Because perhaps, thinking back, you shouldn't have done what you did. But it was a different time. Everyone had to get by as best they could. You the same as her. She knew she was breaking the law, so what did she expect? If you hadn't done it, someone else would have.

The man in the fleece is at the counter now ordering. He wants a Hawaiian. Pineapple on a pizza. Madness. The server is a fresh-faced young Asian woman with a sleek black ponytail. He's all smiles with her, and she parries his jokes with the grinning professionalism that is one of your least favourite imports from America.

You were never into Russian culture. You could never be bothered with the compulsory Russian lessons in school. But now sometimes you think those blank Komsomol faces with their contained dignity were better than the glossy superficiality of what followed.

Look at this place. So much better before. In your day. You remember how it was so well. The curling cigarette smoke. The greasy smells. The rinsed-out people. The clattering white crockery stencilled with the word 'MITROPA.' The stubby coffee pots with their rimmed lids. The coffee spoons embossed with an Art Deco 'M' atop a railway wheel.

Another person brushes past. A woman this time, young and bustling. She smiles at you with, you think, the pity that young women reserve for older women, not realising that they are their destiny.

This place is so red and plasticky and cheap now. God, how you hate it. If this is indeed the place. You glance behind you. Could you have got it wrong? You came here so often. But it's been so very, very long. You've stayed away for so long. Didn't want to see certain faces. Didn't want to go certain places.

People like to judge others. It makes them feel better about their own shortcomings. Magda made it very easy for them to judge you. Made everything public. Her trauma. Her shattered life. Turned it into *art*. Photographs of your young spying face in a fashionable gallery in East Berlin. The words you wrote in her file plastered all over the walls. Not your words anymore. Hers. How can that be? Well, that's the artist's privilege, isn't it? To tell their truth. To splash it all over everything. No right of reply.

You look along the concourse. You think you have made a mistake. You think it was further down. Perhaps where that bookshop is.

You grab your stick and turn yourself around. These days, you have the turning circle of an oil tanker. Your legs inside your billowing black velvet trousers are cumbersome and swollen. Everything is hard. Any movement makes you breathless. And this is all your own work. You don't have an underactive thyroid. You don't have anything. The doctor told you so, a slight edge in his voice, after he'd run all the tests you asked for. Then he used that nice new term that your daughter likes so much. 'It's a question of self-care.'

But how can you care for yourself when others care so little for you? How can you like yourself when no one else does?

It was all over the papers. Because of the reviews. It made her reputation – and destroyed yours. But do you bleat on about your shattered life? No.

The bookshop has massive wood and glass doors. Old style. Not like the doors on the pizzeria. You see yourself reflected in the glass. The sagging skin on your face. The brittle hair that you can't stop dyeing. What did your daughter say when she saw Magda on the television? *She looks good.* The reproach in that statement. The surprise. Subtext: not like you. Why have you given me this shabby image of my future when I could have had that?

It's ridiculous to say that a woman of Magda's age is beautiful, so let's not say it. But she's presentable. She's looked after herself. Kept her figure, whereas you've mislaid yours. And those cheekbones, they're still there. Your grandmother used to say that true beauty was in the bone structure and endured forever. But what is true beauty?

Her hair is grey, yes it is, but glossy. Styled and chic. 'You see, Mama,' your daughter said, 'that's what I've been saying. Your hair would look much better if you'd just leave it.

Just leave it. The arrogance of youth. What she means is stop embarrassing me with that four-centimetre corridor of grey at your parting that you just can't get under control and that gives the game away. If you can't be like that cool lady artist on the TV whom you used to know but who's out of your league now, in so many ways, just give in, please, stop trying, and be the old bag, the *drink-addled* old bag, let's be honest, that you are.

No wonder Papa left you. Look at you. She never said that but she thought it. She said, 'You've had him for 17 years. Seriously, what more do you want?'

She was very young. Still, it hurt. Your boy, your darling boy, he told her to leave Mama alone. You heard him whispering to her. 'There's no need to be cruel.' Always your champion. But faraway now. In America. A son's a son until he gets a wife, but a daughter's a daughter for life. So true. For better or for worse.

Inside, the bookshop smells of polish and warm cinnamon pastries. Yes, this is it. Isn't it? This is where it was. There are the broad wooden stairs leading to gallery. The tall windows. The decorative glass ceiling. The parquet floor. The Art Deco chandeliers.

You loved it here. So much. You loved sitting here amidst all the lonely hearts and the drunks and the people who were just passing through.

'A pot of coffee,' you'd say to the puffy-faced waiter, and he'd exhale in that loud, exasperated way that said I know your game, young lady. You're going to be in here all day, aren't you, reading your books about ancient history and scribbling down your notes. This isn't a library, you know. This isn't your living room.

Well, fuck him. The Mitropa was your sanctuary. Open all hours, even on Christmas Eve. How many times did you pile in here with friends when you wanted one for the road and everywhere else was shut? How many times did you sit here with her in the early hours of a cold Sunday morning, waiting for the first tram home?

You can still see the menu. Soljanka. Pork cutlet. Broiler. Still feel the glamorous haze that clung to the place. Something to do with a faint whiff of international travel. Those restaurant cars that trundled westwards with their special menus. Radeberger Pilsner. For export. What kind of a country saves its best products for export? Doesn't that say it all?

This bookshop, though. What the Hell? Everything so glossy. Clean. Boring.

You lay your hand on the display table to steady yourself. Your swollen hand. You still paint your nails and wear rings on every finger. Your daughter doesn't like that either.

The display table is devoted to local history. Books about the City of Heroes. No, they turned that name down, didn't they? Good for them. Not them. Us. You're still from here, even if you never come here. Lots of books about the heroes in this shop, though. The people who took a different path from you. Or perhaps just didn't get found out. Books about the changing city. The once crumbling buildings that are now all spick and span. All neatly painted in lovely colours and full of happy capitalists who work in marketing and HR and other meaningless functions. Books about 1989. The Monday demonstrations. You can't bear to look at those. You were there. She was there. You were together. Later in Berlin, you crossed the border together. You hugged each other, and you thought, well, that's it. It's all over. Because you saw straightway that it was. So, I don't need to worry anymore about those stupid scribblings that I handed over. To them. They count for nothing now. That's all history. Meaningless rubbish. Scrap paper. You even convinced yourself that she knew. Because everyone knew really, didn't they? People reported on each other. That was just how it was. It didn't mean anything. It wasn't – such a big, ugly word – a *betrayal.*

And for the longest time, she didn't want to see her files. And you forgot all about it.

Then she did want to see them.

God, how you miss her.

You look around you, remembering the crazy people who used to hang out here. It was here, wasn't it? Drinking. Smoking. Cursing. Laughing too loud in that zoned-out way. Driven mad by a crackpot regime. Sometimes crashing to the floor and pissing their pants.

You saw that once. You and she. A man in his fifties fell off his chair when he stood up to go to the toilet. He pissed himself there on the floor of the Mitropa. You remember watching the stain seep across the crotch of his trousers. A pool of steaming urine spread beneath him. You tittered, putting a hand to your mouth. Magda jumped up.

'Come on. We'd better make sure he's okay.'

She got you to help her wrestle the man into a seated position away from the pool of piss. 'Anyone there?' she asked, patting his cheeks with her elegant artist's hands.

'Yeah, me,' he grunted.

'Good,' she laughed. 'That's exactly who I was expecting.' She stood up, brushed some dust from the skirt of the green dress she was wearing and shouted to the waiter behind the bar to bring her a bucket of hot, soapy water and a mop.

'I was just coming,' he barked. That tone. The hysterical edge that invades a person's voice when they are piling all the frustrations of their day, of their life, into yelling at someone because they can. It's one of the things you remember most about that time. The way servers screamed at their customers in frustration because they could.

Still, Magda had a way with her. The waiter cursed her but he slid into the backroom and reappeared with a bucket and mop.

She said she'd mop up the piss. 'It's all right,' she told the waiter. 'I'll do it.' She wanted it done quickly. Properly. The way she wanted everything done.

He thrust the mop into her hand. 'Suit yourself.' His forehead glistened, as he lurched back to the bar, muttering something about bloody fucking bossy women. The tail of his white shirt had escaped from his black trousers, revealing a wad of grey flesh and the waistband of his underpants.

'Another beer,' a middle-aged woman in a raincoat called as he passed, but he just ignored her.

Magda, in her green cocktail dress that she loved so much because it had been her mother's, mopped the floor. It was October. The start of a new year of study. The year when everything changed for her. And, though you didn't know it at the time, for you. She wore heavy black lace-up boots with the dress and patterned tights. She always knew how to mix things up like that and make it work. She was so beautiful with her pale skin and grey-green eyes. Maybe that is the most beautiful she ever was. That night when she'd decided what she was going to do but had not yet put the wheels in motion. A moment in time when everything was possible, when she was excited about her plans but hadn't yet committed to anything. You had, though. You'd already taken your decisive step.

Everyone in the room was watching her, especially the men, especially one man. He was sitting in the corner, smoking a cigarette, rolling a beer mat between his fingers. He was probably in his thirties, which seemed old to you then. Less wasted than the others in the room, he wore a dark blue donkey jacket. On the table in front of him was a half-drunk beer and a packet of Camel cigarettes. He stood up and came over.

'Sweetie,' he said to Magda, just loud enough for everyone to hear, 'want to come and do my housework for me?' A bank note was visible in his clenched right fist. Deutsche Mark. Magda didn't even look up as she told him where to go. He glanced then at you, raised an eyebrow. That's how it always was. First her, then you. Oh, you were attractive enough in those days with your dark hair and your Kohl-rimmed eyes. But not like her. You shook your head. What else could you do? What would she have thought of you? You'd done it before. A couple of times during the annual trade fair. And she'd done it. She'd prostituted herself. But not for money. It was never for money with her. Always for some higher purpose, some important goal. Like getting the fuck out of that shithole of a country once she'd realised what a shithole it was. The end justifies the means.

She told you that once. 'I'd do anything to get out of here.'

You wrote it down later. Like you wrote down everything she said.

When Magda had mopped up the piss, she handed you the mop and bucket. 'Give those back, will you? I'm going to find someone to help this man.' What were you? Her sidekick? Her factotum? Yes, sometimes. She went outside and came back with a young policeman, a Vopo in his grey winter coat and black cap. Maybe she flirted with him to get him to help. Who knows? Who cares, right? She got him to check the drunk man over and then she got him to take him home in his green and white Wartburg.

That's what she was like. She got things done. She knew how to handle people. When to shout like she did at the waiter. When to tell people, usually men, where to shove it. And when to lay on the charm.

You sat back down at the table you'd been sharing with her and watched her help the Vopo manoeuvre the drunk man towards the door. He had one arm slung around Magda's shoulder and the other around the Vopo's. His eyes were half-closed and he was cursing softly. The Vopo was supporting him by the waist. Magda issued instructions to him. Watch out for that chair. Hold him more firmly. 'Walk,' she said to the drunk man. 'Come on, mister. You can walk.' She stood straight, despite the weight of the drunk. She held her head high, though she must have known that everyone was watching her, judging her because she'd done what you weren't supposed to do. She'd made a spectacle of herself and in so doing had made everyone else look bad.

She's a phenomenon, you thought as you finished your beer and then hers. When she came back, she was glowing from the cold air outside and the satisfaction of a job well done. 'He'll be all right now.' She flopped down in the chair beside you and stared at the empty glasses on the table. 'You drank my beer. I don't believe it.' She grabbed your cigarettes, took one and lit it. 'Bitch!' she said. But she was only joking.

'Do you want another?'

She shook her head, tilted it back and blew out the smoke she'd inhaled. 'The first tram's due soon. Let's just go home. There's beer there.'

It was the wee small hours of the morning. You'd been to a party at the student club. It was hard for her because the students who'd been to England were back, and they were holding court, sitting on the stairs telling everyone about their experiences in the non-socialist abroad. She should have been one of them but she hadn't been. Politics were more important than grades. You could tell from her face how she hated them, how she thought she'd have made much more of it than they had. Which she would have done.

'And Madame Tussauds,' said Jana, the scrawny little technocrat whose job it had been to watch Magda before you, 'it was so expensive. An unbelievable amount.'

'Why did you go, then?' Magda flicked her cigarette ash on to the floor. 'It's not compulsory.'

They looked at her like she was mad. Not go to Madame Tussauds on a once-in-a-lifetime trip to London? Impossible. For they were just as beguiled by those capitalist trinkets as any American tourist. Whereas Magda wasn't. She didn't care about those things. That wasn't why she wanted to leave. She loved the apartment on Shakespeare Street. She loved her homemade clothes. She loved her

Praktica SLR, which she said was the best camera you could buy anywhere. Wasn't the GDR the first country in the world to manufacture an SLR for professional photographers? She loved her trips to Prague and Budapest. She was happy in the Workers' and Farmers' State. Or she could have been if she hadn't lifted that stone – the stone that covered all the bad things that had happened in her family – and looked at all the creepie crawlies squirming about beneath it.

Later, in the attic at Shakespeare Street, you both drank your final beer of the night and smoked a last cigarette. She sat on the leather sofa with her feet tucked up under her and laughed about it all, mimicking the man in the Mitropa. *'Sweetie, want to come and do my housework for me?* What an arsehole.' And you said, 'He had a packet of Camel cigarettes.' For Camel were her favourites. She looked up and met your gaze. She looked at you so intently that you felt yourself blinking uncomfortably fast. That was the first time that happened but not the last. 'Did he? Kerstin, you really do notice everything, don't you?'

The next day, you wrote it all down. Every little detail. That was what they wanted. They wanted to know everything. Now you think: why? What did they do with all that information? But then you just wrote. You filed your reports and you got your little bit of extra money. Sometimes you spent it on her. There was a Cuban restaurant she liked. You took her there sometimes. Once – and this was a risk because you had to make up a story to explain it – you bought her a packet of the Camel cigarettes she liked so much from the Intershop with a Forum check that your handler had slipped you.

That ghastly little man. He loved Magda and hated her at one and the same time. He was so pleased when he recruited you. His cheeks shone. 'Well,' he smiled. 'Well, well. Miss Magdalene will have to be more careful now, won't she?'

'She's already very careful,' you said, without thinking.

'Hmm.' He stood up and walked to the window of the safe house. 'Is she? I don't doubt it.' He looked down at the city below. Your city. His city. Crumbling under brown coal dust. But still great somehow. Still cool. Then as now. Or so you're told. He swung around and smiled at you again, but this smile had a different quality. It was sly. Knowing. 'But we've got her now, haven't we?' He came back to the table where you were sitting and picked up the document you'd just signed. As he did so, he let his fingers graze your breasts. He cocked his head and gave you a long look, daring you to protest, which of course you didn't. Because it was too late. Because you saw that he was right. They'd got her. You weren't just going to be giving him little titbits of information here and there 'for our records,' as he'd said at the beginning. You were going to help him bring her down. You were his creature now, and he could touch you if he wanted. You deserved it. Like you deserved her anger later.

They should have nurtured her, the regime. She was a rare talent. And a true socialist. Not like you. Not like you at all. What did she say to you all those years later when she knew what you'd done? 'You're one of those people, Kerstin, who believes in nothing. You would survive in any regime. It's just as well you weren't alive during the Third Reich. Your crimes might have been much worse.'

What a thing to say. So cruel. Because she knew about your family history. You still think about it sometimes. Was she right? Is it in the blood? What a stupid notion.

That's the trouble with people who believe in things. They can be cruel in pursuit of their beliefs. Magda had socialism right there in her heart. Red. Beating. She truly believed. That's what they never understood about her. The bureaucrats and snitches. That's why she was how she was. She wanted the Workers' and Farmers' State to be a gleaming socialist paradise. And so, she couldn't take it. All the shit that she found out. All the lies and cover-ups. The preferential treatment for those and such as those. The strings that were pulled. In her own family too. There shouldn't have been so much shit for her to find out.

Less shit, please. That would have been your wish for her. Not that you have any right to make wishes for her. You don't even have the right to phone her. Or write to her. She's made that very clear. And yet, you loved her. You did. She'll never believe it, but it's true.

People like her are dangerous, most of all to themselves. Believers are a liability. Belief clouds your judgement. But it's attractive. You should know. You were attracted to it. Cold pragmatism isn't attractive. It's useful, though. You were useful to the regime that you didn't believe in half as much as her with your sensible desire to make the best of things. To lead an ordinary life, to study and work, and perhaps have a little bit of extra money. You didn't ask too many questions because you didn't really care. And what's wrong with that, eh? We can't all be heroes. You didn't know how it would turn out. You didn't know she would go to prison, for God's sake. How could you have known that?

There's a café on the gallery. Perhaps you should drink a coffee. That would be nice. Drink coffee in the Mitropa again. If this is where it was. You're still not 100 percent sure.

At the broad wooden stairs that lead to the gallery, you grab the handrail to pull yourself up. You collapse into a seat at a table that faces out towards the bookshop, towards the Mitropa. You consult the menu. Half of it's in English. That's normal. Your daughter says there are bars in East Berlin where the bar staff can't speak German. A waitress comes, all togged out in waitress gear with a little white frilly apron. You order an Americano. In honour of your son who phones every Sunday from Providence, Rhode Island, where he teaches mediaeval history at Brown University in the same department as his wife.

The coffee comes with a cinnamon biscuit in a cellophane wrapper. You tear open a sachet of sugar, drop the sugar into the cup and stir.

She should have known really, shouldn't she? Perhaps she did. Somewhere deep down inside. It's not like she was stupid. Far from it. That's what she said to you. When she found out. 'It's not like you're stupid, Kerstin, is it?' So, no excuses; that was the message. An intelligent woman who informs on her best friend is inexcusable. Would it have made a difference if I'd been stupid, you wanted to ask. Perhaps not stupid. But, you know, not the brightest bulb in the box. Not the sharpest knife in the cutlery drawer.

But of course, you didn't ask. You couldn't. You no longer had the right to ask her impertinent questions. The way you can when you know someone really well. When you're best friends. Best girlfriends. That was over. You were of no more significance to her than a fleck of dirt. You could call it victor's justice but you'd better not.

You'll never forget how she was when she came out of prison. Her hollow eyes. Her hollow heart. She came to you, and you tried to help her. They've broken her, you thought, and a part of you was glad. She could be broken, just like anyone else. Another part of you hated it. No, not her. Not my darling Magda. If she can be broken, anyone can.

Well, anyone can be broken. You know that now. But they hadn't broken her. She recovered. Perhaps they didn't try hard enough. Perhaps they were scared of her.

Like you are.

You sip your coffee. Your bitter, black coffee. Why didn't you order a flat white? Just because it was written in English on the menu, and you hate that. How stupid.

You pick up your phone. Check your messages. There are six messages in your building's WhatsApp group and a text from your electricity provider. Otherwise, nothing. You look at Google Maps. How far to the centre of town, to the other places you want to see on your nostalgia trip? But you're just messing about. Looking at your phone for the sake of it, like your daughter does when she visits you. Scrolling, scrolling, scrolling.

You're not going into town. Not today. Too much for the old legs. Too much for the old heart. This is far enough.

Second Glances: Retrospective Approaches to the 'Second World'

Ulrich Busse

Who is – or rather was? – the Second World? A lexicographical and meta-communicative approach to a twentieth-century keyword

Introduction

In history classes, students are told that mere names, dates, or figures are much less important than the understanding of developments, relationships, and so on. But numbers can have a socio-historical impact. This insight serves as a link to the topic of the present volume on 'contemporary British writing whose narrative focus lies on Central and Eastern Europe of the Cold War period – the so-called "second world."'[1]

To specialists in the field it is perfectly clear what *second* means in this context. However, many uninitiated people might wonder: Why second? Who is first? How many worlds are there? Therefore, the starting point for the present paper is to put the term *Second World* in relation to its field members *First World*, *Third World* and *Fourth World*, and to provide an in-depth study of the lexical set. Methodologically, the study is corpus-based, combining three different linguistic approaches: lexicography, meta-pragmatics, and corpus linguistics.

We can regard vocabulary in general – to quote Fowler – 'as a representation of the world for a culture; the world as perceived according to the ideological needs of a culture.'[2] More particularly, the terms under discussion are meta-communicative lexemes, as they 'encapsulate cultural models of communication rooted in particular practices of socio-culturally defined people.'[3] Furthermore, they can be regarded as keywords in the sense of Williams's classic study insofar as

---

1 Katrin Berndt and Andrew Wells. 'Introduction.' *The 'Second World' in Contemporary British Writing*. Ed. Katrin Berndt and Andrew Wells. Göttingen: V&R unipress, 2024. 11.
2 Roger Fowler. *Language in the News: Discourse and Ideology in the Press*. London: Routledge, 1991. 82.
3 Axel Hübler and Ulrich Busse. 'Introduction.' *Investigations into the Meta-communicative Lexicon of English: A Contribution to Historical Pragmatics*. Ed. Ulrich Busse and Axel Hübler. Amsterdam and Philadelphia: Benjamins, 2012. 8.

particular words reflect ideas or ideologies of (Western/British) society in different periods.[4]

Since the study uses various English dictionaries as its primary source of information, meta-lexicography, often also called dictionary criticism, serves as a further base from which to pursue this inquiry. As the term *Third World* seems to have been coined as *tiers monde* in French, it is also essential to shed light on the itineraries of this and the related terms in order to investigate their origin and their dissemination into English.

The objective of this integrative approach is to analyse how historical circumstances after the Second World War and political agendas succeeded in reifying political and economic divisions in the collective use of these lexemes.

The lexicographical history of *Second World* and its associates

As the term *Second World* stands in close lexical relationship to its immediate 'neighbours' *First World* and *Third World*, and, to a lesser degree, to *Fourth World*, it seems advisable to investigate their individual histories first and then compare them to each other.

Thus, as a first step of the analysis the meanings of these terms shall be defined. The dictionaries selected for this purpose are the *Oxford English Dictionary* [OED] as a representative of a comprehensive dictionary of the English language built on historical principles and the *Barnhart dictionaries of New English* [DNE I, II] as specimens of dictionaries of neologisms, which record and monitor new words over a limited time span. The presentation of the results follows the numerical order of the four terms under scrutiny from *First* to *Fourth World*.

First World

A view into the OED shows two different senses that are far apart from each other in time and mental space. Sense 1 takes us back to the Middle Ages and to the realms of mythology and religion. While such spiritual or theological senses are not documented for *Second* and *Third World*, they have a parallel in the historical development of senses for *Fourth World*.

1. In various mythologies and religions: the first age of the world, as distinct in some way from the present human realm; the first era of human or earthly history; (*esp.* in

---

4 Raymond Williams. *Keywords: A Vocabulary of Culture and Society*. Glasgow: Fontana/Croom Helm, 1976.

Theology) the antediluvian or (less frequently) the prelapsarian world. Now chiefly *poetic*.

*c*1384 God..sparide not to the first world [Latin *originali mundo*], but kepte Noe. *Bible* (Wycliffite, early version) *(Royal MS.) (1850) 2 Pet. ii. 5* (OED, s.v. 'First World, n., sense 1')

Sense 2 below defines its present meaning in geo-politics:

2. With *singular* agreement. The industrialized, developed, relatively wealthy and powerful nations of the world (collectively); *spec.*[ifically] the industrialized capitalist countries of Western Europe, North America, Japan, Australia, and New Zealand.[5]

The second part of the definition and the first citation from 1974 (below) draw attention to a shift of meaning in the course of time, because in early use *First World* was frequently 'opposed both to the communist nations (formerly) regarded as constituting the Second World and to the less-developed and poorer nations regarded as constituting the Third World; now more usually only as opposed to the latter.' (OED, s.v. 'First World, n., sense 2')

The term was formed by compounding within English after the model of *Third World*.

The word is in frequency band 5. That means it occurs between one and ten times per million words in typical modern written English. From 1950 to 2010 it occurs six times per million words on average with a peak of 6.8 in 1950.[6]

Seven citations ranging from 1967 to 2005 illustrate the meaning. The following five do not only mention the term, but offer defining information.

1967 Studies which attempt to survey world trends and to characterize the major attributes of the First World (the United States), the Second World (the U.S.S.R.), and the Third World, are courageous undertakings. *Political Science Quarterly* vol. 82, 155

---

5 All information from the OED online was retrieved in early September 2023. Since the OED is under constant revision, the information is liable to change. Except where otherwise indicated, emphases in quotations from dictionaries are as in the original.

6 'Historical frequency series are derived from Google Books Ngrams (version 2), a data set based on a corpus of several million books printed in English between 1500 and 2010. The Ngrams data has been cross-checked against frequency measures from other corpora, and re-analysed in order to handle homographs and other ambiguities. The overall frequency for a given word is calculated by summing frequencies for the main form of the word, any plural or inflected forms, and any major spelling variations. Smoothing has been applied to series for lower-frequency words, using a moving-average algorithm. This reduces short-term fluctuations, which may be produced by variability in the content of the Google Books corpus.' ('Frequency,' OED, n.d. Oxford University Press. Date of access 16 Feb 2024, <https://www.oed.com/information/understanding-entries/frequency/>.)

1974   Mr Teng announced that the 'socialist' camp no longer existed, and that the planet was divided into the First World, consisting of the two superpowers, the Second World, consisting of the other developed countries, and the Third World, which included the developing countries. *Times* 13 April 5/7

1974   The conventional image of recent years has been of a first world of developed market economies, a second world of 'socialist' states, and the 'third world' of the developing nations. *Economist* 18 May 66/1

1980   The already industrialized countries of the capitalist and communist blocs (respectively the 'first world' and 'second world'). *Scientific American* September 107/2

1990   A world view different to that of Washington (the First World) and Moscow (the Second). S. Elseworth, *Dictionary Environm.* 264 (OED, s.v. 'First World, n., sense 2').

The 'First World' entry in the *Second Barnhart Dictionary of New English* [DNE II] (1980) emphasises the semantic feature 'chief industrialised countries' as a defining characteristic, but unlike the OED entry includes the Soviet Union: 'the chief industrialized countries within the political power bloc of the world, including many of the countries of Western Europe, the United States, Japan, and the Soviet Union.'

According to the DNE II the term was coined in 1974, and patterned on the earlier *Third World* (1965).

Second World

For the entry *Second World*[7] two closely related definitions – indicated by the letters (*a*) and (*b*) rather than numbering – are given in the OED:

(*a*) (Following the outlook of the Chinese leadership) the developed countries apart from the two 'superpowers';

(*b*) (possibly reflecting the original implication of the term *Third World*) the Communist bloc.

Regarding its etymology it is formed within English by compounding after the model of *Third World*. It belongs in frequency band 5. From 1970 to 2010 its frequency is quite constant, ranging between 7.6 and 7.8 items per million words of written English in each decade.

The two meanings are amply illustrated by the following six citations ranging from 1974 to 1980.

---

7 A note says that this entry has not yet been fully revised. The OED is currently updated four times a year, most recently in September 2023.

1974 Mr Teng announced that the 'socialist camp' no longer existed, and that the planet was divided into the First World, consisting of the two superpowers, the Second World, consisting of the other developed countries, and the Third World, which included the developing countries. *Times* 13 April 5/7

1974 The conventional image of recent years has been of a first world of developed market economies, a second world of 'socialist' states, and the 'third world' of the developing nations. *Economist* 18 May 66/1

1975 The 'Second World' of the Socialist countries will make a show of complete support. *Time* (Canada edition) 8 September 20/2

1978 The scene was dominated by the post-war tension between the First and Second Worlds. *Church Times* 25 August 4/2

1979 In this approach, Europe would be seen as playing the role of what Chinese diplomacy likes to refer to as 'the second world.' *Dædalus* Spring 124

1980 The already industrialized countries of the capitalist and communist blocs (respectively the 'first world' and 'second world'). *Scientific American.* September 107/2 (OED, s.v. 'Second World').

According to the DNE II (1980) the term *Second World* was coined in 1974 and was patterned on the earlier model of *Third World*. Two different definitions, which are underpinned by illustrative citations and also a long explanatory note for the change of meaning, are provided.

1. the industrialised countries of the world not including the United States and the Soviet Union.
As far as "Second World" countries are concerned (in Chinese terminology, this refers to nations half-way between the Superpowers and the Third World), the Chinese no longer give priority to relations "between peoples," but are concentrating on links "between states." The most obvious example of that new policy is their rapprochement with the Japanese. *Philippe Pons, "Reshuffling Asia's Political Pack," The Manchester Guardian Weekly (Le Monde section), Nov. 19, 1978, p 12*
2. the socialist or Communist countries of the world.
The Smithsonian official called for involvement in global conservation efforts of the "second world – the socialist states, whose influence can be equal to our money, and whose active participation would go a long way to rationalize the apparent disparity in motivation between the 'have' and 'have not' nations." *Gladwin Hill, The New York Times, Dec. 1, 1976, p A-18*

For the division of meanings the following explanatory note is given:

The two meanings of the term correspond to two methods of classification. *Definition 1* resulted from the division of countries according to their economic power. Under this classification the most developed countries (especially the U.S. and the U.S.S.R.) constitute the FIRST WORLD and the least developed countries constitute the FOURTH WORLD.

Definition 2 corresponds to the original quasi-political scheme of Communist, non-Communist, and Third World countries. (DNE II, s.v. 'Second World')

Third World

The OED provides one meaning for the entry *Third World*:[8]

> The countries of the world, esp. those of Africa and Asia, which are aligned with neither the Communist nor the non-Communist bloc; hence, the underdeveloped or poorer countries of the world, usually those of Africa, Asia, and Latin America. (OED, s.v. 'Third World, n.')

In terms of frequency, *Third World* is in frequency band 6; it typically occurs ten times per million words on average. However, its usage varies over time with a frequency of just one token per million in 1960, a peak of 17 tokens in 1980, and a decline to 6.8 in 2010.

Unlike *First World* and *Second World*, *Third World* did not originate within English by means of compounding, but translates the French term *tiers monde*. This is illustrated by quoting a French source as a first citation in square brackets.

> [1956 La conférence tenue à Bandoeng en avril 1955, par les délégués de vingt-neuf nations asiatiques et africaines..[*sic*] manifeste l'accès, au premier plan de la scène politique internationale, de ces peuples qui constituent un 'Tiers Monde' entre les deux 'blocs,' selon l'expression d'A. Sauvy. G. Balandier, *Tiers Monde* 369][9]

Its meaning and use in English are illustrated by nine citations ranging from 1963 to 1980. Out of these, the following can be considered as a defining citation.

> 1974 The First World Development was Capitalist... The Second World was Communism, in particular Russian Communism. The Third World takes in all the other countries that are not developed. Everyone counts China in the Third World... It includes the whole of Africa, Asia, Latin America. It has to do with income and low standard of living and so this takes in such countries as Greece, Yugoslavia, and some include Spain and Portugal. *Globe & Mail* (Toronto) 29 January 13/1

A consecutive development of two different senses is recorded in the DNE I (1973):

---

8 A note says that this entry has not yet been fully revised.
9 'Through the involvement of delegates from twenty-nine Asian and African nations, the conference held at Bandoeng in April 1955 marked the admission of these peoples, who constitute the "third world" between the two "blocs" (after the expression of A. Sauvy), to the highest level of international politics.' [translated by the editors].

a collective name for the group of underdeveloped countries, especially of Africa and Asia, that receive aid from both the Communist world and the non-Communist world and therefore cannot be aligned with either. (s.v. 'Third World')

An explanatory note says that *Third World* is a 'translation of French *tiers monde*, in which *tier* is an archaic form instead of the normal *troisième* because the French expression, in use since the late 1940s, was based on the eighteenth-century *tiers état*, the Third estate, i. e. the commoners as against the other two estates of nobles and clergy.'

This definition is slightly changed to the following in DNE II (1980): 'the underdeveloped countries of the world, especially those in Africa, Asia, and Latin America, without regard to their political alignment.' (s.v. 'Third World')

The 1970s saw an important change in Chinese foreign and economic policy, whose background was longer-standing 'differences' with the Soviet Union. Ideological differences on the role of communism in the world go back to the Moscow conference of communist parties in 1960. As a result of the Warsaw Pact occupation of Czechoslovakia in August 1968 and a military confrontation with Russia on the Ussuri River in March 1969, which fuelled Chinese fears of a Soviet attack, Sino-American diplomatic relations improved, resulting in so-called ping-pong diplomacy, 'the establishment of trade and other relations between the United States and the People's Republic of China, begun when an American table tennis team went to China in 1971' (DNE II, s.v. 'ping-pong diplomacy'). This event was followed by a secret visit of Henry Kissinger in July 1971 and a later visit of US President Richard Nixon in February 1972. A number of economic reforms in China and the newly established relationships to non-socialist countries resulted in a new self-image of Chinese policy in the mid 1970s. In the following citation China presents itself as a developing, non-aligned socialist Third World country:[10]

In a keynote address to the Special Session of the UN General Assembly in April, Vice-Premier Teng Hsiao-p'ing declared that in the Chinese view the socialist camp no longer existed. The world was now divided into three. The First World was that of the two superpowers, the Second was that of the other developed countries and the Third was that of the developing countries. China was a socialist country belonging to the Third World. The Third World was described as the motive force for propelling history forward in the world today. *Michael Yahuda, "China" The Annual Register of World Events in 1974 (1975), p 318* (DNE II, s.v. 'Third World')

---

10 For more detailed historical background information see John Garver. 'Chinese Foreign Policy in 1970: The Tilt Towards the Soviet Union.' *The China Quarterly* 82 (June 1980): 214–249 and Philippe Lionnet. 'Anpassungen in der Wirtschaftspolitik in der Volksrepublik China: die Scharnierjahre 1974/1975.' *Jahrbuch für Historische Kommunismusforschung* (2020): 155–171.

As year of origin for this newer sense, 1968 is given. The first occurrence of the older sense (given in DNE I) is 1965.

Fourth World

The OED provides four senses. For the present purpose, sense 3 is relevant. However, the whole spectrum of senses is interesting for cultural and also linguistic reasons. The oldest sense is attested from 1833 onwards.

> 1.a. A distant, mysterious, or otherworldly place, *esp.* one inhabited by magical or supernatural beings. In later use, *gen.:* a supernatural, fantastic, or imaginary realm.
> 1.b. The present world, or the human realm, regarded as a distinct cosmological era or plane. (OED, s.v. 'Fourth World, n., sense 1')

This mythological sense shows a direct parallel to the semantic development of *First World*, which also had its origins in mythology. Sense 2 is attested from 1967 onwards and takes us from the spiritual word to real-world problems of people, territory and governance.

> 2. A loose or notional confederation of territorial or political units without sovereign statehood, often consisting of established regions or peoples which have distinct cultural identity or partial administrative autonomy within a larger state; Indigenous minorities living in or subject to another nation. (OED, s.v. 'Fourth World, n., sense 2')

For the topic of the present investigation sense 3 is pertinent:

> 3. A group of nations considered distinct because of common characteristics not shared by those countries regarded as belonging to the First, Second, or Third World. Now: *spec.*[ifically] those developing countries and communities, esp. in Africa, Asia, and Latin America, considered to be the poorest and least developed, typically heavily dependent on foreign economic aid and having very low per-capita GNP, and often as distinguished from wealthy neighbouring nations possessing oil resources. (OED, s.v. 'Fourth World, n., sense 3')

Sense 4 is semantically closely related to sense 3. It is documented from 1976 onwards. In contrast to sense 3, the emphasis is not on economically poor countries, but on deprived people:

> 4. (A category of) people living in a relatively wealthy nation, yet in conditions of extreme deprivation or poverty, *esp.* an urban underclass; the phenomenon of poverty in wealthy nations. (OED, s.v. 'Fourth World, n., sense 4')

Etymologically, this sense differs from all the others. While the entry's etymology section tells us that *Fourth World* was formed within English by compounding, sense 4 originated as *quart monde* in French 'in the name of the Mouvement ATD (Aide à Toute Détresse) *Quart Monde*, an international non-governmental agency founded in 1957 by the French priest Joseph Wresinski (1917–88) to relieve poverty worldwide' (OED, s.v. 'Fourth World, n., sense 4').

Fourth World belongs in Frequency Band 4, and 'typically occurs about 0.2 times per million words in modern written English.'[11] The description of this frequency band states that '[s]uch words are marked by much greater specificity and a wider range of register, regionality, and subject domain than those found in bands 8–5.'[12]

Four citations ranging from 1967 to 1996 illustrate the meaning and use of Sense 3. The two citations below do not only attest the term, but provide defining features.

> 1977 A disaster for developed countries, OPEC was an unmitigated tragedy for the abysmally poor nations of the 'Fourth World,' those nations of Africa, Latin America, and Asia unblessed by oil or other riches. *New York Review of Books* 12 May 39/3
>
> 1996 A 'fourth world' has emerged, inhabited by more than 1 billion souls who survive on less than $400 dollars a year. *Times Union* (Albany, New York) (Nexis) 21 April e1 (OED, s.v. 'Fourth World, n., sense 3')

According to the DNE II (1980) the term denotes 'the world's poorest and most underdeveloped countries in Africa, Asia, and Latin America.' Its first attestation stems from 1974, and it is classified as an analogical formation to *Third World*, 'coined by Robert McNamara, president of the World Bank, to distinguish such countries from the oil-rich nations of Asia, often grouped with the THIRD WORLD.' (DNE II, s.v. 'Fourth World')

In order to reveal the relationships of the terms to each other, and their dependencies upon one another, the information from the different dictionary entries shall now be compared and summarized in a second step of the investigation.

Comparison of results from the dictionary entries

Originally, the set comprised three interrelated terms, out of which *First World* denoted the industrialized western countries on the one side, as opposed to the communist countries (i.e. the *Second World*) on the other side, and the economically less-developed poorer nations constituting the *Third World*.

---

11 'Frequency,' OED.
12 'Frequency,' OED.

However, the positioning of China was – and still is – controversial. According to the Chinese view in the 1970s, the two superpowers (the US and the USSR) constitute the *First World*, the other developed countries the *Second World*, and the developing countries make up the *Third World*. As outlined above, China viewed itself, despite being a socialist country, as part of the third world.

Even today, the status of China is heavily contested, as the quotation from the *Voice of America* shows:

> The U.S. House of Representatives has voted unanimously to challenge China's status as a developing nation, a classification made by organizations such as the World Bank and the United Nations that gives the world's second-largest economy special treatment for trade and low-interest loans.[13]

The term *Third World* is an umbrella term for the economically less-developed countries, and *Fourth World* designates the poorest and least developed countries of the world. Table 1 below summarizes the major findings from the OED and DNE I, II.

Table 1: Synopsis of the relevant lexicographical data on *First*, *Second*, *Third* and *Fourth World*

TERM	ORIGIN	FIRST ATTES-TATION	PATTERN	CREATOR	FREQUENCY per million words
First World	Engl.	1967 OED 1974 DNE II	after *Third World*	unknown	6
Second World	Engl.	1967 OED[14] 1974 DNE II	after *Third World*	unknown	8
Third World	French	1963 OED 1965 DNE I	from French *tiers monde*, 1952	A. Sauvy	10
Fourth World	Engl.	1967 OED 1974 DNE II	after *Third World*	R. McNa-mara	0.2

The French term *tiers monde* seems to have been the source for all the other terms. The first written attestation of *tiers monde* appears in an article by the French demographer Alfred Sauvy from 1952.[15] The article finishes by comparing the *Third World* to the third estate in pre-revolutionary France and echoes the

---

13 Lin Yang. 'China: We're Still a Developing Nation. US Lawmakers: No Way.' *Voice Of America: China News*. 8 April 2023. <https://www.voanews.com/a/china-we-re-still-a-developing-na tion-us-lawmakers-no-way/7041814.html> (accessed 16 Feb 2024).
14 OED, s.v. 'First World, n., sense 2.'
15 Alfred Sauvy. 'Trois mondes, une planète.' *L'Observateur* 118 (14 Aug. 1952): 14.

famous question of Abbé Emmanuel Joseph Sieyès (1789) 'Qu'est-ce que le Tiers-État?'[16]

In an explanatory footnote Sauvy comments on the origin of the term:[17]

En 1951, j'ai, dans une revue brésilienne, parlé de trois mondes, sans employer toutefois l'expression "Tiers Monde".

Cette expression, je l'ai créée et employée pour la première fois par écrit dans l'hebdomadaire français "l'Observateur" du 14 août 1952. L'article se terminait ainsi: "car enfin, ce Tiers Monde ignoré, exploité, méprisé comme le Tiers Etat, veut lui aussi, être quelque chose". Je transposais ainsi la fameuse phrase de Sieyès sur le Tiers État pendant la Révolution française.

Je n'ai pas ajouté (mais j'ai parfois dit, en boutade) que l'on pourrait assimiler le monde capitaliste à la noblesse et le monde communiste au clergé. (Sauvy, 'Trois mondes')[18]

The information on (changes of) meaning over time and documentation of use gathered from dictionaries shall now be complemented by consulting corpora. To this end, usage frequencies, extracted by using Google's Ngram Viewer shall be presented next, followed by the results from the query 'Second World' in the *British National Corpus*.

First, Second, Third and Fourth World in the Google corpora

Google's Ngram Viewer is a tool that is available for free and easy to handle; it provides usage frequencies for words on the basis of Google Books. 'When you enter phrases into the Google Books Ngram Viewer, it displays a graph showing how those phrases have occurred in a corpus of books (e.g., 'British English,' 'English Fiction,' 'French') over the selected years.'[19] For English a number of corpora are available. Figure 1 displays the results for the corpus *English* (2019).

---

16 Emmanuel Joseph Sieyès. *Qu'est-ce que le Tiers-État?* [Paris], 1789. A facsimile of the original text and a modern transcription can be found under <https://gallica.bnf.fr/ark:/12148/bpt6k 97743407/f1.item>.

17 For more information on the coinage and development of the term *Third World* see Jean Lacouture. 'Bandung ou la fin de l'ère colonial.' *Le Monde diplomatique* (Apr 2005): 22–23; Marcin Wojciech Solarz. '"Third World": the 60th anniversary of a concept that changed history.' *Third World Quarterly* 33.9 (2012): 1561–1573.

18 'In a Brazilian review of 1951, I spoke of three worlds without however using the expression "third world". I created and employed this expression for the first time in writing in the French weekly *l'Observateur* of 14 August 1952. The article ended thus: "because finally, this third world, ignored, exploited, despised like the Third Estate, also like it wants to be something". I thus transposed the famous phrase of Sieyès on the Third Estate during the French Revolution. I did not add (but I sometimes said as a witticism) that one could liken the capitalist world to the nobility and the communist world to the clergy.' [translated by the editors].

19 'What does the Ngram Viewer do?' *Google Books Ngram Viewer.* n.d. Date of access 25 Nov 2023, <https://books.google.com/ngrams/info>.

This corpus contains '[b]ooks predominantly in the English language published in any country.'[20] By contrast, Figure 2 shows the results for the corpus *English Fiction* (2019). It contains English books 'that a librarian or publisher identified as fiction.'[21] Unfortunately, no bibliographical references for individual titles are available.

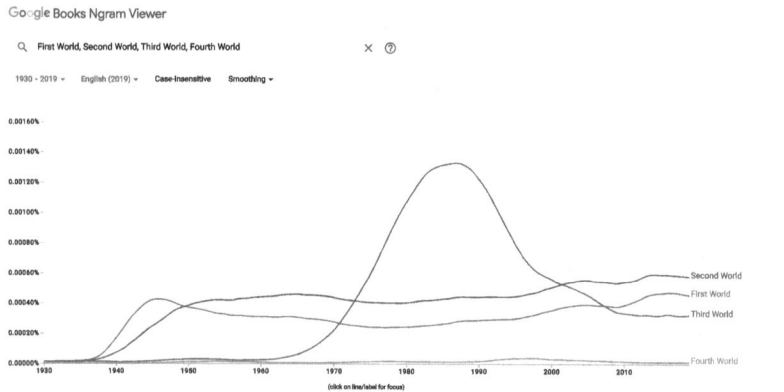

Figure 1: Google Books Ngram Viewer *English* (2019)

Figure 1 shows the combined usage frequencies for *First, Second, Third* and *Fourth World* in Google's corpus *English* (2019). The lines for *First* and *Second World* run roughly parallel to each other; they do not show large differences in usage. By contrast, the values for *Third World* begin to rise in the 1960s, reaching an all-time high in the 1980s and 1990s and then drop below the usage frequencies of *First* and *Second World*. Throughout the entire time span from 1930 to 2019, *Fourth World* is only marginally attested.

By and large, these results, unsurprisingly, confirm the usage frequencies provided in the OED, since the OED bases its frequency data on the Google Books Corpus and then corrects them by using other corpora (see footnote 5).

In comparison to Figure 1, the graph for the same query – but this time run in the Google Books corpus of *English Fiction* (2019) – looks different (Figure 2). The curves for *First* and *Second World* are again fairly parallel to each other, but especially from the 1960s to the 1990s they show a higher frequency with a flattened peak. The curve for *Third World* looks similar to that in Figure 1, again with a more pointed peak in the mid 1980s. *Fourth World* is as marginal as in *English* (2019).

With all necessary care, one can conclude that the two complementary terms *First* and *Second World* played an important role in anglophone fiction, espe-

---

20 'What does the Ngram Viewer do?'
21 'What does the Ngram Viewer do?'

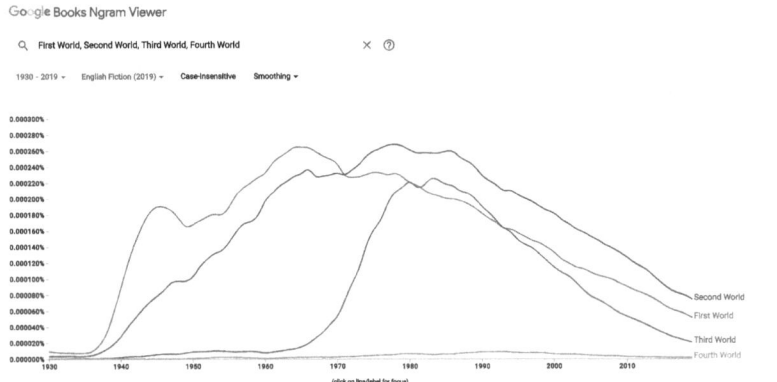

Figure 2: Google Books Ngram Viewer *English Fiction* (2019)

cially during the Cold-War period, reaching a peak – almost a plateau – from the 1960s to the 1990s, and from then on decline in their usage frequency. However, due to lack of information, we can only say that the result pertains to fiction written in the English language and not verify whether the texts come from British, American, Australian (etc.) literature.

Second World in the *British National Corpus*

In addition to the information on the meaning(s) of *Second World* retrieved from dictionaries, and information on usage frequencies based on the OED and Google Ngrams, a query was run in the *British National Corpus* [BNC][22] in order to find out how *Second World* is used in British English. All samples below fall into the time span from 1985 to 1993. They are all written and come from different parts of the United Kingdom.

Entering *Second World* as a simple query resulted in just eight hits from six different sources, once the many irrelevant hits for *Second World War*, and *Second World Cup*, had been removed. Thus, in terms of numbers *Second World* only plays a very marginal role. Since the corpus is parsed and tagged, background information on text type, medium, domain (etc.) is available.

Text (1) below stems from a periodical. The text type is classified as 'Other written material,' and the text domain as 'Informative: Arts.'

---

22 '*The British National Corpus* (BNC) is a 100 million word collection of samples of written and spoken language from a wide range of sources, designed to represent a wide cross-section of British English from the later part of the 20th century, both spoken and written.' 'What is the BNC?' *BNC*. Jan 2009. Date of access 16 Feb 2024, <http://www.natcorp.ox.ac.uk/corpus/inde x.xml>.

(1) 2435 NOW THAT the <u>Second World</u> of formerly communist countries is falling over itself to join the First World, the name 'Third World' suits the rest of the planet less well than ever. 2436 Whatever it's called, though, one of the most gloomy facts about it is that it now spends more on weapons than on health and education put together (No. 191, ACP 2435, BNCweb CQP-edition)

Text (2) stems from a book entitled *White mythologies: writing histories and the West* (text type: Academic prose; text domain: informative, World Affairs).

(2) 174 For the 'Third World' was invented in the context of the 1955 Bandung Conference, on the model of the French Revolution's 'Third Estate,' and incorporating equally revolutionary ideals of providing a radical alternative to the hegemonic capitalist-socialist power blocks of the post-war period. 175 The Third World as a term needs to retrieve this lost positive sense – even if today the political order has changed so that to some extent the various forms of Islamic fundamentalism have taken over the role of providing a direct alternative to First and <u>Second World</u> ideologies. 176 'Third World' will, therefore, be used in this book without (further) apology, or scare quotes, as a positive term of radical critique even if it also necessarily signals its negative sense of economic dependency and exploitation. (No. 747, CYT 175, BNCweb CQP-edition)

Text (3) comes from a book, entitled *Introduction to politics* (text type: Academic prose, text domain: World affairs).

(3) 1465 Thus this period saw the division of the global system into three 'worlds': the first world of developed capitalist states; the communist bloc, or <u>second world</u>; and the less developed third-world states of the southern hemisphere. The image of three distinct worlds dominated thinking about global politics for almost forty years (see chapter 7). 1467 Such a conflictual, yet relatively stable, world-view has been shattered by events since the late 1980s. 1468 The end of the Cold War has invalidated the three-world image, although 'third-worldism' retains relevance as an ideological position supportive of third-world interests. 1469 Of more immediate significance to the practice of global politics, however, was that the end of the three-world view also heralded the end of the duopoly of superpower domination of the global system. (No. 1096, GV5, BNCweb CQP-edition)

Text (4) below comes from a periodical, *New Internationalist* (text type: Non-academic prose and biography, text domain: Informative, World affairs).

(4) 15074 Each year, without fail, a new set of alienating words and phrases is put into currency. 15075 One of the most infectious was 'Third World.' 15076 It was first used by Alfred Sauvy, a French demographer, in an article published in Le Monde in which he referred to two industrialized worlds, one capitalist, one communist, and a tiers monde which remains largely agricultural. 15077 The developmentalists grabbed it and used it to make distance between the materially rich and poor nations so that very soon 'Third World' universally connoted poverty, overpopulation, disease, disorder, illiteracy, violent social upheavals and every imaginable human horror. 15078 Tacitly interpolating a <u>second world</u> as a buffer between

the first and third, served to emphasize the non-relationship between the rich and the poor. (No. 1188 HH3, BNCweb CQP-edition)

Text (5) comes from a periodical, *Spare Rib* (text type: Other published written material, Text domain: Arts).

(5) 227 AND THEN OF course I see great differences in feminisms in different countries – in first world, third world, whatever, and also principally between third world countries themselves and I think that's a point we haven't really touched on yet. 228 And that's because the third world is bigger than any other section whether you call it the first world or <u>second world</u> or whatever, and I think the first and second put together. 229 And in fact, I think in recent years what we know as the third world is the fourth, because those oil producing countries in the third world retained the status of being third and everyone got pushed to the fourth. (No. 1389, HSL 228, BNCweb CQP-edition [emphasis in the original])

Text (6) stems from a book, entitled *Sociology of the global system* (text type: Acdemic prose, text domain: Information, Social science), which yielded two further hits for the query.[23]

(6) 119 The experiences of some of the <u>Second World</u> (communist) countries, those who had escaped from the grip of global capitalism, particularly the Soviet Union and then China, seemed to lend support to the argument. 120 The theory was most exhaustively worked out for countries in Latin America, where it swept the board among academics, politicians, bureaucrats and militants for some time under the general rubric of the dependency approach. 121 It did for a time seem to explain the trajectories of development and underdevelopment in some countries of Latin America, but when it was applied to Africa and Asia it was much less successful. 122 This led some writers to suspect that the Third World, like the First World, was not of a piece, but that there might be substantial differences of kind as well as the obvious differences of degree between countries. (No. 1401, HVT 119)

The findings from the BNC can be summed up as follows. All in all, the query for *Second World* yielded eight attestations from six different sources, all of them written – either from books or periodicals. As text type, most of the sources are classified as informative (non-) academic prose on world affairs or social science, directed to a general, or to a more specialised audience.

The texts reveal that the terms under investigation are indeed relational. *First, Second, Third,* and even *Fourth World* often occur in the same stretch of text. In most cases the focus of the text is on *Third World,* rather than on *First* or *Second World.*

In order to control, and possibly underpin, these results, queries were also run for *First, Third* and *Fourth World.* The hits did confirm that the terms are relational. The following patterns of usage can be discerned:

---

23 No. 1405, HVT 930 and No. 1406, HVT 1053. BNCweb CQP-edition.

Pattern 1: *First World* and *Third World* are used as binary opposites. In this case the distinguishing semantic feature is 'wealth'; i. e. industrialised and rich vs. not industrialised and poor:

> 587 To be sure, the modern West has turned into a corrupt and greedy Scrooge, with each affluent nation ever-reluctant to share its gross national product with a starving and emaciated Third World. 588 The <u>First World</u>'s miserly materialism is enough to make any honest seeker yearn for a new alternative or age. (No. 270, B2G 588, BNCweb CQP-edition)

Pattern 2: In addition to the difference in economic status, the organization of the economy (capitalist vs. non-capitalist) can be important:

> 428 Dependency theorists, therefore, were still trying to answer the question that had troubled Marxists since the turn of the century, namely 'can capitalism develop the <u>Third World</u>?' 429 Frank, and those who agreed with his theory of the development of underdevelopment, unequivocally denied that capitalism could ever develop the Third World. 430 The best it could do would be to permit a small degree of enclave development, which only reproduced First World-Third World exploitation within the Third World. 431 Dependent development theorists, on the other hand, acknowledged capitalist development in the Third World, particularly in the NICs, but it was development of a peculiar kind, namely dependent development. (No. 1329, HTV 428, BNCweb CQP-edition)

Pattern 3: *Third* and *Fourth World* are contrasted. The most salient semantic feature being 'poor' vs. 'very poor':

> The term 'Third World' came to seem rather outmoded as developing countries divided into many different characters and degrees of prosperity. [...] 66 Meanwhile the poorest nations of all were left even further behind as an effective '<u>fourth world</u>.' (No. 9, HH3 66, BNCweb CQP-edition)

The texts from the BNC show that semantically the four terms often function as binary opposites alongside the most salient semantic features:

First World	(non-socialist)	vs.	*Second World*	(socialist)
First World	(industrialised)	vs.	*Third World*	(non-industrialised)
Third World	(poor)	vs.	*Fourth World*	(very poor)

Summary and conclusion

The original three-term partition of the world into *First*, *Second* and *Third World* is a result of the separation and confrontation of the US and the Soviet Union and their respective allies during the Cold War, resulting in a capitalist *First World*, a socialist *Second World*, and the developing countries as the *Third World*.

This geo-political division of the world according to economic power and/or capitalist/socialist economy has dominated public discourse in English (and other languages) from the 1960s to the present. Even the four points of the compass developed new economic meanings:

East   (industrialised, socialist economy) West   (industrialised, capitalist economy)
North   (industrialised, affluent)   South   (not industrialised, poor)[24]

The northern patronizing attitude towards the less affluent southern third-world countries has resulted in a consecutive amelioration or replacement of words designating the status of these countries from *underdeveloped*, via *developing countries* to *emerging countries*, or, more recently, to *Lesser/Least Developed Countries* (used by the United Nations) or *Low-Income Countries* (used by the World Bank).

Countries on the threshold to the industrialised countries are currently subsumed under the acronym BRICS (namely, Brazil, Russia, India, China and South Africa).

Thus, after the collapse of the USSR and the disintegration of the Eastern Bloc, i. e. the *Second World*, all the four terms no longer reflect the current geo-political power blocs and spheres of influence of the early twenty-first century. Interestingly enough, these developments are not matched by providing corresponding pragmatic labels in the OED such as, for example, *dated, historical, offensive* (etc.). Admittedly, the notes on *First* and *Second World* in the OED[25] say that these articles are not yet fully revised. The documentation for *Second World* ends in 1980.[26] However, the Google Ngrams and the results from the BNC show that the terms are still in use.

Work on the German Dictionary of Anglicisms [AWb][27], has shown that the terminology is politically loaded. In this context Lehnert[28] comments that some loan translations, such as *Dritte Welt* and *Vierte Welt*, originating in the Western capitalist world, do not correspond to the Marxist ideology of the GDR, but that

---

24 *North* and *South* as economic designations first appeared in the expression *North-South dialogue* (1976). See DNE II, s.v. 'North.'
25 See footnotes 7 and 8 in this chapter.
26 Revison work on the OED began in 1990, after the publication of OED 2 (1989), starting with letter 'M.' 'With the release of our March 2022 update, just over half (54%) of the entries are new or fully revised. If you count in terms of senses (as dictionary editors tend to), 55% of senses currently in *OED* are either new or updated.' [Michael Proffitt, current Chief Editor]. 'OED Annual Report 2022.' *OED*. Date of access 16 Feb 2024, <https://www.oed.com/informa tion/about-the-oed/history-of-the-oed/preface-to-the-third-edition-of-the-oed/oed-annual-report-2022/>.
27 See the entries for 'Dritte Welt' and 'Vierte Welt.'
28 Martin Lehnert. *Anglo-Amerikanisches im Sprachgebrauch der DDR*. Berlin: Akademie-Verlag, 1990. 154.

for reasons of international communication they cannot not be avoided or replaced easily.

The information that the whole concept and its terminology are of Western origin (and hence mirror the western/capitalist world view) is not explicitly mentioned in the dictionaries.

When Raymond Williams worked on his dictionary *Keywords* in the early 1970s, he complained that the OED reflected the state of affairs of its compilation from the 1880s to the 1920s and also the ideology of its editors. Fifty years later, the OED is more up-to-date and less biased, but one important caveat postulated by Williams for studies in historical semasiology is still relevant today:

[I]ndividual words should never be isolated; [...] the area of signification is not confined to the system itself, but in one dimension necessarily extends to the users of language and to the objects and relationships about which language speaks [...].[29]

References

Barnhart, Clarence L., Sol Steinmetz and Robert K. Barnhart. *A Dictionary of New English 1963–1972*. Bronxville, NY: Barnhart Books and Berlin: Langenscheidt, 1973. [DNE I]

–, – and –. *The Second Barnhart Dictionary of New English*, Bronxville, NY: Barnhart Books, 1980. [DNE II]

British National Corpus, <http://www.natcorp.ox.ac.uk>. [BNC]

Carstensen, Broder and Ulrich Busse. *Anglizismen-Wörterbuch. Der Einfluß des Englischen auf den deutschen Wortschatz nach 1945*. 3 vols. Berlin: de Gruyter, 1993–1995. [AWb]

Fowler, Roger. *Language in the News: Discourse and Ideology in the Press*. London: Routledge, 1991.

Garver, John. 'Chinese Foreign Policy in 1970: The Tilt Towards the Soviet Union.' *The China Quarterly* 82 (June 1980): 214–249.

Hübler, Axel and Ulrich Busse. 'Introduction.' *Investigations into the Meta-communicative Lexicon of English: A Contribution to Historical Pragmatics*. Ed. Ulrich Busse and Axel Hübler. Amsterdam and Philadelphia: Benjamins, 2012. 1–16.

Lacouture, Jean. 'Bandung ou la fin de l'ère colonial.' *Le Monde diplomatique* (Apr 2005): 22–23.

Lehnert, Martin. *Anglo-Amerikanisches im Sprachgebrauch der DDR*. Berlin: Akademie-Verlag, 1990.

Lionnet, Philippe. 'Anpassungen in der Wirtschaftspolitik in der Volksrepublik China: die Scharnierjahre 1974/1975.' *Jahrbuch für Historische Kommunismusforschung* (2020): 155–171.

Oxford English Dictionary, <www.oed.com>. [OED]

Sauvy, Alfred. 'Trois mondes, une planète.' *L'Observateur* 118 (14 Aug. 1952): 14.

---

29 Williams, *Keywords*, 20.

Solarz, Marcin Wojciech. '"Third World": the 60th anniversary of a concept that changed history.' *Third World Quarterly* 33.9 (2012): 1561–1573.

Williams, Raymond. *Keywords: A vocabulary of culture and society.* Glasgow: Fontana/Croom Helm, 1976.

Yang, Lin. 'China: We're Still a Developing Nation. US Lawmakers: No Way.' *Voice of America: China News.* 8 April 2023. <https://www.voanews.com/a/china-we-re-still-a-developing-nation-us-lawmakers-no-way/7041814.html> (accessed 16 Feb 2024).

Paul D. Morris

Representing the Historical and Imaginative 'Truth' of the *Holodomor:* Malcolm Muggeridge's *Winter in Moscow* (1934) and Agnieszka Holland's *Mr. Jones* (2019)

Despite the drama implicit in the terrible loss of human life during the Great Ukrainian Famine of 1932–1933, the *Holodomor* has received comparatively little artistic representation in the West.[1] Various reasons why this is so may be surmised, with some less benign than others. For one, prior to transformation into art, Ukraine's tragedy required recognition as a simple fact of historical reality, something unconscionably long denied. The *Holodomor* seems to have suffered from the 'perceptual' distance separating Ukraine from the information centres of Western Europe and North America in the first half of the twentieth century. The convulsions of the First World War, the fall of the Russian and Austro-Hungarian Empires, the Russian Revolution and the establishment of the Union of Soviet Socialist Republics rendered Ukraine a conceptually distant and politically ambiguous geo-political entity. Ukraine also posed obstacles in terms of cultural and linguistic remoteness for most western commentators who lacked familiarity with the region and its languages. Significantly more consequential than such cultural and geographical impediments, however, were the ideological barriers purposefully established by various actors whose first allegiances were not to historical fact but to the success of the Soviet Union, a political system highly contested in ideological debates extending far beyond its borders. The *Holodomor* occurred as a direct result of Soviet state policy. In the effort to protect the image of the fifteen-year-old experiment in revolutionary governance, the Soviet state invested extensive resources of repression and persuasion to deny the reality of a devastating famine. A large number of the few western commentators in a position to reveal the reality of that tragedy refused to do so. While some may have been reticent due to fears of their ignorance regarding the precise scale of the famine, far too many others wilfully chose to deny the destruction for overtly ideological reasons. Committed from personal conviction to

---

1 Compare, for instance, with the literary depictions of the holocaust in Ukraine, the subject of a recent 'special dossier': Helena Duffy. 'The Holocaust in Ukraine: Literary Representations.' *Eastern European Holocaust Studies* 1.1 (2023): 79–87.

the success of the communist experiment in social engineering, these *popuchiki* (fellow travellers) participated in a campaign of disinformation promoted by Soviet authorities. Hence, as a matter of historical reality, belated awareness of the *Holodomor* in the West was not a result of ignorance but, far more importantly, an ideologically motivated effort to suppress knowledge of the naked truth of mass death.[2]

Two journalists who refused to participate in this collective act of ideological self-deception – and two works of art associated with them – are the focus of the present chapter. In March–April 1933, Gareth Jones and Malcolm Muggeridge were amongst the very first to break the conspiracy of silence exercised by their journalist peers by offering eye-witness newspaper reports on the famine.[3] Both men subsequently became the objects of fictional representation of the *Holodomor*. In early 1934, Muggeridge published his novel *Winter in Moscow* as a fictional account of his personal experiences in the Soviet Union amongst the representatives of Soviet power and their western fellow travellers.[4] Gareth Jones was murdered under mysterious circumstances in Inner Mongolia in 1935 and was thus never able to transform his experiences into artistic expression.[5] In 2019, however, the Polish-Ukrainian-British feature film directed by Agnieszka Holland, *Mr. Jones*, was released. *Mr. Jones* is a bio-pic that depicts the life of Gareth

---

2 Important exceptions to this ignorance were to be found in the diasporic Ukrainian (and Mennonite) communities that immediately organised to inform western governments of the famine taking place. The emergence in English of widespread awareness of the *Holodomor* is outlined in such publications as James Mace. 'The American Press and the Ukrainian Famine.' *Genocide Watch*. Ed. Helen Fein. New Haven: Yale University Press, 1992; Stephen Oleskiw. *The Agony of a Nation: The Great Man-Made Famine in Ukraine 1932–1933*. London: The National Committee to Commemorate the 50th Anniversary of the Artificial Famine in Ukraine 1932–1933, 1983; and, especially, Robert Conquest. *The Harvest of Sorrow: Soviet Collectivization and the Terror-Famine*. New York: Oxford University Press, 1986.
3 See Teresa Cheras. 'Forgetting Stalin's Famine: Jones and Muggeridge: A Case Study in Forgetting and Rediscovery.' *Kritika: Explorations in Russian and Eurasian History* 14.4 (2013): 775–804 for an excellent account of the chronology and events surrounding Jones's and Muggeridge's near simultaneous disclosure of first-hand knowledge of the *Holodomor*.
4 Malcolm Muggeridge. [1934] *Winter in Moscow*. Grand Rapids: Wm. B. Eerdmans, 1987. *Winter in Moscow* is amongst the first English-language works of fiction to depict the Soviet dictatorship of the proletariat. Written in what Muggeridge described as 'a mood of anger' (*Chronicles of Wasted Time: 1 The Green Stick*. London: Collins, 1972. 274), *Winter in Moscow* fared poorly while contributing to Muggeridge's ostracization from his liberal intellectual milieu: 'the financial results of this [publication] were relatively meagre, and the professional consequences disastrous' (*Chronicles of Wasted Time: 2 The Infernal Grove*. London: Collins, 1973. 18). Contemporary reviews (in *Pacific Affairs* and *Time*, for instance) were largely dismissive. A more positive account of *Winter in Moscow* would have to await Michael Aeschliman's 'Introduction' to the edition of 1987.
5 The circumstances of Jones's death and the possible, even probable, involvement of the Soviet NKVD are recounted in Margaret Siriol Colley. *Gareth Jones: A Manchuko Incident*. Newark: Nigel Linsan Colley, 2001.

Jones; it focuses on his experiences in the Soviet Union and, in particular, the 1933 journey through the Ukrainian countryside prior to filing his reports on the famine later that spring.[6] Thus, amongst the vanishingly few artistic works dedicated to the *Holodomor* are a satirical, autobiographical novel from 1934 and a biographical feature film from 2019, both centred on the two principals responsible for the earliest reporting on the famine. Separated by 85 years and their respective artistic media – film and prose fiction – the two works are very different in terms of the conventions of artistic representation at their disposal and yet very similar in terms of a core motivation that transcends the reporting of historical fact: how to serve both historical and imaginative truth; how to satisfy the witness-reporter's responsibility to observable fact while acknowledging the myriad issues that transcend empirical commentary. In the preface to his novel, Muggeridge concedes that his recourse to fiction derived from his identification of this dilemma and his realisation that only art was adequate to capture both forms of truth: 'I had to be a bit of novelist as well as a reporter. Thus the episodes of my book are truth imaginatively expressed, and the characters real people imaginatively described' (*Winter* 8). In the following chapter, I wish to discuss several overlapping and yet distinct strategies employed by the two works to recount the historical, empirical reality of the *Holodomor* while – equally importantly – also depicting the dangers of enthralment to an ideology whose essence found terrible metonymic expression in the organised starvation of millions.

History, artistic representation and the *Holodomor* – *Winter in Moscow* and *Mr. Jones*

Both *Winter in Moscow* and *Mr. Jones* derive their primary force as representations of the *Holodomor*. As works of art, the philosophical and aesthetic value of each is dependent upon the fundamental 'truth' of this foundational historical reality. An unusual, additional feature of these works, which substantially enhances their truth function, is that they contain substantial (auto)biographical elements in their depictions of an historical event. Muggeridge and Jones both conducted real-time, non-fictional reportage that contributes significantly to the plots of both works of art, but which also exists independently of the novel and

---

6 *Mr. Jones*. Dir. Agnieszka Holland. Perf. James Norton, Vanessa Kirby, Peter Sarsgaard. Film Produkcja, 2019. *Mr. Jones* has received mixed but in general positive reviews; in 2019, it won the 'Grand Prix Golden Lions' award at the Gdynia Film Festival in Poland: Ola Salwa. '*Mr. Jones* Tames the Golden Lions at the Polish Film Festival in Gdynia.' *Cineuropa*. 23 Sept 2019. <https://cineuropa.org/en/newsdetail/378608/> (accessed 14 Feb 2024).

film in the realm of historical documentation. In Muggeridge's case, apart from his contemporary newspaper reports, there are his diary entries, published in 1981 as *Like It Was*, and the two volumes of his memoirs, *Chronicles of Wasted Time*, published in 1972 and 1973. The historical experiences that provide the material for *Mr. Jones* are also amply authenticated in various forms of documentation, including in Jones's reporting and in his diaries from the 1930s.[7] Further independent documentation is provided by external actors of the period who also figure as active participants in *Winter in Moscow* and in *Mr. Jones*.[8] I would like to argue that each work shares three common goals which derive from, but ultimately surpass, the representation of history and fact: (i) to depict the foibles and ideologically motivated deception of those westerners who refused to acknowledge the truth of the Soviet regime; (ii) to offer an accurate, if necessarily partial, account of a catastrophic historical event, the *Holodomor*; and lastly (iii), to intimate the broader dangers – political and moral – of a governmental system capable of engineering a famine. Artistic representation – as intimated by Muggeridge – offers a means to attain a form of imaginative truth that transcends mere facts, terrible as those facts may be. Beyond these shared concerns, of course, the two works differ in accordance with the separate historical contexts of production and with regard to the representational techniques available to their respective genres.

A corrupted ideology and corrupted intellectuals

The first of these goals is the depiction of a sordid, ultimately decadent milieu, wherein moral and ideological corruption is depicted through representation of the behaviour and motivation of key characters. *Winter in Moscow* is a broadly satirical *roman à clef* divided into seven chapters that together offer a comprehensive depiction of a range of characteristics specific to the Soviet Union and the culture it fostered. Written in the third person – apart from a brief section that introduces an unspecified first-person narrator – the novel depicts episodic moments and set scenes revolving around a collection of western intellectuals and journalists as well as a variety of Soviet officials during the winter of 1932–

---

7 A comprehensive selection of materials related to Gareth Jones – including his newspaper articles and transcribed diaries – are accessible at www.garethjones.org. Jones's legacy has been admirably curated in a growing number of publications by, in particular, Margaret Siriol Colley, Nigel Colley and Ray Gamache.

8 An important case in point is that of Eugene Lyons, the UPS correspondent to the Soviet Union, who documented the atmosphere amongst the foreign journalists in Moscow as well as the suppression of reporting on the *Holodomor*: Eugene Lyons. *Assignment in Utopia*. London: George G. Harrap & Co., 1937.

1933. Each of the characters seems based on real-life individuals that Muggeridge had known during his several-month sojourn in Moscow as a replacement for the *Manchester Guardian*'s regular Russian correspondent, W.H. Chamberlin. Some of the figures are clearly identifiable, for example Ouspenski (Konstantin Aleksandrovich Umanskii, Head of the Press and Information Department of the Soviet Ministry of Foreign Affairs), Jefferson (Walter Duranty, Anglo-American bureau chief of the *New York Times* in Moscow), Paul (Louis Aragon, the French poet), Prince Alexis (Prince D.S. Mirskii, critic and historian of Russian literature). Others are caricatures of the fellow-travellers who (in)famously travelled to the Soviet Union during the period – assorted progressive intellectuals, trade union representatives and cultural icons (e.g. G.B. Shaw, Sidney and Beatrice Webb). And finally, there are the composite figures, those who retain significant and yet unverifiable traces of their actual character: for instance, Wilfred Pye (Gareth Jones) and Wraithby (Muggeridge).[9] The author Muggeridge subjects his characters to satiric scorn in order to highlight the chasm existing between their lofty aspirations in supporting what they naively believe are the ideals of Soviet society with the pettiness and even perversions of their thoughts and actions. Here, sexual peccadilloes and prurient obsessions feature prominently as illustrated by the figure of Mr Trivet in the first chapter, mockingly entitled 'Revolutionaries':

> In another part of the room Mr. Trivet looked about him. He was as wizened as his wife was fluid, and had come grudgingly on their tour of investigation, comforted only by the thought that the enlightened Russian proletariat bathed in the nude, and that he might find a comsomolka; slim and ardent; red kerchief round dark hair, who would tell him about her sexual life. His Intourist guide (not, it is true, dressed for the part – silk stockings, smart hat and fur coat; trophies of past category A travellers) might have met his requirements except that Mrs. Trivet shared her with him. He wanted a comsomolka all to himself. There were private, bitter questions he wanted answered before he could decide whether all was well or not with the Dictatorship of the Proletariat. (*Winter* 23)

Intimations of intellectual and moral corruption are sharpened further in the depictions of those who *could* understand the reality of the Soviet system but choose not to for reasons of ideology and egoism. In both instances, Muggeridge

---

9 The identity of many of these characters may be gleaned through comparison of the events in *Winter in Moscow* and Muggeridge's diary entries and memoirs of the same period. Curiously, Muggeridge – although a relatively intimate acquaintance of Jones as evidenced by their exchange of letters – *never* referred to Jones in any of his subsequent writings. In *Winter in Moscow*, facets of Jones's personality appear in the figure of Pye, who is at the centre of chapter four, 'Ash-Blonde Incorruptible,' but also in the journalist Ferdinand Stoope 'blond and boyish and ardent; a recognised authority on European affairs, and a journalist with a reputation for originality and sprightly writing' (*Winter* 90). In contrast, the film *Mr. Jones* makes but a brief reference to Muggeridge, as Jones is seen greeting him glancingly at a party for journalists.

suggests an evil that comes from the brutal utilitarian calculus of accepting innumerable acts of injustice – the arrest of innocent people or the starvation of millions – in the name of abstract ideological goals. Amongst the journalists, the most explicit example among many is that of the American journalist Jefferson, the fictional representative of Walter Duranty, bureau chief of the *New York Times* in Moscow.[10] The 1932 Pulitzer Prize laureate for his reporting on the Soviet Union, Duranty's reputation has subsequently been tarnished under suspicions of complicity with Soviet authorities. In chapter 3, 'Heavy Industry,' which recounts the public relations spectacle surrounding the opening of the Dnieper Hydroelectric Station in October 1932, Muggeridge has Jefferson-Duranty respond to a question by a fellow journalist about the reports of famine. In the course of his prevaricating answer, Jefferson uses what was to become Duranty's repeated formula 'you can't make omelettes without cracking eggs' (*Winter* 90).[11] In Muggeridge's account, Jefferson-Duranty's corruption is representative of failings amongst the entirety of the foreign press corps; it is perhaps most explicitly described in a narratorial comment on the journalist's efforts to report on a famine that all know is occurring, but only with a view to protecting his journalistic reputation (*Winter* 171). The level of cynical malignity attributed by Muggeridge to the (historical) characters of his novel is most apparent, however, in the case of the Soviet officials depicted. Through the access granted to personal thoughts by the third-person narration, Muggeridge suggests moments of doubt in some officials regarding the legitimacy of their actions in the name of the dictatorship of the proletariat. Others, however, serve to reveal the ultimate source of evil in the system – a naked pursuit of power. In chapter seven of the novel, entitled 'Who, Whom?,' Muggeridge takes up Lenin's famous slogan of 1921 *kto kogo*, to exemplify dominance as the guiding principle of Bolshevik ideology.[12] In this final chapter centring on Wraithby, the character closest to

---

10 Muggeridge's characterization of Jefferson-Duranty in *Winter in Moscow* is damning – particularly with regards to his observance of the standards of journalism – although not as unsparing as the more unstinting portrayal offered in volume one of his memoirs: 'I suppose no one – not even Louis Fischer – followed the Party Line, every shift and change, as assiduously as he did. ... No, he admired Stalin and the régime precisely because they were so strong and ruthless. 'I put my money on Stalin,' was one of his favourite sayings. It was the sheer power generated that appealed to him' (*The Green Stick* 255).

11 On 31 March 1933 – the same day that Gareth Jones published in the *Evening Standard* his first signed newspaper article on the famine – Walter Duranty published a story in the *New York Times* which dismissively addressed Jones and his story directly while denying the existence of famine. In the text of his hastily filed denial, Duranty again deployed the very metaphor referenced by Muggeridge in his novel: 'But – to put it brutally – you can't make an omelette without breaking eggs' [Walter Duranty. 'Russians Hungry but Not Starving.' *New York Times* (31 March 1933): 13].

12 First used by Lenin in 1921, both Trotsky and Stalin subsequently adopted the expression 'who, whom' to express a radical understanding of all political relations as a contest between

Muggeridge, Wraithby has a lengthy discussion with Ouspenski (the official responsible for the foreign journalists in the Soviet Union) in which he seeks an answer to the essential Bolshevik question, 'who, whom':

> 'No, but seriously,' Wraithby interrupted, 'Who whom?'
> Ouspenski's voice dropped confidentially. 'The broad masses are like children. They need a father. A dictatorship of themselves. A force that is them but that, working apart from them, makes it possible for everything to be subordinated to their interests. Any other force must, by its very nature, deceive and enslave them. It alone...'
> 'Please,' Wraithby pleaded, 'Who whom?'
> 'I they,' Ouspenski whispered.
> Wraithby beamed. 'Now I understand,' he said. (*Winter* 215)

The illumination achieved by Wraithby in this exchange places in perspective all the machinations of each of the characters of the novel, from the self-deluded to the corrupt. Protestations of disinterested concern for the welfare of the masses were merely a mask for the will to power.

Like *Winter in Moscow*, *Mr. Jones*, too, focuses on a representation of the journalistic milieu of Moscow in 1933 that emphasises moral squalor and intimations of sinister dishonesty. Upon his arrival in Moscow and prior to his journey in the Ukrainian countryside, Gareth Jones's experiences are depicted in the film as singularly menacing. The murder of a journalist colleague who had been working on a story about disquiet in Ukraine is suggested, interactions with Soviet bureaucracy and officialdom are at once Kafkaesque and ominous, and conversations with fellow westerners are conducted in an atmosphere of fear and repression.[13] The dark, sparse and threatening atmosphere depicted in the film's visual portrayal of Moscow are vocalised and confirmed in a series of conversations with, in particular, Ada Brooks – a non-historical character – who indicates the depth of the falsity, corruption and both moral and physical danger posed by the Soviet system. Brooks also identifies an important source of the malaise afflicting the regime and those supporting it: a willingness to entertain compromised, negotiated perceptions of the truth in the interests of ideological calculation. Just prior to his departure for Ukraine, Jones and Brooks engage in an important exchange highlighting a crucial distinction:

---

dominators and dominated. For a discussion of *kto kogo* / 'who, whom' as the 'operational code in politics' of Bolshevism, see Daniel Bell. 'Ten Theories in Search of Reality: The Prediction of Soviet Behaviour in the Social Sciences.' *World Politics* 10.3 (1958): 340.

13 The film's inclusion of a murdered journalist into the events of March 1933 is not part of the historical record and seems motivated by a desire to suggest the repressive nature of the régime and to foreshadow the intensity of the efforts to hinder reporting of the famine. Interestingly, *Winter in Moscow* for similar reasons also imagines the probable murder of a journalist, Cooley (*Winter* 162–165).

Brooks: What's the agenda now?
Jones: I don't have an agenda, unless you call truth an agenda.
Brooks: Yes, but whose truth?
Jones: The truth, there is only one kind. (*Mr. Jones* 0:42:45)

Brooks is depicted as a foreign journalist working with the historical Walter Duranty, someone willing to compromise the truth for what she (and he) considers a greater good (the struggle against fascism). Later in the film, Duranty presents Brooks with what he terms a 'choice' (*Mr. Jones* 1:40:09), offering her a position in New York in return for a signed article denouncing Jones and confirming the love of the peasantry for Stalin. Brooks refuses the 'choice,' in implicit, belated acknowledgement of Jones's position that truth is singular, independent of either personal or ideological calculation.

Mr. Jones presents various obstacles to Jones's understanding of the truth, from the complacency and arrogance of British politicians through the timidity and collaboration of certain journalists to the brutal exercise of power by Soviet officials. It is Duranty, however, who provides metonymic representation of the decadence of disregard for the truth in the interests of an 'agenda.' It is he who presides over an orgiastic party for Moscow's foreign journalists at his private residence in an arresting set scene of seven minutes (*Mr. Jones* 0:23:00 to 0:30:00). In *Winter in Moscow*, Pye, the figure representing Jones, is depicted as the 'ash-blond incorruptible,' and at Duranty's party in *Mr. Jones*, he is likewise 'incorruptible,' remaining impervious to the cynical banter of other journalists (Eugene Lyons), declining the invitation to share opium (Rhea Clyman), and refusing Duranty's offer of women and alcohol.[14] The off-focus, jerky and discordant manner in which this visually lavish scene is filmed recapitulates Jones's confusion as one unwilling and unable by nature to participate in the antics orchestrated by Duranty. Duranty, who re-occurs throughout the film as a cynical reporter but also an influencer with insider access to sources of Soviet power, is presented – literally – as naked, his corrupted, morally crippled essence laid bare to reveal an individual willing to compromise the truth for a 'cause' that is a mere cover for his base personal desires.

---

14 Despite the quality of Beata Poźniak's portrayal in *Mr. Jones*, it is unfortunate that the depiction of Rhea Clyman was limited to a scene of her injecting herself with opium. The Polish-Canadian journalist merits considerably more awareness. For an account of her independent, 3,000-kilometre journey through the grain producing regions of the USSR, her subsequent expulsion from the country and her extensive reporting on the famine shortly after the reports by Jones and Muggeridge, see Jars Balan. 'Rhea Clyman: A Forgotten Canadian Witness to the Hunger of 1932.' *Women and the Holodomor-Genocide: Victims, Survivors, Perpetrators*. Ed. Victoria Malko. Fresno: The Press at California State University, 2019. [Online]. Available: https://holodomor.ca/wp-content/uploads/2020/04/3.5.2_Jars-Balan-Rhea-Clyman-English.pdf. Accessed 14 Feb 2024.

Telling the truth – reporting the *Holodomor*

The second, and ultimately foundational, motivation of the two works under discussion is the revelation of the truth of the famine in the Soviet Union. The journey into the Soviet countryside occurs at the end both of *Winter in Moscow* and of Muggeridge's actual stay in the Soviet Union, providing the narrative with a terminus and culmination. The journey is preceded in the final chapter – 'Who Whom?' – by a series of encounters by Wraithby (Muggeridge) with several interlocuters who represent various dimensions of Soviet life and society. The actual descriptions of Muggeridge's voyage through Ukraine to the North Caucasus (Rostov-na-Dony) were famously smuggled out of the Soviet Union via British diplomatic bag to be published – without attribution – on 25, 27 and 28 March 1933. In *Winter in Moscow*, the passages recounting Wraithby's voyage are minimal; the effects of the famine on the Soviet individuals are laconically expressed. Of greater relevance than the events of his journey – such as the sight of peasants begging for food – is the effect on Wraithby-Muggeridge, which creates a moral imperative to leave the country but also never to obfuscate reality in the interests of ideology:

> They [starving peasants] knelt down and wept and pleaded. Whatever else I may do or think in the future, he [Wraithby] thought, I must never pretend that I haven't seen this. Ideas will come and go; but this is more than an idea. It is peasants kneeling down in the snow and asking for bread. Something I have seen and understood. (*Winter* 244–245)

The earlier chapter devoted to the Jones-like character Pye made explicit references to Pye's journeys in the countryside and his reporting, including several experiences unmistakeably identifiable to Jones, as will be discussed below. Even while drawing on the historical Jones, however, Muggeridge masks and contorts the actual provenance of Pye's experiences (in Jones's real-life journey) by having his fictional journalist conform to type. Rather than acknowledging the empirical truth of the famine before his eyes (and in contrast to Jones's real-life posture), Pye adopts the approach favoured by the journalists depicted by Muggeridge to content himself with the comforting explanations of Soviet officialdom. Momentarily suspending the satiric treatment of the foreign press corps, the third-person narration of *Winter in Moscow* subsequently leaves the subjective thoughts and conversations of Pye and all of the other journalists satirized in the novel to offer a synthesizing, objectively framed commentary on the specificity of the famine:

> The famine now raging in Russia is different from any that has hitherto happened because it is organised from within. No external cause like bad weather or a blockade can be blamed for it. People feel it to be a consequence of an inward corruption. It seems to them innate in Bolshevism and a fruit of the Dictatorship of the Proletariat. (*Winter* 138)

In contrast to *Winter in Moscow*, the physical depiction of the famine is far more extensive and graphic in *Mr. Jones*. Rather than serving as a narrative terminus,

Jones's witness to the famine serves as a fulcrum to his life as presented in the film; it is the film's centre of gravity portrayed in an almost 30-minute segment (*Mr. Jones* 0:48:40 to 1:20:28) filmed in stark near-monochrome. This segment recounts Jones's experiences travelling to Kharkiv, then the capital of Ukraine. Rather than complete his journey, prior to his arrival in Kharkiv Jones jumps off the train to travel on foot, unaccompanied, through the countryside. Just as his actions in England and Moscow were driven by the desire to confirm what he (correctly) assumed was the truth of Stalin's forced requisition of grain, so, too, the remainder of his life shown in the film was influenced by his expedition and subsequent reporting. Significantly, in this pivotal segment, the film departs from a narration of historical fact to depict experiences Jones never had, such as his supposed deception of a Soviet chaperone, his inadvertent consumption of human flesh, and his arrest by the OGPU. These distortions of historical fact have been criticized, although it may also be plausibly argued that the film's director, Agnieszka Holland, and the script writer Andrea Chalupa chose this approach in order to transcend the specifics of Jones's reporting and represent the broader realities of the *Holodomor* and the system that caused it (see below).

Of the telling details presented in the film's segment on the famine-stricken countryside, one that seems almost certainly to have derived from Jones's historical experiences concerns an orange. During an emotionally tumultuous scene prior to his departure from Moscow, Ada Brooks presents Jones with an orange (*Mr. Jones* 0:47:08) which he subsequently unpeels while travelling through Ukraine with starving passengers. The peel, innocently deposited into a spittoon, is immediately snatched up and consumed, prompting Jones to share the remainder of his orange with a child. In the film, this event – depicted as Jones's first concrete experience of the famine – transpires wordlessly; its morose profundity is communicated by the eerie silence of the watching fellow passengers and the astounded realisation on Jones's face (*Mr. Jones* 0:53:55 to 0:55:38). Testimony to the illustrative force of this modest incident is offered elsewhere, including in *Winter in Moscow*. Upon the completion of his journey and his departure from Russia, and prior to his return to London, the historical Jones organised a press interview in Berlin on 31 March 1933 to inform the world of his recent confirmation of the famine. Several of the reports filed from Berlin on the basis of Jones's press interview – beginning with H.R. Knickerbocker's posting for the *New York Evening Post* – included repeated reference to the same incident: 'I threw an orange peel into the spittoon and the peasant again grabbed it and devoured it.'[15] The same anecdote, with further details gleaned from the several

---

15 H.R. Knickerbocker. 'Famine Grips Russia Millions Dying. Idle on Rise, Says Briton. Gareth Jones, Lloyd George Aid, Reports Devastation. Tours Farm Areas, Finds Food Gone.' *New York Evening Post* (29 March 1933): 1.

posts filed on Jones's press interview, also finds its way in satiric form into *Winter in Moscow*. In Muggeridge's novelistic re-telling, the relevance of the incident is inverted in service of his generalised depiction of the foreign press corps as corrupt. Rather than serve as a horrifying proof of the famine for a discerning journalist, it becomes an illustration of the insouciance of a foreign journalist unable to comprehend the reality before his eyes due to his desire to believe Soviet ideology:

> Three peasants on the opposite seat; one old and the others not so old; perhaps his sons, watched Pye eat an orange. He peeled it slowly and threw the peel piece by piece into a spittoon. The peasants seemed fascinated by the spectacle of Pye eating an orange, and followed each of his movements with their eyes. He finished the orange and dried his fingers and mouth with a hand-kerchief.
> 'Food shortage?' the young man [Pye's Soviet travelling companion] said. 'Not at all. Very big business, but no food shortage [....]' [...] 'No food shortage,' he went on, smiling reassuringly.
> 'Quite so. Quite so,' Pye nodded.
> The peasants were looking now at the orange peel. The one nearest to the spittoon leant forwards; not deliberately, but casually [...] As he leant forwards his hand went nearer to the spittoon; suddenly made a dart and clutched the orange peel. He ate it up ravenously, giving none to his two companions.
> 'I think I'll read a bit now,' Pye said; (*Winter* 140–141)

Beyond this experience with the orange, the 30-minute segment devoted to the famine offers several sequences which are designed, in terms of subject matter, dialogue and filming technique, to elicit a range of extreme responses. Jones's responses as a participant and witness, from astonishment through disgust and revulsion to pity and fear, effectively become those of the film viewer, rendering the *Holomodor* an emotionally affective experience. The segment ends with Jones's violent (fictional) arrest, which likewise recapitulates the violence perpetrated on the populace and, secondarily, the film audience.

The *Holodomor* and beyond

As indicated in the introduction, *Winter in Moscow* and *Mr. Jones*, although insistent upon the need to acknowledge the historical fact of the *Holodomor*, are also concerned with realms of truth that transcend the historically verifiable, the third motivational factor shared by the two works. Both *Winter in Moscow* and *Mr. Jones* contain facets of imaginative truth intended not to supplant the primacy of each work's factual objective, but to deploy the creative potential of art to amplify it in suggestive though necessarily non-definitive ways. As discussed above, *Winter in Moscow* represents the reality of the famine of 1932–1933 (in part via an inverted depiction of Jones's historical journey). In this depiction, the famine itself becomes the culminating illustration not only of the worldly corruption engendered by an ideology, but of the evil it represents. Thus, beyond the satirical depiction of the foibles and failings of self-deceiving fellow-travellers is a deeper realisation about the epistemological and moral dangers of subordinating truth to ideology. In the novel's concluding chapter, 'Who Whom?,' Wraithby understands that his experiences in the Soviet Union – from the repression of individuals through the falsification of reality and the creation of a famine to the delusions of western 'useful idiots' – have revealed to him the essential truth of the system Bolshevism had created. What was presented as the triumph of a noble idea was revealed – in echo of the chapter's title – as an amoral will to power. The consequences of this realization lead Wraithby (as they led Muggeridge) to a stark but simple choice between good and evil:

> He knew that he had reached an epoch in his life. There were two alternatives; clearly marked; unmistakable; and he had to choose between them. … Every tendency in himself, in societies; the past and the future; all he had ever seen or thought or felt or believed, sorted itself out. It was a vision of Good and Evil. Heaven and Hell. Life and death. There were two alternatives; and he had to choose. He chose. (*Winter* 225–226)

Wraithby's framing of his choice in the existential binaries of 'Good and Evil. Heaven and Hell. Life and death,' offers a final, non-verifiable and yet eminently truthful totalising assessment of the Soviet Union and its supporting ideology.

The strategies deployed by the director and screen-writer of *Mr. Jones* to surpass the historically verifiable events of Gareth Jones's life in depicting the broader dimensions of the *Holodomor* are more controversial. *Mr. Jones* includes events and interactions that did not occur historically as depicted in the film, but which imaginatively represent facets of the historical reality of Gareth Jones's experience and the *Holodomor*. For instance, there is no record of Gareth Jones entering into contact with a journalist murdered by the OGPU; he was not involved in an intimate affair during his 1933 visit to the Soviet Union; he did not engage in inadvertent cannibalism during his travels through the Ukrainian countryside, nor did he report personally witnessing dead bodies in the streets of villages; he was not imprisoned by the OGPU with a group of six British engineers from Metropolitan-Vickers, nor was he induced to sign a confession to secure their release; and finally Jones is not known to have been a personal acquaintance of Eric Blair/George Orwell. For these and other embellishments, the film has been censured by critics and members of Jones's family.[16] From the perspective

---

16 For a critique of the introduction of historical inaccuracies into the film, see, for example Philip Colley. 'My great-uncle's legacy must be preserved, but not at the expense of the truth.' *Le Monde*. 11 Sept 2023. <www.garethjonessociety.org/_files/ugd/ec6902_5fdee9e3c3534a9 2802a793767f6f83b.pdf> (accessed 14 Feb 2024) and Ned Thomas. '*Mr. Jones*: Not the Only

of the strictest standards of empirical truth (a standard seemingly professed by the producers of a film claiming to be 'the most important true story you will ever watch'), these criticisms are justified. From the perspective of the prerogatives of imaginative art claimed by Muggeridge to depict 'real people imaginatively described,' the exaggerations are less egregious, particularly if they are 'read' as a means of shifting focus from Gareth Jones the individual to the *Holodomor* and the ideological system that created it – and which the eponymous historical character was committed to exposing. Viewed in this way, each of the 'embellishments' to Jones's life contributes to a fuller understanding of the historical reality of the *Holodomor*.

Individuals, particularly Soviet citizens, were repressed by the state for seeking to divulge the truth of the *Holodomor*. Jones's love-interest in the film, Ada Brooks, is fictional, but her perspective on the Soviet Union expresses a tragic dilemma shared by many at the time who were not – like Muggeridge's journalists – either delusional or sinister, but rather saw communism as an alternative to fascism. In the film, Brooks is depicted for reasons of personal history to have close links to Nazi Germany. She offers qualified support to the Soviet Union not as a matter of ideological capture, but in the context of a struggle with fascism which she perceives as a still greater evil. It is also a terrible truth that in the misery of famine, numerous victims were driven to cannibalism.[17] Jones himself need not have seen dead bodies in the street; such things undeniably occurred. Jones was not arrested with the British engineers from Metropolitan-Vickers, although his fictional inclusion in this affair resonates on two levels. Firstly, the briefly referenced historical trial of the British engineers offered the film the opportunity to invoke one of the most grotesque yet representative travesties of Soviet society – the perversions of justice in the show trials that came to define the Stalinist justice system and, ultimately, the debasement of the very notion of truth as witnesses were compelled to confess to fantastical crimes planned or committed at the behest of putative enemies of the Soviet state. Secondly, Jones's fortunes as a journalist and the foreign press corps' equivocal response to his revelations about the famine were linked to the Metropolitan-Vickers affair. In *Assignment in Utopia* (1937), which detailed his experiences as UPS correspondent in Russia, Eugene Lyons offers a brief précis of the historical Jones, described as the 'conscientious' journalist who provided the 'first reliable report on the Russian famine'; Lyons also describes the collective decision to downplay the accuracy of Jones's reporting about the *Holodomor* so as to curry

---

Gareth Jones.' *Planet extra*. [no date]. <https://www.planetmagazine.org.uk/planet-extra/mr-jones-not-only-gareth-jones> (accessed 14 Feb 2024).

17　Martin Fornusek. 'Interior Ministry Discloses Archived Files on Holodomor Cannibalism Cases.' *The Kyiv Independent*. 25 Nov 2023. <https://kyivindependent.com/interior-ministry-publishes-documents-on-cannibalism-during-holodomor/> (accessed 14 Feb 2024).

favour with Soviet authorities as a precondition to accessing coverage of the trial: 'Throwing down Jones was as unpleasant a chore as fell to any of us in years of juggling facts to please dictatorial regimes – but throw him down we did, unanimously and in almost identical formulas of equivocation.'[18] The historical Jones was not arrested with the Metropolitan-Vickers engineers, although the fate of his career as a journalist and the reception of his reporting on the *Holodomor* was implicated in their historic trial.

Finally, there is the inclusion of George Orwell in the film. Orwell was not a participant in the historical events the film represents. He functions as a framing device, an individual whose spirit animates – and shapes – character Jones's and the audience's understanding of the totality of the events. Recently, attempts have been made to link Jones to Orwell's creative efforts, particularly in *Animal Farm*.[19] It seems more likely, however, that Orwell's presence in the film is to offer indirect reference to many of the issues of relevance to Jones's experiences, beyond the specifics of his reporting on the *Holodomor*. Orwell the figure is associated with injustices of Soviet totalitarianism, but also with necessity of adhering to the truth, of refusing the pressures of ideological conformity and of combatting the obfuscations of the fellow-travellers of the period. While there is no record of Jones ever meeting Orwell, as depicted in the film, it seems none-theless true that both were shaped by direct experience of Soviet ideology and (consequently?) animated by a similar spirit of incorruptible, non-dogmatic understanding of the world.

Winter in Moscow and *Mr. Jones* are thus two works of art separated by genre and historical time, but which are remarkably similar in their attempt to docu-ment the historical reality of the *Holodomor* while also depicting some of the imaginative truths related to it. Both works, in keeping with the representational means made available by their respective genres, draw upon the imaginative potential of art to serve, while transcending, the facts of history. Each work establishes a common social and intellectual setting in the context of fellow-

---

18 See Lyons, *Assignment in Utopia*, 575 for the collective press corps' betrayal of Jones and his reporting in exchange for journalistic access to the Metropolitan-Vickers trial.

19 For a summary of some of the arguments connecting Jones and Orwell, see Nigel Colley. 'Was Gareth Jones's Surname behind George Orwell's Naming of "Farmer Jones" in *Animal Farm?*' *GarethJones.org* (April 2007) and Mirosław Wlekły. *Gareth Jones: Chronist der Hungersnot in der Ukraine 1932–1933*. Transl. Benjamin Voelkel. Hamburg: Osburg Verlag, 2022.While interesting, and although further research may reveal more conclusive evidence, at present the evidence linking Jones and Orwell remains circumstantial. Orwell incontestably read (and reviewed) Lyons's account of the period with its account of the deplorable treatment of Jones and it seems all but certain that he would have been aware of Jones's revelations about the famine. However, he would also have very likely read *Winter in Moscow*, a novel that includes (perhaps inaugurates) characterization of Stalin as Napoleon, a comparison later taken up in *Animal Farm* (*Winter* 44). Muggeridge and Orwell subsequently developed a relatively close acquaintanceship as attested to in Muggeridge's diaries and memoirs.

travelling westerners wilfully blind to the truth of the Soviet regime; they each feature personal witness and empirically verifiable reportage of the *Holodomor*; and lastly each proposes an understanding of the *Holodomor* as more than a catastrophic human tragedy, but as a representative consequence of the ideological system that engineered it.

References

Balan, Jars. 'Rhea Clyman: A Forgotten Canadian Witness to the Hunger of 1932.' *Women and the Holodomor-Genocide: Victims, Survivors, Perpetrators.* Ed. Victoria Malko. Fresno: The Press at California State University, 2019. [Online]. Available: https://holodomor.ca/wp-content/uploads/2020/04/3.5.2_Jars-Balan-Rhea-Clyman-English.pdf. Accessed 14 Feb 2024.

Bell. Daniel. 'Ten Theories in Search of Reality: The Prediction of Soviet Behaviour in the Social Sciences.' *World Politics* 10.3 (1958): 327–365.

Buckley, William F. 'Uncovering Stalinism.' [Review of *Winter in Moscow* by Malcolm Muggeridge]. *National Review* 19 February (1988): 56.

Cherfas, Teresa. 'Forgetting Stalin's Famine: Jones and Muggeridge: A Case Study in Forgetting and Rediscovery.' *Kritika: Explorations in Russian and Eurasian History* 14.4 (2013): 775–804.

Colley, Philip. 'My great-uncle's legacy must be preserved, but not at the expense of the truth.' *Le Monde.* 11 Sept 2023. <www.garethjonessociety.org/_files/ugd/ec6902_5fdee9e3c3534a92802a793767f6f83b.pdf> (accessed 14 Feb 2024).

Colley, Nigel. 'Was Gareth Jones's Surname behind George Orwell's Naming of "Farmer Jones" in *Animal Farm?' GarethJones.org.* April 2007. <https://www.garethjones.org/soviet_articles/farmer_jones.htm> (accessed 14 Feb 2024).

Conquest, Robert. *The Harvest of Sorrow: Soviet Collectivization and the Terror-Famine.* New York: Oxford University Press, 1986.

Duffy, Helena. 'The Holocaust in Ukraine: Literary Representations.' *Eastern European Holocaust Studies* 1.1 (2023): 79–87. <https://doi.org/10.1515/eehs-2022-0026>.

Duranty, Walter. 'Russians Hungry but Not Starving.' *New York Times* (31 March 1933): 13.

Fornusek, Martin. 'Interior Ministry Discloses Archived Files on Holodomor Cannibalism Cases.' *The Kyiv Independent.* 25 Nov 2023. <https://kyivindependent.com/interior-ministry-publishes-documents-on-cannibalism-during-holodomor/> (accessed 14 Feb 2024).

Gamache, Ray. *Gareth Jones: Eyewitness to the Holodomor.* Cardiff: Welsh Academic Press, 2013.

Jones, Gareth. 'Famine Rules Russia.' *Evening Standard* (31 March 1933): 7.

Knickerbocker, H.R. 'Famine Grips Russia Millions Dying. Idle on Rise, Says Briton. Gareth Jones, Lloyd George Aid, Reports Devastation. Tours Farm Areas, Finds Food Gone.' *New York Evening Post* (29 March 1933): 1.

Lyons, Eugene. *Assignment in Utopia.* London: George G. Harrap & Co., 1937.

Mace, James E. 'The Politics of Famine: American Government and Press Response to the Ukrainian Famine, 1932–1933.' *Holocaust and Genocide Studies* 3.1 (1988): 75–94. <https://doi-org.uml.idm.oclc.org/10.1093/hgs/3.1.75>.

–. 'The American Press and the Ukrainian Famine.' *Genocide Watch*. Ed. Helen Fein. New Haven: Yale University Press, 1992. 113–132.

Mr. Jones. Dir. Agnieszka Holland. Perf. James Norton, Vanessa Kirby, Peter Sarsgaard. Film Produkcja, 2019.

Muggeridge, Malcolm. [1934] *Winter in Moscow*. Grand Rapids: Wm. B. Eerdmans, 1987.

–. *Chronicles of Wasted Time: 1 The Green Stick*. London: Collins, 1972.

–. *Chronicles of Wasted Time: 2 The Infernal Grove*. London: Collins, 1973.

–. *Like It Was: The Diaries of Malcolm Muggeridge*. Ed. John Bright-Holmes. New York, William Morrow and Company, 1982.

–. [unattributed]. 'The Soviet and the Peasantry: An Observer's Notes.' *The Manchester Guardian* (25 March 1933): 13–14.

–. [unattributed]. 'The Soviet and the Peasantry: An Observer's Notes.' *The Manchester Guardian* (27 March 1933): 9–10.

–. [unattributed]. 'The Soviet and the Peasantry: An Observer's Notes.' *The Manchester Guardian* (28 March 1933): 9–10.

Oleskiw, Stephen. *The Agony of a Nation: The Great Man-Made Famine in Ukraine 1932–1933*. London: The National Committee to Commemorate the 50th Anniversary of the Artificial Famine in Ukraine 1932–1933, 1983.

Salwa, Ola. '*Mr. Jones* Tames the Golden Lions at the Polish Film Festival in Gdynia.' *Cineuropa*. 23 September 2019. <https://cineuropa.org/en/newsdetail/378608/> (accessed 14 Feb 2024).

Siriol Colley, Margaret. *Gareth Jones: A Manchuko Incident*. Newark: Nigel Linsan Colley, 2001.

–. *More Than a Grain of Truth. The Biography of Gareth Richard Vaughan Jones*. Newark: Nigel Linsan Colley, 2005.

Thomas, Ned. '*Mr. Jones:* Not the Only Gareth Jones.' *Planet extra*. [no date]. <https://www.planetmagazine.org.uk/planet-extra/mr-jones-not-only-gareth-jones> (accessed 14 Feb 2024).

Wlekły, Mirosław. *Gareth Jones: Chronist der Hungersnot in der Ukraine 1932–1933*. Transl. Benjamin Voelkel. Hamburg: Osburg Verlag, 2022.

Andrew Wells

The Stasi, the Self, and the Socialist Past: Timothy Garton Ash's *The File* (1997) and Historical Methodology

Introduction

In one of the most quietly eloquent scenes of *Das Leben der Anderen* (*The Lives of Others*, DE 2006), the main protagonist Georg Dreyman reads through the pages of his extensive Stasi file – its size is a minor joke – and pauses over the minutiae recorded in coldly functional terms. A description of the aftermath of his birthday party, for example, reads: 'Laszlo [his codename] and CMS [his girl-friend, Christa-Maria Sieland] unwrap presents. Then follows presumably sexual intercourse.' The German word, clinically descriptive, *Geschlechtsverkehr.* Acclimatising to the nature of this text, Dreyman begins to notice discrepancies between his own recollection and the events recorded in the file. The Stasi officer responsible for his case, Captain Gerd Wiesler, reported events that never occurred, such as Dreyman co-writing a play to celebrate the 40th anniversary of the GDR. Puzzled, he moves to the end of the file, in which Christa-Maria's arrest for drug abuse is recorded, along with her (coerced) agreement to work as an informant and subsequent release from custody. Following her accidental death within hours of release, the operation against 'Laszlo' was terminated.

The file's final pages also explain, by means of a red fingerprint at the end of the closing report, the miraculous disappearance of incriminating evidence. Dreyman had written a subversive article smuggled to West Germany using a small typewriter that he hid under his floor. Yet when his apartment was searched by the Stasi, the typewriter, which had only a red ink ribbon, was gone. The fingerprint showed Dreyman that the author of this final report, Wiesler, had removed the typewriter himself, saving his prey from the clutches of an ambitious and corrupt superior, as well as concealing his own sabotage of the operation.[1] For inventing a case in which a 'good' officer saved a citizen, *Das Leben der Anderen* was strongly criticised, and the attempt to justify this device by pointing

---

1 *Das Leben der Anderen.* Dir. Florian Henckel von Donnersmarck. Perf. Ulrich Mühe, Martina Gedeck, Sebastian Koch. Buena Vista International, 2006. DVD.

to Oskar Schindler's story was dismissed summarily by the director of the Hohenschönhausen memorial: 'there was a Schindler. There was no Wiesler.'[2] Yet this scene insightfully demonstrates several of the historical and autobiographical processes on which this chapter will focus in its analysis of Timothy Garton Ash's book, *The File* (1997).[3]

The File explores the Stasi's investigation of Ash during his time in East Germany, and is an extended meditation on memory, on the recording of and reconciliation with the past, and on their fusion into what may be termed a 'personal history'; this is, tellingly, the subtitle of the book.[4] Such processes are captured in miniature by Dreyman's struggle to reconcile the contents of the file with those of his own memory. Of course, in his case, this task is made more difficult by the fact that Wiesler had extensively fabricated whole sections of the file to cover up Dreyman's dissident activities: *die Akten lügen*. Ash too points to discrepancies between what his Stasi file records and what was actually happening in his and the other lives interwoven through its pages. He ultimately concludes however that the facts recorded are generally reliable, even if their interpretation is typically paranoid (*File* 32). His text is an autobiographical work but not, as he makes clear, one with self-indulgent intent: he hopes that his experience of reading through his file, comparing it with his own memories and his diary, tracking down and interviewing the informants and case workers 'may even teach us something about history and memory, about ourselves, about human nature. So if the form of the book seems self-indulgent, the purpose is not. I am but a window, a sample, a means to an end, the object in this experiment' (*File* 23).

In the following pages, I will examine those aspects of Ash's book which focus on the roles and responsibilities of the historian. Indeed, while *The File* is certainly autobiographical, it is also an important work of contemporary history and historical methodology. It is arguably the case that Ash's most insightful reflections on historical method stem directly from the fact that his is a work of contemporary history: only in this period is the large-scale deployment of oral history sources feasible, and with them come inevitable issues of memory and the

---

2 Hubertus Knabe. 'Interview. Historiker Hubertus Knabe: "Das Leben der Anderen" zeigt ein falsches Bild der Stasi.' *Leipziger Volkszeitung* 6 Apr 2006: 19.

3 Valuable reviews of the film include Anna Funder. 'Tyranny of Terror.' *The Guardian*. 5 May 2007. <https://www.theguardian.com/books/2007/may/05/featuresreviews.guardianreview12> (accessed 11 Mar 2024); Anna Funder. 'Review of *Das Leben der Anderen*.' *Sight and Sound*, 17.5 (2007): 16–20; and Timothy Garton Ash. 'The Stasi on Our Minds.' *The New York Review of Books*. 31 May 2007. <https://www.nybooks.com/articles/2007/05/31/the-stasi-on-our-minds/> (accessed 11 Mar 2024).

4 Timothy Garton Ash. *The File: A Personal History*. New York: Random House, 1997.

narrativization of one's own remembered past.[5] At the same time, where the historian is also the object of study, but one that is embedded in a history beyond him/herself, memory can interact with a range of sources (in Ash's case his file, diary, and the research notes he took while in East Germany), and provoke a set of broader insights into the historical craft that are otherwise only tenuously possible. These broader topics – particularly memory and history – are the focus of this chapter, in which I hope to show that Ash's embarrassment of riches stems not only from his unusual diligence in 1980–81 but also from the very nature of the societies he set out to explore and describe.

The Book and its Literary Aspects

The File is a relatively short, highly readable 'thick description' of Ash's Stasi file. After offering a taster of the book by exploring one incident in his file – which causes him in more ways than one to blush and leads him to speculate on the reasons why the Stasi chose his codename, 'Romeo'[6] – he introduces his project, the Staatssicherheitsdienst (Stasi, run by the Ministerium für Staatssicherheit or MfS), and the so-called 'Gauck Behörde.' Unofficially named after its first head, the later German President Joachim Gauck, this authority in charge of the Stasi files bore (before its absorption into the Federal Archives in 2021) the official but unwieldly title, 'Federal Commissioner for the Documentation of the State Security Service of the Former German Democratic Republic.'[7] The next couple of chapters offer a memoir of Ash's time in Germany between 1978 and 1980, first in West Berlin and then, between January and October 1980, in the East. There follows a number of chapters, each devoted to a particular Stasi informant that appears in the file, which describe the information they provided on Ash and his efforts to track down and interview them. Although this is technically a 'confrontation,' Ash deals very sensitively with each of the individuals involved, refraining from judgement until one is justified. The confrontations offer Ash the scope to explore memory more deeply, this time extending beyond his own to those of his interviewees and the complicated processes by which they sup-

---

5 See in particular the special issue of *Journal of Contemporary History* on 'Collective Memory' 39.4 (Oct 2004), especially Joanna Bourke. 'Introduction: "Remembering" War.' *Journal of Contemporary History* 39.4 (Oct 2004): 473–485.
6 The actual reason for this choice of codename is probably more mundane than the romantic liaison Ash describes: he drove an Alfa Romeo sports car during his time in Germany. See Ash, *File*, 25, 250.
7 'Der Bundesbeauftragte für die Unterlagen des Staatssicherheitsdienstes der ehemaligen Deutschen Demokratischen Republik,' often abbreviated 'BStU.'

pressed or reconstructed their recollections into an autobiographical narrative with which they could live.

The book then returns to a memoir for the next couple of chapters in which Ash describes the immediate aftermath of his stay in East Germany, especially his time in Poland, his burgeoning courtship with Danuta, and their shared horror at the introduction of martial law in Poland in December 1981, which they were forced to experience from afar. A lengthy chapter then follows in which Ash describes his efforts to trace the Stasi officers who worked on his case, from General Günther Kratsch, head of Department II (responsible for counter-espionage in Berlin) and one of the lieutenants of the head of the Stasi, Erich Mielke, to lowly Lt. Heinz-Joachim Wendt, the case officer and the only former member of the Stasi involved in Ash's case who refused to talk. The remainder of the book oscillates between further memoir (of Ash's activities across the 1980s in Eastern Europe and occasionally the GDR, from which he had been banned in early 1982), investigative journalism (as he probes the British security services on their files and activities), and ethical, moral, and historical considerations of the opening and use of secret police files, efforts to deal with the past, and on the people involved in his case.

This description of its contents fails to do justice to the book itself. For one thing, Ash wears his erudition lightly in a text that deals with a dark yet dreary theme – his review of *Das Leben der Anderen* talks of its failure to capture an evil 'so banal, so unremittingly, mind-numbingly boring' as the Stasi.[8] Yet in its pages he makes direct and indirect references to a range of European authors, from English and German (Shakespeare, Samuel Johnson, Thomas Hobbes, CS Lewis, Oliver Goldsmith, Goethe, Nietzsche, Thomas Mann) to Polish and French authors, above all Proust. Shakespeare plays an unexpectedly pivotal role, quite apart from a stray reference to *A Midsummer Night's Dream*, in which Ash 'sighs for a chink in the Wall'[9] (*File* 213): it was during the annual Shakespeare festival in Weimar (the *Shakespearetage*) in 1980 that Ash met a close friend who features prominently in *The File*.

Ash's wide range of literary reference is perhaps only fitting for a book that straddles a number of textual genres, being at once a memoir, autobiography, history, and work of investigative journalism (among potentially several others). Diaristic conventions appear in *The File* through the knowing repetition of phrases (such as 'and so to bed') associated with perhaps the most famous historical diarist in English, Samuel Pepys. But the most fascinating tie with diaries comes from Ash's reflections on the Stasi's perversion of the intimacy that

---

8 Ash, 'Stasi on Our Minds.'
9 Added by the editorial team of the *Spectator* for an earlier article but one which Ash repeats in the book.

a diary entails. For example, when confronting Colonel Alfred Fritz, a typical *Wendehals* (the East German term for someone who rather too easily adjusted to the fall of the GDR and reunification), Fritz discussed the attempt to blackmail a woman having an affair into working for the Stasi. Ash notes with disgust that 'I sense from the crooked smile on his face how he misses that side of the job: the voyeurism, the intimate details, the games they could play with a woman's life' (*File* 190).

As an autobiography, the book contributes to a sub-genre that has been labelled 'file-based autobiographies.'[10] These are autobiographical texts that have an official file (often compiled by a secret police or security service) as their focus or that use such as a structuring element. Such autobiographies rarely stray beyond the segment of a life for which the file is relevant. In like manner, Ash says very little about his life before his arrival in Germany or after the fall of the system that produced his file, and at one point he hints at the nature of this sub-genre by making a pointed anagrammatical juxtaposition of 'file' and 'life' (*File* 23). Indeed, it may even be justifiable to state that his book is a biography or 'personal history' less of himself than of his file.

Having said that, Ash does reflect in autobiographical fashion on subjectivity, and particularly on how his experiences in both Germanies transformed him. By the time he and Danuta are forced to watch the horrors unfolding in Poland from the sidelines in Oxford, he recognised that in contrast with his wife,

> I ... was back in my own country, in the same old city. But if the city was the same, the 'I' was different. Until this moment of commitment I had still essentially lived, I suppose, with a peculiarly English – and altogether peculiar – ideal of self, an ideal of emotional invulnerability, self-control and self-sufficiency ... But now I thought quite differently. (*File* 157)

This is not the only place where the 'I' came to be questioned. Only a few pages earlier, Ash had spoken of the typical question people born and living in western democracies ask themselves when confronted with authoritarian systems, especially totalitarian dictatorships: how would I have behaved? Or in his words, 'as an Englishman I have often thought to myself, If Britain were a communist police state, would we have lots of informers?' (*File* 134). Ironically, one of the Stasi informants on Ash was in fact British. Codenamed 'Smith,' this Briton had moved to East Germany, married and had children, and was a busy operative, even if he

---

10 See, in particular, Catherine Karen Roy. 'Ash's Stasi File as a Script of Life.' *COLLOQUY text theory critique* 18 (2009): 318–329 and her doctoral dissertation, 'File-Based Autobiographies After 1989.' Ph.D. dissertation, University of British Columbia, 2011. Examples of such autobiographies include Katherine Verdery. *My Life as a Spy: Investigations in a Secret Police File.* Durham, NC: Duke University Press, 2018; Vera Wollenberger. *Virus der Heuchler: Innenansicht aus Stasi-Akten.* Berlin: Elefanten, 1992; Anke Jauch. *Die Stasi packt zu.* Frankfurt am Main: August von Goethe Literaturverlag, 2007.

had been coerced into working with the Stasi. He was recruited after being told that he was suspected of working for a Western secret service; terrified that he would be deported or imprisoned, leaving his wife and children behind, he agreed to work for the MfS to show he was trustworthy. As Ash states, this was 'the wrong decision, of course, but completely understandable. All my sympathy is engaged' (*File* 137). A few months after Ash had questioned him about his involvement, 'Smith' turned up to a lecture given by Ash in Berlin and handed him an envelope containing a brief letter and three pages of detached, half-scholarly reflections on the Stasi. As Ash concluded the chapter, 'The word "I" does not appear once in his text' (*File* 139).

Memory

Another feature, particularly of 'file-based autobiography,' is the role accorded to memory. Autobiographies tend to rely heavily on the personal memories of the subject, while their file-based counterparts strongly feature records created and used by others.[11] The role of memory in autobiography is one aspect that makes historians' biographies particularly interesting, since those working in different traditions tend to approach memory as a more or less reliable source, and this often influences the choices they make about the wider period and themes they incorporate in such writing. French historians, for example, have argued that memory is a poor guide to the past that can be used only in conjunction with other material, which however in the case of official papers remains sealed in archives for 30–50 years, so their autobiographies have concentrated on a more distant period.[12] However, Anglo-American historians in particular have few such scruples and some seem to take the view that personal memories are a particularly valuable kind of source.[13] They have faced, however, some stiff opposition in taking this stand. Ash and his fellow file-based autobiographers are in the unique position of being able to adopt the more intellectually responsible French perspective while also having a range of written documentation from the recent past at their disposal. In Ash's case, this documentary evidence stems from his personal and an institutional archive, allowing him to interrogate and explore his memories and those of the people he interviews.[14]

---

11 Roy, 'Ash's Stasi File,' 321.
12 Examples include Daniel Cordier and Anne Kriegel. See Richard Vinen. 'The Poisoned Madeleine: The Autobiographical Turn in Historical Writing.' *Journal of Contemporary History* 46 (2011): 551.
13 Examples include Eric Hobsbawm and Norman Stone. See Vinen, 'Poisoned Madeleine,' 551.
14 Vinen. 'Poisoned Madeleine,' 550–552; Luisa Passerini and Alexander C. T. Geppert. 'Historians in Flux: The Concept, Task and Challenge of *ego-histoire*.' *Historein* 3 (2001): 13.

This leads him to the first really important historiographical theme of *The File:* memory in the writing of contemporary history in general, and the history of society under a totalitarian dictatorship in particular. He not only has his own fallible memory to deal with, but he also has to navigate his way along the treacherous paths laid down by the memories of others, particularly those who have a vested interest in forgetting, suppressing, or otherwise reconfiguring their memories of betrayal or oppression. Spatial metaphors of memory are abundant in Ash's text, as they arguably are in any noteworthy meditation on memory: we have all taken a stroll down memory lane or tried to unlock – that is, gain access to – hidden or otherwise inaccessible memories. Ash uses the lock-and-key metaphor productively to cover both memory and his own project: in describing the modest size of his file, for example, he offers the consoling reflection that 'small keys can open large doors' (*File* 22). Metaphors of space, especially closed and inaccessible spaces, are particularly potent ways to link human recollection, the Stasi, and the GDR, a country that had more than its fair share of places that were actually and metaphorically 'off limits.' The first entries in most Westerners' files will involve an initial border crossing and tailing once the target has entered East Berlin, and such is the case with Ash. And his file comes to an end with a document that records that his re-entry to the country is prohibited until 31 December 1989, a ban that was only ever partially enforced and was lifted for good in June of that year.

Also important to remember is that spatial metaphors of memory almost invariably consist of two aspects: a place/space and an action that is undertaken within or to gain access to it. Recent work on oral history has highlighted the active nature of memory, which should be understood less as a repository of facts, a hard drive that can be straightforwardly accessed for reliably consistent information, than as an active, subjective process in which memories are narrated and re-narrated to create meanings in a range of contexts. Memories are generated and selected for storage based on their importance for the individual at a given moment, and are consolidated and reconsolidated, told and re-told as narratives that are never completely identical, for the same reason that Heraclitus stated it is impossible for a person to step into the same river twice: even if the river were the same, the person would not be.[15]

Ash's metaphors of memory emphasise not only its active nature but also its inherent flux. In one of his most vivid – and oft-quoted – images, he reflects on how a Stasi file 'opens the door to a vast sunken labyrinth of the forgotten past, but how, too, the very act of opening the door itself changes the buried artifacts, like an archaeologist letting in fresh air to a sealed Egyptian tomb' (*File* 108). Our

15 Alistair Thomson. 'Memory and Remembering in Oral History.' *The Oxford Handbook of Oral History*. Ed. Donald A. Ritchie. Oxford: Oxford University Press, 2010. 78–95.

past experiences are not accessed in a pristine state but are rather decayed or honed, they mellow or sharpen with the passage of time and change of circumstances. In another telling set of images – for Ash's book is about people, above all – he explains this continual process of revising memory through an analogy with divorce, 'where today's bitterness transforms all the shared past, completely, miserably, seemingly forever. Except that this bitter memory, too, will fade and change with the further passage of time' (*File* 108–109). Early on in the book, Ash feels that his inability to recollect the romantic liaison described in the file's earliest pages is also a form of betrayal, not of the woman in question, but of his own past, to which he feels disloyal.

But loyalty, like disloyalty, involves a conscious act of will and the Proustian metaphor of the madeleine, to which Ash refers repeatedly throughout the book, has been taken to be the locus classicus of involuntary memory. That is, a memory involuntarily evoked by a sensory or mental cue, such as the flavour of a madeleine, previously dunked in tea, on Marcel's tongue in the first part of *À la recherche du temps perdu* [*In Search of Lost Time*] (1913). Unlike Marcel, however, who is unable to locate the memory evoked by the flavour of the madeleine until after he has both repeated this sensory cue ten times and then tried to clear his mind of it, Ash has a range of memory technologies at his disposal. His diary, contemporary notes, and published writings come to his aid when even the blacked-out portions of his file, his 'poisoned madeleine,' prompts the awareness of a memory whose content he cannot, without their help, reconstruct.[16]

History

Another of these technologies of memory are the individuals whom he interviews. Indeed, their status as such is consciously used by Ash as a means of trying to persuade them to talk. Especially in the case of the former Stasi officers whose initial reluctance to speak is partly based on the excuse that 'it's all there in the documents' (*File* 183), Ash invariably replies that the documents can only tell us so much, and that it is important to have a first-hand account 'for understanding the background and the motives of those involved' (*File* 183). Here is the second major historiographical theme in *The File*, for it is precisely this ability to interview those involved that sets apart contemporary history from those less fortunate periods in which this is not possible. Indeed, it is alone thanks to his discussion with living witnesses that he can establish the innocence of one informant and fully understand the activities of another. In her fascinating memoir

---

16 Marcel Proust. *Remembrance of Things Past.* Transl. C. K. Scott Moncrieff and Terence Kilmartin. 3 vols. New York: Random House, 1981. 1: 48–51.

of working in Soviet archives in the 1960s, the Australian scholar Sheila Fitzpatrick also spoke about the benefits of being in contact with living witnesses to the phenomena she studied:

> It's a wonderful thing to have archives, especially if nobody else has used them. But untapped archives plus a primary informant willing to give you a running commentary on what you read in the archives the day before is something that only happens once in a lifetime.[17]

But this possibility of working simultaneously with archives and those intimately involved in their production and use is not necessarily one shared by all contemporary historians. Ash also interviewed members of the British intelligence services and managed to discover that MI5 held a file on him, but as a living, working government agency – and an intelligence agency to boot – he had no access to this archival material; only under the circumstances of a defunct agency or an arbitrary system (such as the USSR, in Fitzpatrick's case) was it possible to combine written and oral testimony in this way.

Yet the results of such a combination are incredibly fruitful, and Ash exploits this potential to the full, especially to explore questions of ethics and motivation. Ethical doubts are largely and understandably limited to Ash himself. Unlike the Stasi officers he interviews, he regards the secret police *system* under the GDR as indefensible – indeed, it is only in this context that he uses the word 'evil' – and his ethical considerations focus purely on whether he should confront, publish, or name those involved in his case. His decisions to confront and publish, but not to name, are based on the straightforward question of utility: what good would it do? It furthers the purpose of the book to explore the stories of these individuals, but naming would satisfy little except a grasping curiosity that could be devastating for those concerned (*File* 126–127). The palpable relief Ash conveys when he discovers that his erstwhile adviser from the Humboldt University was not a direct informant is clear, as is his conscientious recognition that being deemed 'Gauck positive' is a social and professional kiss of death. (To be 'gaucked' is to have one's past relationship with the Stasi checked with the Gauck Authority, and someone found to have worked willingly and closely with the Stasi is said to be 'Gauck positive'; as Ash notes in the book and elsewhere, to have collaborated with the secret police is a civil equivalent of HIV.[18])

17 Sheila Fitzpatrick. *A Spy in the Archives: A Memoir of Cold War Russia*. London: I. B. Tauris, 2014. 170.

18 Ash, *File*, 86–87. See also a talk given by Ash to the Chicago Council on Foreign Relations on 29 Nov 1997 'Public talk on *The File*.' *C-SPAN*. 9 Oct 1997 <https://www.c-span.org/video/?92619-1/the-file-personal-history> (accessed 5 Feb 2024); he makes these comments at 00:16:30–00:16:58 and 00:27:41–00:28:12. Ash's analogy with HIV is made more poignant by his reference to an actual death from AIDS among his circle of Berlin friends. See Ash, *File*, 40.

But his sensitivity to these issues in no way means that Ash shies away from questions of motivation, which are deeply and thoroughly explored in his book. These questions are very familiar to students of twentieth-century German history, and the answers are remarkably consistent – 'we were at war' (albeit a cold one in the more recent case); 'I was just following orders'; 'if I didn't comply, my loved ones would be hurt' – and are just as inadequate. Yet as with the scholarly consensus concerning low-level perpetrators of national socialist crimes, there are only ordinary men in *The File*.[19] Evil exists in the shape of the system rather than the individuals, about which Ash almost expresses regret: 'If only I had met, on this search, a single clearly evil person. But they were all just weak, shaped by circumstance, self-deceiving; human, all too human. Yet the sum of all their actions was a great evil' (*The File* 252). He proceeds to lay out in agonising detail the likely manner of their corruption, which leads him to the conclusion that the absence of especially parental (paternal) love played a decisive role in the process whereby Stasi officers and informants were led astray.

The Stasi archives are, Ash concludes, 'a vast anthology of human weakness' (*File* 252), and for that reason provide yet another example of the 'banality of evil.' Banality and boredom are chords that have been repeatedly struck in historical writing on the GDR, notwithstanding the work of Mary Fulbrook, Katja Hoyer, and others (including Ash himself) who have sought somewhat to counter the 'Stasiland' narrative of East German history as an undifferentiated grey mass of oppression.[20] Yet the overpowering tedium of life in the GDR, certainly by the late 1980s, was well captured in one oppositional song released in 1988, entitled 'Boredom' (*Langeweile*) by the rock group Pankow:

> Dasselbe Land zu lange gesehen
> Dieselbe Sprache zu lange gehört
> Zu lange gewartet, zu lange gehofft
> Zu lange die alten Männer verehrt
>
> *For too long we've seen the same country*
> *For too long heard the same language*

---

19 See the analyses of Police Battalion 101 in occupied Poland and of denunciators to the Gestapo in the Reich that feature in, respectively, Christopher Browning. *Ordinary Men: Reserve Police Batallion 101 and the Final Solution in Poland*. Rev. edn. New York: Harper Perennial, 2017 and Robert Gellately. *Backing Hitler: Consent and Coercion in Nazi Germany*. Oxford: Oxford University Press, 2001. Chs. 6, 7.

20 Anna Funder. *Stasiland: Stories from Behind the Berlin Wall*. London: Granta, 2003; Mary Fulbrook. *The People's State: East German Society from Hitler to Honecker*. New Haven: Yale University Press, 2008; Katja Hoyer. *Beyond the Wall: East Germany, 1949–1990*. London: Allen Lane, 2023; Timothy Garton Ash. *"Und willst du nicht mein Bruder sein…": Die DDR Heute*. Hamburg: Rowohlt, 1981.

For too long waited, for too long hoped
For too long honoured the old men[21]

This song holds up an ironic mirror to Ash's project to use the various technologies of memory to reconstruct a history beyond himself, for it emphasises that memory has no place where boredom reigns: nothing has the chance to pass into history because it is continually repeated, every time without apparent meaning; words are intoned without understanding.

Conclusion

Such a rich meditation on history and memory under a totalitarian system as *The File* has a wide range of powerful lessons, and not only for historians: important for us all to bear in mind as we approach such complicated pasts are aspects such as the ordinariness of the individuals involved, or the unique prerogative of victims alone to forgive. I will however conclude with two of the most important and useful lessons for practitioners of history to be gained from Ash's book. The first is to be humble in the face of the past, and to reserve judgement until the kind of thorough investigation exemplified by Ash is complete. While it might not be the case that '*Die Akten lügen*' ('the files lie'), as had been claimed by many opposed to opening up and using the Stasi files, there are certainly moments where they can mislead. Words are misquoted, information received by word-of-mouth is incorrectly attributed, and individuals are named as informants when they were not, or at least not knowingly. This humility must extend to one's own recollections, and by extension to our somewhat presumptuous claim to understand the thoughts of others. Ash realises early how difficult it is to reconstruct how he thought and felt; by contrast, he remarks, 'how much easier to do it to other people!' (*File* 42).

Related to this, we must realise what a blessing and a curse Stasi – and other secret police – files really are. Beyond being a poisoned madeleine for the individual subject, they offer historians an object lesson in the importance of diligence in their craft. Only then is the humility of the kind just described possible. Bias has many surprising and subtle ways by which it can creep in. Sheila Fitzpatrick has remarked that historians tend to absorb the bureaucratic perspective of the institutions they work on, and she wondered if the Soviets might have had more success in winning Western historians over to their point of view if they had only opened the files of their security service and no other. Perhaps then

---

21 Pankow. 'Langeweile.' *Aufruhr in den Augen.* [East] Berlin: Amiga, 1988. LP.

Western historians would also have seen enemies and subversion everywhere they looked.[22]

These points emphasise the importance of the historian's self and the inescapable 'I' that is at the heart of all historical scholarship. This is perhaps captured in a dimension of Benedetto Croce's dictum that 'all history is contemporary history' that has only lately attracted attention: present political and cultural priorities obviously influence the writing of history, but all history writing is also autobiographical, shaped by the personal interests, prejudices, and peccadilloes of the individual historian.[23] If this in turn highlights a certain arbitrariness in historical research, that is all to the good, for we do frequently forget just how arbitrary history as an activity can be: which archives have survived and who is still alive to interview shapes history quite profoundly. As indeed can the mood swings of archivists or librarians. Fitzpatrick tells of how archivists in the USSR judged the historians who worked in their archives: if you put in the hours, they would be helpful; if you ordered a bunch of material and left it all week, they were less so. Fitzpatrick once unexpectedly received a file concerning convict labour in the USSR, an absolutely taboo topic. She thought this was a simple error, but she took extensive notes before returning the file. Only years later, during Glasnost, did an archivist ask her if she was pleased with the file they had slipped in, as a treat to reward Fitzpatrick's diligence. As the latter remarked, 'Perhaps the Stasi man's affection for his surveillance object in the film *The Lives of Others* wasn't so far-fetched after all.'[24]

References

Ash, Timothy Garton. *"Und willst du nicht mein Bruder sein…":Die DDR Heute*. Hamburg: Rowohlt, 1981.
–. *The File: A Personal History*. New York: Random House, 1997.
–. 'Public talk on *The File*.' Chicago, 29 Nov 1997. *C-SPAN*. 9 Oct 1997. <https://www.c-span.org/video/?92619-1/the-file-personal-history> (accessed 5 Feb 2024).
–. 'The Stasi on Our Minds.' *The New York Review of Books*. 31 May 2007. <https://www.nybooks.com/articles/2007/05/31/the-stasi-on-our-minds/> (accessed 11 Mar 2024).
Bourke, Joanna. 'Introduction: "Remembering" War.' *Journal of Contemporary History* 39.4 (Oct 2004): 473–485.

---

22 Fitzpatrick, *Spy in the Archives*, 185–186.
23 Benedetto Croce. *History as the Story of Liberty*. Indianapolis: Liberty Fund, 2000. 8; Vinen, 'Poisoned Madeleine,' 531–554; Special issue on 'European Ego-Histories: Historiography and the Self, 1970–2000.' *Historein* 3 (2001): 7–178; Pierre Nora (ed.). *Essais d'ego-histoire*. Paris: Gallimard, 1987.
24 Fitzpatrick, *Spy in the Archives*, 208–209.

Browning, Christopher. *Ordinary Men: Reserve Police Batallion 101 and the Final Solution in Poland.* Rev. edn. New York: Harper Perennial, 2017.

Croce, Benedetto. *History as the Story of Liberty.* Indianapolis: Liberty Fund, 2000.

Das Leben der Anderen. Dir. Florian Henckel von Donnersmarck. Perf. Ulrich Mühe, Martina Gedeck, Sebastian Koch. Buena Vista International, 2006. DVD.

Fitzpatrick, Sheila. *A Spy in the Archives: A Memoir of Cold War Russia.* London: I. B. Tauris, 2014.

Fulbrook, Mary. *The People's State: East German Society from Hitler to Honecker.* New Haven: Yale University Press, 2008.

Funder, Anna. *Stasiland: Stories from Behind the Berlin Wall.* London: Granta, 2003.

–. 'Review of *Das Leben der Anderen.*' *Sight and Sound* 17.5 (2007): 16–20.

–. 'Tyranny of Terror.' *The Guardian.* 5 May 2007. <https://www.theguardian.com/book s/2007/may/05/featuresreviews.guardianreview12> (accessed 11 Mar 2024).

Gellately, Robert. *Backing Hitler: Consent and Coercion in Nazi Germany.* Oxford: Oxford University Press, 2001.

Hoyer, Katja. *Beyond the Wall: East Germany, 1949–1990.* London: Allen Lane, 2023.

Jauch, Anke. *Die Stasi packt zu.* Frankfurt am Main: August von Goethe Literaturverlag, 2007.

Knabe, Hubertus. 'Interview. Historiker Hubertus Knabe: "Das Leben der Anderen" zeigt ein falsches Bild der Stasi.' *Leipziger Volkszeitung* 6 Apr 2006: 19.

Nora, Pierre (ed.). *Essais d'ego-histoire.* Paris: Gallimard, 1987.

Pankow. 'Langeweile.' *Aufruhr in den Augen.* [East] Berlin: Amiga, 1988. LP.

Passerini, Luisa and Alexander C. T. Geppert. 'Historians in Flux: The Concept, Task and Challenge of *ego-histoire.*' *Historein* 3 (2001): 7–18.

Proust, Marcel. *Remembrance of Things Past.* Transl. C. K. Scott Moncrieff and Terence Kilmartin. 3 vols. New York: Random House, 1981.

Roy, Catherine Karen. 'Ash's Stasi File as a Script of Life.' *COLLOQUY text theory critique* 18 (2009): 318–329.

–. 'File-Based Autobiographies After 1989.' Ph.D. dissertation, University of British Columbia, 2011.

Thomson, Alistair. 'Memory and Remembering in Oral History.' *The Oxford Handbook of Oral History.* Ed. Donald A. Ritchie. Oxford: Oxford University Press, 2010. 78–95.

Verdery, Katherine. *My Life as a Spy: Investigations in a Secret Police File.* Durham, NC: Duke University Press, 2018.

Vinen, Richard. 'The Poisoned Madeleine: The Autobiographical Turn in Historical Writing.' *Journal of Contemporary History* 46 (2011): 531–554.

Wollenberger, Vera. *Virus der Heuchler: Innenansicht aus Stasi-Akten.* Berlin: Elefanten, 1992.

Katrin Berndt / Andrew Wells

Interview with Katja Hoyer, author of *Beyond the Wall: East Germany, 1949–1990* (Penguin: London, 2023)[1]

Eds [Katrin Berndt and Andrew Wells]: We would like to start with a few questions on your aims and methodology in *Beyond the Wall*. It strikes us that it seems especially difficult to study the history particularly of the later GDR in the 1980s without allowing the knowledge that the Berlin Wall is about to fall from intruding on your consciousness. Do you think there are ways in which we can write history that allow us to recapture the contingent nature of the past? Is it ever possible entirely to filter out hindsight?

KH [Katja Hoyer]: I think what especially helps is to immerse oneself as much as possible in sources written at the time, be it newspaper articles or exchanges of letters (etc.), in order to catch a glimpse at people's hopes and fears without too much hindsight creeping in. Empathy here is an important skill, which is probably a bit underrated in academic historical studies that often tend to focus on large structures and processes over the long term. Analysing these things is obviously important and we have an advantage here over people living in the midst of them, but equally it requires a good degree of empathy to be able to read somebody's private or public writings and to try to glean from them how that person may have felt or thought at a particular moment without the knowledge of what was coming next. I think it is a combination of these two – the hindsight-influenced 'big picture' and the empathetic understanding of individuals in the moment – that allows us to reconstruct to a certain extent what was happening without being too tempted to read it all through the lens of the (from our perspective, inevitable) outcome that was about to change the world of these people. I think that is the key aspect. For me, it is particularly difficult to do this for a historical setting in which many individuals are still living today, because they think they still remember exactly what happened at the time from the perspective of what they did then, which of course they do not. So it is also a case of challenging – to a certain extent – what people are telling you because they are

1 The interview was conducted on 20 November 2023.

convinced that they still remember exactly how they acted or thought at the time without the knowledge of what happened to them later. And there is the additional big challenge for someone like me, who was not there at the time, to come along and say, 'well, actually, there's also this, that, and the other that was going on at the time, which you may have forgotten or don't think about as important for you any more, but that's also what happened.' Putting all these perspectives together is not easy, but it is a task incumbent on us as historians to try and capture these moments at the time without conceding too much to hindsight.

Eds: Do you think there are particular written or literary techniques that we can use in the writing of such histories to allow the reader to have a sense of that contingency, or is it best that we rely on the contemporary documents and the sorts of evidence that you have just mentioned?

KH: I try to reconstruct, from documents, interviews, and other sources, the sort of stories that happened to people at the time, and so I start all of my chapters with a short anecdote or a personal angle on a particular theme, which I think helps. These stories do not necessarily come directly from personal recollections but I use other sources which I then bundle together to create a sort of mini-vignette or a narrative that makes the topic to be discussed more accessible for the reader. It also allows them to develop the sort of empathy I was just talking about, which is difficult enough for historians who study this material in depth to develop, and a real challenge is to transfer that understanding and empathy to readers, students, and the wider public. This was the reason why I chose to seek a personal angle, even for bigger political questions and structural themes, and then begin the discussion with a story through which the reader can read and think, 'oh, OK; I get that now: the impact that this had on people or the impact that it had on a group of people as well as the person who is exemplary for a particular aspect or a part of society.' I think that using individuals or groups to exemplify certain aspects of the past is a good way to communicate this sense of contingency to the modern reader.

Eds: The technique of using personal anecdotes to provide an introduction to each major topic also relates to your use of oral history. Were the reasons you have just given for your decision to use personal stories the only ones that were relevant for you, or did you feel that it offers something missing from other techniques of narrative history?

KH: Another reason was that I was writing for an audience mainly that did not consist of the people directly affected. I was writing about East Germans and their society for people in the West who had never experienced either these things or the entire world behind the Iron Curtain: what it meant to live in a socialist dictatorship and what such a system looked like. I think it is pretty difficult to understand for somebody who grew up, say, in Britain or the US or even West Germany, or my generation too, which has not really experienced it. So my other aim was to try and (excuse the rather hackneyed expression) 'humanize' that history in a way that makes it more comprehensible. I tried to highlight this goal in the introduction to the book, particularly using a quotation from Angela Merkel, in which she said – I think in 2005, just before she became Federal Chancellor – that 'it is obviously incredibly difficult to understand and make comprehensible how we lived back then.' (Hoyer 2) I took that as a challenge and asked myself, 'is it? Let's try!' I wanted to reconstruct this past across time as well, not only looking at the people still living today – which is where the oral history element comes in – but also for people who lived through the events of the 1950s, 1940s, or even 1920s. I try to find a similarly personal approach, despite the fact that I was not always able to talk to people who were around at the time any more.

The oral history component was important for me because it adds an element of the voice of East Germans today that has previously been somewhat neglected: there is a particular group of East Germans who speak in public about the GDR but they do not reflect the entirety of society, whereas there are plenty of individuals who would not see themselves as experts or even as *Zeitzeugen* [witnesses of a particular era] of that time, because they don't think they have experienced anything extraordinary, when of course they are witnesses to the period in which they have lived. They are, however, not the sort of people who would independently come forward and talk about themselves. For me it was also important to add a group of people that I found was under-represented in the whole archival and museum landscape, which has tended to interview a fraction and individual pockets of society rather than a cross-section.

Eds: How did you strike a balance between the oral history and the documentary history sources that you used, and how did you locate and identify your interviewees?

KH: I had to be careful in managing my resources as effectively as possible, because I undertook all the research for the book myself and did not have research assistants at my disposal, so I could not have interviewed, say, 200 people. I also did not want to replicate what was already out there, so I consulted the relevant databases that are available (and these are detailed in the footnotes and bibliography to *Beyond the Wall*) and did not feel the necessity to interview the same people again, with only a couple of exceptions such as Egon Krenz. Now there are obviously a lot of interviews with him available, but I did think it was helpful for me to actually sit there with him on a sofa and have a long conversation for me to gain enough insight into his own mindset and into what was going on behind the political scenes from his point of view. Other than in this instance, I tried to concentrate on individuals and sorts of people and aspects of society that had not been well covered. For example, I was interested in what drove somebody to work on the gas pipeline in the East for two or three years, because I suspected it was an opportunity for people to get out of the stuffiness and constriction of the GDR in the 1980s, given that so many people volunteered for it. But I was not certain and I could not locate any existing interviews, at least none of any length, with people who had done that where they had been genuinely asked, 'why would anybody do that?' So I then asked around – and this is an advantage of coming myself from eastern Germany – I asked friends, family, colleagues, neighbours, 'does anybody know anybody with that particular experience or from this particular group of people?' Another example derives from my wish to speak to a range of older people about what it was like in the 1950s, so I simply asked around if anybody knew people in their eighties or nineties who had lived in the GDR for the entire time it existed and who could tell me a little bit about what it was like for them. I had no idea what I would get from such interviews because the selection criterion for this one was simply interviewee age. I also wanted to speak to a female member of the *Nationale Volksarmee* [NVA, National People's Army], and ask what it was like as a woman to join that, so again I just asked around: 'does anybody know anybody, a woman, who was once a soldier or an officer in the NVA?' I wanted to know what it was like first-hand because you can find snippets in the post-*Wende* [literally 'turning point,' used to describe the events of 1989/90 in Germany] period, where such women talk about what it was like to be made unemployed or to change your profession, but nobody had really spoken to them about what it was even like to be one of the first women in the army where there were no gender-specific facilities or anything of that kind set up. I had not even thought about the fact that, at first, they had no changing rooms or uniforms tailored for the female body, all those kinds of things. So that was the kind of approach I took and from which I got a fairly good picture, but there was also a random element always present, because I was never entirely sure what people would actually tell me: I was looking more for types of people and individual experiences as opposed to feeling that I needed to interview a specific person about a specific matter, with the exception of a few, such as Egon Krenz or Frank Schöbel, where I had an idea what I was going to get out of it.

Eds: This brings us back to a point that you raised earlier and is especially interesting, particularly when it comes to dealing with contemporary history in general: obviously memory plays a very important role, certainly in the oral history method, but memories, as you recognise, whether individual or collective, are always complicated by subsequent experiences, the knowledge that you gain after the event, and so on. How do you think this will affect future histories of the GDR, as people who lived through it die off and living memory shifts, decade by decade until in perhaps 30–40 years' time the 80- or 90-year-olds are the only ones with memories of the 1980s? Do you think that this passing on and also this greater knowledge about the GDR that is being continually produced are going to affect future histories of the GDR and how will they affect them?

KH: There is a saying that the *Zeitzeuge* is the biggest enemy of the historian: I do not subscribe to that! But there is a lot less acrimony around what you say when talking of the more remote past, say the 1950s. There is disagreement, of course, but it is on an academic level, so people will politely say, 'Oh, I don't quite agree with what you say about x, y, or z.' For example, I talk in the book about [the rising on 17 June] 1953 as a sort of rebellion against poor living standards and the lack of participation of the people in the state, and that shifts the focus away from the purely political somewhat. I can discuss this with other people without them getting personally angry about it, because it is not their own experience any more. Those who get a lot more angry about what I say concerning the 1980s than about the 1950s are those who were dissidents in the 1980s, and this sometimes gets in the way of having a calm discussion about the GDR: people will attack you for your personal history, for your background, it becomes very emotional and leads away from the actual analysis. So I think there is an opportunity in that, in the future, fewer people will be directly connected to the topic. I think an additional issue with having not just *Zeitzeugen* around is that they are also often at the same time historians. There will come a point where they retire and leave the profession but will still be around as *Zeitzeugen*, only no longer actively writing the history any more.

I think a further shift will come as people expand the range of topics of interest in the GDR. So far, particularly because of our proximity to the fall of the Berlin Wall, we have concentrated a lot on 1953 almost as if it were a direct precursor to 1989, and in between there was just a period that people do not talk about very much with the exception of the building of the Berlin Wall. In academia, of course, people deal with this period but the focus is often on drawing associations between these two high points of discontent, as well as on the process of political decay and on economic issues. We always look at the GDR with a view to proving that it could never have worked, and we place everything in that context rather than looking at it in its own right. I think that this will change as fewer people are around who were there at the time, because they do tend to view this history strongly influenced by hindsight and their personal involvement. This is not something that ever entirely disappears – in Britain, some people are still invested in one side or another in the English Civil War! – as people become interested in a particular time period or in a particular person because they have a cognitive connection. But this is still different from having actually been there, so I think the focus will shift to broadening out the research into new areas. For instance, people have looked a lot at the way gay people were treated in the GDR because that is an aspect of particular interest in our society today.

Finally, I think the GDR will cease to be viewed as an 'active enemy': people still see the GDR as somehow a counter-model to the *Bundesrepublik* [Federal Republic of Germany] and there is still this tendency to talk about the *ehemalige DDR* [former GDR] as if by saying simply 'the GDR' instead of adding 'the former,' it would magically still be around. Because there are still many people living who experienced the GDR, many still see it as an active thing and the moment you highlight any aspect of it that does not talk it down or make it the enemy, people are frightened that you are conjuring it back up as an alternative model of doing things. At the moment, it is not possible to say something like, 'women were able to do their jobs and have children at the same time,' without somebody shouting in, 'Oh! But they [the GDR regime] only facilitated this because they needed the workers,' or 'it was only done to repress women further because they still then had to do the household chores and this at the same time.' It is not possible at the moment to raise this issue without somebody feeling uneasy and thinking, 'does this mean we now have to provide extensive childcare facilities and all the women will be out working?' Of course it does not, and I think this misperceived danger will fade into the background the further history slips into the past.

Eds: Totalitarian ideology is a recurrent subject in your book. For example, you describe political leaders' belief that difference of opinion was 'factionalism,' which posed a dangerous threat to communism. How much did the demand for ideological subordination shape everyday life in the GDR?

KH: I think it seeped down from the top and also has to do with the psychological aspects I mention in the book, above all this sort of paranoia. All of these experiences can be traced back, one the one hand, to the formal training received in the Soviet Union, where factionalism was highlighted as one of the great evils, cited as the reason why Western societies and multi-party systems deliberately divide the population into different camps that will fight each other, in what I suppose is the entire 'divide and conquer' logic. On the other hand, children were raised in Kindergartens and schools where they learned this as a key concept: that our society cannot afford to have internal dissidents, which is the principal idea of socialism. I do think it is how the GDR was supposed to function, and this was in the minds of those returning to Germany after 1945, having survived the Soviet Union. This seeps down to every level, so in a factory, school, or university, the same logic applies because people from the cadre system were in charge of these organizations and shared the same ideology.

But I also think it only went so far: people were encouraged to highlight problems and to voice their discontent, particularly in the workplace. An example would be when the regime decided that women should be equal partners in society but discovered from its own sources that this was not working out, so it encouraged women to inform on their colleagues and employers and state when they were not being treated equally or being told that, for example, they could not do their job properly. This was also a way of enforcing ideas and directing from above while involving people in the process. Yet it was another case of everybody pulling in the same direction: it was not possible to voice concerns more tailored to individual circumstances, such as a working mother complaining that she could not afford to work part-time, but wished to do so in order to look after her children.

There was also the problem that an open discussion in society, with differing voices and views, was not possible because there existed no public sphere. Within the SED [*Sozialistische Einheitspartei Deutschlands* – Socialist Unity Party of Germany – the ruling party in the GDR, formed from the 1946 merger of the Communist and Social Democratic parties in East Germany], this was also a source of frustration as you can see when you look at the criticisms that were hurled at Walter Ulbricht after 1953, when people dared to voice that criticism because he was in a weak position. It also meant that there was no internal renewal within the SED itself, which produced a great deal of the frustration visible later, in the 1980s, when people were demanding participation and a voice, but this did not emerge. I think therefore that this demand for ideological sub-ordination is something that seeped down but left gaps as well, more so than, for instance, was the case in the Nazi system. I do think there were niches and room for people to do their own thing within certain parameters.

Eds: Taking up the aspect of ideological purity demanded by the regime and people's struggle to make personal adjustments: would you say that this encouraged a rift between the government and the general population that increased over the years of the GDR's existence? We are thinking in particular of the many stories you have included in your book that people shared with you about political oppression and harsh punishments they received for minor transgressions.

KH: I am glad you noticed them – some of my German readers did not! I believe that is right but that it also backfired. At the top of the regime you see more and more people ossified in their ways of thinking, yet particularly in the early years, strangely enough, you do see Walter Ulbricht being at times quite flexible and reacting to criticism he has been given (not necessarily directly: he was always obstinate when it came to responding to people themselves in the early 1950s). But as the GDR became more settled there was a limited desire to hear people's voices and to respond to them. In part, even the Stasi was also tasked with informing the regime where there were elements of discontent and identifying areas where it needed to improve. But as this elite got older – and there was hardly any renewal – the more set in its ways it became, and the more it became paranoid about foreign and outside influences, and about young people as well. It was in part as a result of this that opposition grew, since there was less and less of a feeling that improvement was possible from the inside: it quickly became obvious that this was not the case. It was also a result of the GDR's education system, in which young people were made to read and think about society and politics and become politicized: this is also an underemphasised aspect. I think it was quite possible, for instance, to emerge from the West German school system and not be political but rather seek after a prosperous, decent life in which you do your own thing. It was difficult to emerge from the GDR school system without a political mindset because pupils were constantly talking about society, politics, and class struggle. And a society was created that was talking about these things and understood something about the social structures about which it was taught, but which found it impossible to effect change despite this education and knowledge because there was no public sphere to voice opinions. The more the 1980s went on, the greater the conflict became as young people in particular became in-credibly frustrated, for example when they were told that the party system didn't work sideways but from the ground up and top down. This one-dimensional structure led to growing frustration among an increasing number of people and produced the wider movements and uprisings in the later 1980s. The issue of change therefore differs somewhat across time: it becomes more stringent at the top, but people at the bottom feel more empowered to do something about it.

Eds: One aspect that seemed to be, if not missing then certainly underemphasised in the account that you offer, was this question of the arbitrariness of power, of the *Willkür* that made decisions that affected people's everyday lives without any explanation or accountability. Did you deliberately choose not to include so much on this aspect of arbitrariness, and if so, why did you choose not to emphasise that aspect of life under this system?

KH: Yes, it was deliberate and was perhaps a bit of a pushback against the wealth of literature that exists on this aspect of life in the GDR; it is a matter very much on people's minds when they approach this subject and I didn't feel the need to write about it to the same extent. Another reason was that I tried to keep that aspect of the regime in proportion to the way the bulk of society experienced it. I think we have a tendency, because of the generally middle-class, professional background of those who read and write about the GDR, to look at the GDR in a similar way and forget that there is a large number of working-class people out there who experienced the GDR in a slightly different way. This is not to say they all had the same unified experience, but I have heard time and again from people who are frustrated with the idea that they were all constantly subjected to the whims of the regime and had no agency, because a lot of people do not see it that way. So I was trying to keep this theme within the proportions that I saw as I looked at the sources, that I encountered in the interviews I conducted, and that I heard when talking to people over the years. It therefore takes up a smaller share of the book than might have been expected.

People often criticise that there is not more on subcultures in the book, the discussion of which I have largely restricted to the 1980s, and even there as one strand rather than the main focus of the chapter. Again I felt, while talking to people, that an emphasis on subcultures is very much dictated by hindsight because we are looking at all this from after the downfall of the regime. By contrast, what I sought to highlight with the chapter on people's attempts to escape this world was that people were still trying to make their lives work because they did not know it was coming to an end. And yes, there were more and more people trying to escape from the GDR or form opposition groups, but this was still a small part of society overall and I have tried to keep it in its proportion. Another reason for not making more of these aspects was because I am talking to a wider audience in the book, which is not meant to be a contribution to existing scholarly debates: I was trying to provide an overall picture of the GDR that is as representative of that society as I can make it without overemphasising elements that affected certain people very deeply but also a lot of people not as deeply. That was my rationale for the balance of the narrative.

Eds: You describe the GDR in the late 1980s as 'a highly literate, highly skilled and highly politicized society, confident and proud in its achievements and keen to move forward. It was fertile ground for the seeds of reform and democratization.' (Hoyer 328) Leaving the global context aside for a moment, do you mean to imply that a more capable political leadership might have succeeded in reforming the country, and in offering a more promising development?

KH: Not to the point that the GDR would have survived, because of the political and social context, but there is an interesting split: when you look at the in- tellectuals who wanted change before it became a mass movement, many of them were people who wanted reform towards a more democratic socialism. Those people were still sitting at the [Central] Round Table in 1989/90 [*Zentraler Runder Tisch*, the name given to political discussions conducted by opposition and former governing groups in the GDR in the aftermath of the collapse of the SED regime], arguing about some sort of confederation with the *Bundesrepublik*, with some then bitterly disappointed when reunification happened and the GDR disappeared. So, yes, I think that some of the opposition movement, some of the dissidents, were asking precisely for a more democratic and transparent system of politics that remained socialist and left-leaning and which they did not want to get rid of completely. I sincerely doubt, looking at the intellectuals at the time, that the vast majority of them were laissez-faire, free-market capitalists. So from that angle, there could have been renewal of the system, which would have changed and opened it up.

The biggest issue was, of course, the question of travel to the West and the weakening or opening of the border in some shape or form. The moment this was done, the same situation prevailing before 1961 would have been restored. That makes the GDR somewhat unique and distinguished it from other socialist countries like Poland, where it was possible to open the border without such risks because there was no other Poland, no capitalist version of the same country. There is an extent to which concessions might have extended the lifespan of the regime a little longer and produced smaller or fewer demonstrations. But the fact that the economic factors and external developments made it a mass movement that was no longer exclusively about democratizing the GDR meant that these possible areas of change were nullified, ultimately because there was such a large mix of reasons why people took to the streets in the late 1980s. I think that if criticism had been taken up and responded to in the early 1980s, some of the sharpness of the opposition movement could have been blunted, but opposition later gained a momentum that was more difficult for the regime to counter because people participated for so many different reasons, while the international and economic situation applied relentless pressure. With the best will in the world, it is difficult to see how the regime could have survived much longer, even if run in a perfectly democratic form: the moment democracy entered, people's complaints could be met with action, and if they wished to reunify with West Germany or to travel freely, they would have had a democratic mechanism that allowed them to push for these changes. The downfall of the regime was then inevitable.

Eds: We would like to take up the points you have made about economic history and the demand for consumer goods by the GDRs population, various examples of which are discussed in your book. One was the New Economic Policy in the 1960s, which was accompanied by the decision of the Politburo to encourage more independent thinking, especially among younger people. Could you give us a more detailed idea of how this political 'spring' came about, and why was it comparatively short-lived?

KH: I think it simply came about because the system, as it stood, was not working and there existed pressure from the Soviet Union to make it work at all costs. Another factor that played a role, and which I highlight to a greater extent than other authors, was the disaffection of the Soviet Union towards the GDR. The Soviets just wanted the East German system to work, to be stable, and not to require constant interference. They did not mind what particular system the GDR regime chose, as long as it did not involve cosying up to the Federal Republic, which was beginning to re-arm and westernize quite heavily: that, I believe, was the caveat. Otherwise, it was supposed to be stable so that the Soviet Union did not constantly have to get involved. So there was certainly political room for this liberalization.

One problem that German leaders had is that Germany has a long and proud history of engineering and industrial skill, with many companies specialized in particular areas. These enterprises do not like being told how to do things: you can't go to a company like Carl Zeiss [an optical systems manufacturer, founded 1846 and based in Jena, Thuringia] and say, 'You have to meet these production targets by then,' without getting a bit of pushback from them, saying, 'Thank you, we know what we're doing.' I think it was part of the problem that the regime very quickly realized that such companies got very frustrated with the planned economy, not least because of the absurd situation that these highly specialized industrial concerns were asked to produce goods in which they had no expertise. For example, once a target was set to produce so and so many washing machines, the regime might approach, say, a watch manufacturer and say to them, 'can you just change your machines to produce washing machines?' On the one hand, such production is very ineffective, and on the other, these companies become incredibly angry about it, because they know that this is not an effective way of running things. To some extent, due to the greater degree of Soviet interference there, this also occurred in Czechoslovakia, a country that likewise boasted a proud industrial heritage, and in which many industrial concerns were similarly frustrated with the idea of production targets, none of which really matched reality on the ground.

I think there is a period when Walter Ulbricht opens up a little more widely and is genuinely interested in why the people are so disaffected with a system that he sees as the best. Let's not forget that this was the first time that anybody had attempted on German soil what had so far been tried only in the Soviet Union. The leading politicians were sitting there wondering why the workers did not recognise the worker's paradise they found themselves in, and there are moments when Ulbricht – and later, in the 1970s, also [Erich] Honecker – tried to work out what the problem was. This counts also for the economic sphere, and when they tried to identify the problems they were told by the industrial leaders, in no uncertain terms, that the system was not working, and that they needed more economic freedom, including the freedom to innovate. Think of something like an iPhone: this would never have emerged from a socialist system because it is not something that can be dreamt up in a stuffy office somewhere in Berlin with Politburo members who sit around a table, talking about wanting a telephone whereby someone can just tap and choose certain things; that just would not have worked. There was earlier no room for such innovation, and it was obvious that this needed to happen, and there were also people in the SED pushing for it as well.

When this policy worked, it simultaneously frightened a lot of people. Günter Mittag was one of those – although he later did not admit to it – who believed that socialism was being destroyed by stealth when this element of capitalism was allowed in. This idea quickly became something that frightened people, including Erich Mielke [head of the Stasi, 1957–1989] who came up with the idea that any kind of Western influence would slowly worm its way into people's minds and the state's structures, and who convinced politicians and others that this was the case. As a result, the New Economic Policy was quickly abandoned. But it did work, and there was a moment when you can see some kind of 'third way' that might potentially have worked for a certain amount of time.

Eds: The economic history seems to have been informed just as much by the attempt to plan as it was by the various incidents and developments that proved that planning just did not work. The book looks at developments such as the New Economic Policy of the 1960s or the global oil crisis of the 1970s, which contributed to stalling economic progress because the Soviet Union was no longer willing to sell their crude oil at a prearranged price that had allowed the GDR to refine and then sell it on at a profit. You make the argument that as a result of this last crisis in particular, what you describe as 'creating an illusion of progress' (Hoyer 281) became then dominant policy – which meant that instead of pursuing actual progress, measures of so-called *Zersetzung* (decomposition) were introduced: covert methods to psychologically destabilize and denounce individuals who were perceived as critical or who could end up being critical. What was the overall rationale behind such measures?

KH: I think part of the problem was that there existed a central planning system in which very few people had any economic expertise. Günter Schalck-Golodkowski was later said to have been one of the very few who had any economic zeal and ability, and this lack is understandably a development that arises when trying to create a workers' and peasants' state that is led by workers. The state ends up with roofers and carpenters (for example) running the country, and to produce a professionalized economic administration it was necessary to introduce people from a more middle-class background, to whom it had been naturally made very clear that they would have to leave their cultural and familial background behind. Thus where people were interested in economics it was highly unlikely that they were at the same time socialists; it was a difficult group to recruit, in terms of having economic experts in the leadership.

With the entire economy being run in this way, a genuine issue emerges that may sound amusing but is one of the core problems faced by the GDR: there were very few people who could actually predict what would happen if this or that measure were implemented because the economic system was so complex. Indeed, think of how much leaders today rely on think-tanks, experts, and large pools of consultants working together, all of whom still manage often to get things wrong! Then compare this with a country the size of the GDR, whose state apparatus was populated by a group of ideologues who were there because of their ideological loyalty and not because of their economic skill.

A second problem was the ongoing mistrust of the population. Members of the Politburo did not think it was a good idea to trust people with the knowledge that the economy was not running particularly well. Today, leaders try to talk of the economy in an overly positive light, but they have to deal with media on the other side that highlights how inflation is at such a rate and the cost of living is going up – modern politicians cannot avoid that. But in a country where there was strong control over the media, there existed the temptation to pretend that everything was fine and hopefully to fix problems behind the scenes, before saying 'look! We've made progress! Look at what you have!' But it was patently absurd to place three versions of the same thing on the shelf with different prices, pretending that one is better than the others but people can clearly see that it is exactly the same thing, just packaged in a different way. Or look at the Trabant, which is an obvious example: the regime completely misunderstood how important cars are to Germans, whether from East or West, and people could see how their relatives were driving Volkswagens or Mercedes around while they themselves were using the same Trabant that their parents or grandparents had been driving for decades. This was a focus of frustration that the leadership could not understand because there were no auto industrialists or even car enthusiasts involved. The principal leaders thought cars are there for getting from A to B, and people can do that either in a Trabant or they can use the public transport system. They didn't appreciate that this is something that people wanted to work towards, are proud of when they have it, taking care of it by washing it on Sundays, and so on. They didn't understand what was obvious to a capitalist, market-oriented system that undertook consumer research and could make progress in that direction. So I think there was a serious underestimation of how much consumerism in the widest sense meant to people, particular with products like cars. The regime did better with gardens, which might seem like a random example, but Germans are – and have always been – very much into their gardens: they enjoy looking after them and spending time in them. The regime facilitated this by building more and allowing more plots of land to be used for gardens. They responded to the need for leisure, but when it came to consumer goods they managed poorly, principally because the economy was planned by people who were not thinking as the mass of the population was.

Eds: You describe the political elite as not being particularly competent when it came to economic matters. How much was this a structural problem insofar as it also included regional or local party officials, that is, those that were in charge of executing the ideas that were coming from the top? As you just said, they underestimated the actual demand and the agency people wanted to have over their own lives, trying to realize an idea that many people may even have supported, but only in a way that was for them manageable, and where they could see a particular action was producing a particular result and would shape their lives in a way they hoped. How much was the gap between the political idea and the economic realization a structural problem – both for members of the party and ordinary citizens?

KH: I think it was. The GDR is often called a 'complaint society,' and for good reason when you look at the amount of complaints people filed in workplaces or elsewhere. People were given the illusion that they could have a say and they often took the regime at its word and did complain officially about things; unofficially, too, there was a lot of grumbling going on. When speaking to people today, almost everyone – including those who say that they were largely happy in their lives – says that they were frustrated about things, that it was not working for them, and that there was no way of voicing that in any shape or form. Discontent did seep down to all levels including individual workplaces and local politicians, and frustration was vented because people had the illusion that they could do something about it. For example, in the so-called *Aussprachen* [discussions] that were organized, in which people in a factory, workplace, or another context were summoned together in a room and told 'You can now say what you think about something,' party functionaries were often taken aback by how much anger and frustration was coming their way because people did feel that this was a forum to actually say something. I think that this aspect is somewhat underestimated: that there was this illusion that people could contribute at the grassroots level because such forums existed. But the higher echelons of the regime did not act on it, not necessarily the local leaders, who passed on these concerns, for example concerning the attitude of the GDRs youth. I use an example in the book from a report of 1987 that predicted that unless something was done to bring the youth back on board within the next two years, they would turn their backs on the regime – quite an accurate prophecy at that point! There therefore existed mechanisms that could have been used to give people a voice even within a dictatorial regime, but they were not acted upon by the more intransigent people at the top. These problems, I think, did affect all levels.

Eds: You are based in the UK and decided to write the book in English, and its reception in Britain has meant that you have been invited to talk at various events. If you were to look back on the conversations that you have had, for example at the Chalke Valley History Festival, how would you describe the British audience's interest in the GDR?

KH: It is surprisingly large. I sensed from conversations that I have had over the past ten years or so with those around me that there existed interest in Britain. This interest, shared more widely, I think, in the English-speaking world, is also one of the reasons why I thought it might be worthwhile writing this book. But the interest in Britain is surprising. At the Chalke Festival, for example, I was accompanied by a journalist from *Die Welt* who wrote a piece on the event and he said the same thing: he came away saying it was amazing how specific the questions were, with people wanting to know (for example) what Walter Ulbricht was thinking at this particular point in time about this or that policy. Such specific questions had piqued people's interest and there is a genuine desire, I think, to understand how the system worked and how it didn't work; a willingness and an open-mindedness to move away from the sort of 'Stasiland' idea that people had. (John Le Carré has a lot to answer for in the way that British people see the GDR! But people are not wedded to that image.) Such events obviously feature a self-selecting audience, but there is a willingness to understand more deeply, to be open to other aspects, and also just to learn more about the GDR. I meet a lot of British people who have, one way or another, a connection to the GDR: they were either there through the British Council or economic endeavours, or were part of the political left which, in particular during the height of trade union power during the 1970s, showed an interest in alternative models. The GDR was for them the obvious place to go because it was culturally a Western country and the only one that was fully immersed in the socialist system, and so there was a huge interest. There was certainly the famous motorcycle tour of Jeremy Corbyn and Diane Abbott through the GDR, but people also went in study seminars and other groups. Others were stationed in West Germany, and lots of soldiers were interested in the East: many of them joke it was them looking at us, that sort of thing. Many of them are now particularly interested to learn about what it was like on the other side of the Wall. I think there is a wide constituency of interest, and not necessarily for ideological reasons, which helps to explain the reception here as well, such that there are people writing from across the political spectrum – from Peter Hitchens in the *Daily Mail* all the way to the *Guardian* and

Observer – wanting to see the 'human face of socialism' (a phrase that made me cringe somewhat!) in the book. It is for that reason that many people are not shying away, even when they are politically very far removed from the GDR and its ideology, because they are still interested in aspects of its history that do not necessarily conform to their ideas of what it was or what socialism should be like.

Eds: Do you think that this interest might be tinged or even motivated by a sense of nostalgia in the decades after 1990, either for Cold War espionage or just the sort of Cold War era in general, where there existed a set of certainties provided by an overarching ideological competition between West and East, far different from today's perhaps much more complex world?

KH: I am always somewhat careful with this 'nostalgia' term because it is so often used to dismiss those views or sentiments as such. I think there is a fascination with the GDR – that is probably how I would phrase it – and a willingness to immerse oneself in that world. My publisher here has encouraged me to do more in the way of 'world building' to enable this sort of immersion, whether through pictures or anecdotes or whatever, and I am very reluctant to do this. But I do think that is a way for people to allow themselves to be drawn, emotionally and cognitively, to this topic although I would not call it nostalgia as such. People even do this with the 'Blitz spirit' in the UK, which obviously cannot be called nostalgia because most people doing this were not around during the Second World War so they cannot be fondly remembering their own experiences. It is rather almost a kind of willingness to let go of the present and work out what it was like there at the time and also to try to experience some of the emotions that come with that. This is not necessarily a bad thing: it means that people come out of your talk or event having felt some sort of connection with the topic and wanting to find out more about it. So I think in Britain, in particular, this endeavour does have Cold War elements, and this is helped by the fact that there is now a lot more literature on Eastern Europe as well. There is also a greater interest in Polish and Czech history, and Lea Ypi's book *Free* about Albania was also very popular. An interesting contrast, particularly in Germany, comes from the fact that Ypi is far more positive about communist Albania than I am about the GDR, and yet there was no such scandal in Germany about her book because it is not about their history. Likewise in Britain: Ypi is not shy about her sympathies for Marxism and was twelve when communism collapsed in Albania, but she is able to talk in Britain without people openly saying, 'well, hang on a minute, you can't say that!' It is a similarly open approach to just listen to her story and think about it before coming to some sort of judgement.

Eds: What new perspectives can be gained on the GDR from the curiosity of British readers? For example, the British are both fascinated with German history and tend to use humour as a 'default mode' (so to speak) for dealing with the world. Do you think that these two features can interact in the history of the GDR? Is there scope for a humorous treatment of East Germany in the English-speaking world in the same vein as, say, the film *The Death of Stalin* (2017), which was based on a French graphic novel?

KH: Yes, I think so because, first, it is the British way of doing things in any case, not only with other people's history but also their own, and humour sometimes helps because it allows you to distance yourself from the subject matter a little bit. But, second, I think it works in Germany as well. We had a phase where films like *Sonnenallee* (1999) and *Good Bye, Lenin!* (2003) took a humorous approach without being so light-hearted that it could not be done in Germany. I think people would be much more critical if a film like *Good Bye, Lenin!* were made today; it would certainly be more controversial, so we have almost taken a step back. This is certainly something that the journalist I had with me at the Chalke Valley Festival noted: he came out of the event and said that it would not be possible to have something like that in Germany, where 300 people sat in a tent in a field listening to somebody talk about at the GDR. It started, for example, by the host making a mistake while introducing me, and instead of saying about me, 'she's a well-known columnist,' she said, 'she's a well-known communist,' and that led of course to raucous laughter. (I responded, 'finally, someone says it out in the open now, I don't have to hide in my cupboard any more!') Everybody just laughed about that in a way that would not be possible in Germany, where people would immediately think that you are being flippant, or would find it simply embarrassing.

Eds: Are British audiences interested in GDR history because it is definitely *not* British history but, while not being necessarily 'exotic,' still raises curiosity and fascination? Or is it interesting because it is to an extent also one's own history in the broader Cold War context? You mentioned writers like Le Carré, but there are also more recent contributions (not necessarily on the GDR) such as Julian Barnes' *The Noise of Time* about Shostakovich, or Timothy Garton Ash's writing as a historian. These are writers who have experienced the Cold War, but there is also a younger generation who have not, but who are curious about it. So from your point of view, what is the particular attraction of the GDR or the Eastern bloc – the 'Second World' – overall?

KH: I think the GDR hits a sort of sweet spot between the politically remote and the seemingly familiar because you have people from a similar cultural background and, because of the geographical proximity, also lots of direct contact between Britain and the GDR. Having said that, were I to try to write something about communist China, I think that would also be of interest, but I am not sure it would reach as many people because it is too far away and too difficult to relate to, and there would therefore be a smaller pool of people specifically interested in it. Whereas with the GDR, it carries with it some of the fascination that people have in Germany anyway and it offers a number of angles on German history that are difficult to replicate in another context. You can see it in part with the other states in the Eastern bloc, but not as much as with Germany. Take the example of Albania: it is far more difficult to imagine, even geographically, what it looked like where Lea [Ypi] lived; she does try to capture that in the book and it works, but at the same time, people have been to Berlin and have an idea what it looks like. Yes, it is difficult to transport them mentally to somewhere like Görlitz or Rostock, yet they do have an idea of what Germany is, where it is, and you can anchor them in that, which certainly helps and is a reason why other productions have been quite successful. Even pure entertainment like *Kleo* (2022–) on Netflix, with its imaginary Stasi assassin, works because it plays with tropes in a way that allows it not to be too serious. People know very well that they are watching a piece of fiction, and that is fine. Equally with non-fiction, there remains an element that links to much of this spiced-up Cold War atmosphere, the 'exoticness' of it all, but at the same time in such a way that people can actually visualize and empathize with.

Eds: We already talked about the importance of memory: one can obviously have an interest in writing on the GDR as a means of exploring emotionally and intellectually what life was like. In his review of your book [in *The Critic*], David Goodhart welcomed it as an 'attempt to rescue the [GDR] from the condescension of history – to see it as more than a totalitarian blip defined by the Wall, the Stasi and its geriatric leaders.' In your own conclusion, you also make a strong case for approaching the GDR in its complexity and from different angles, and write that it should be considered as a regular part of German history, and not just as a deviation. Would you agree that this has been a main motivation for the book?

KH: Yes, completely. I do think that it needs to be seen as an actual chapter of German history in the same way as, say, the Weimar Republic. We engage seriously with that despite the fact that it failed in the end. There was a very short phase when it was treated with some condescension as a mere prelude to Nazism, but since then the bulk of the literature has said precisely the opposite. We need to deal with it earnestly in its own right notwithstanding that one can very easily argue that it was unsustainable in lots of ways, and there has been much literature that does exactly that, treating it seriously as a political and economic experiment that came with all sorts of problems. You are allowed to highlight those problems, not as an attempt to justify the entire system but in a way that explores them as genuine issues. I have been confronted and even had a long discussion with a politician from the FDP [*Freie Demokratische Partei*, Free Democratic Party, the German liberal party] who had an issue with the fact that I highlight some of the early economic problems of the GDR, and I said, 'but those *were* issues! How can you not talk about the reparations and the economic imbalance between the East and West, by way of explaining why it was so bad?' And she responded, 'well, what about the planned economy?' And I said, 'that was one factor out of five or six reasons why the GDR struggled to get going,' and she just rejected the notion of even mentioning the other factors because she saw it as a means of me saying that the GDR could somehow have worked, which I do not in the book. We do not do this with other aspects of German history, so I think the further we move away from it being part of the immediate past, the easier it will become to treat as a subject in its own right with the good, the bad, and the ugly standing side-by-side without cancelling each other out; that is what I was trying to do. It's remarkable that when I explained this to other Germans before the book came out they said, 'oh, that's a brave approach to take!' And I responded, 'what? You mean that simply describing what actually happened with all its facets is a brave thing to do?' It is just bizarre that we are still in a position where certain things are not supposed to be mentioned or discussed because people worry what effect they will have on the minds of others, here and now, even though they are true. I think that is maybe a way of talking about the GDR as a chapter of German history, as no longer *Zeitgeschichte* [contemporary history] as such: it goes down in history and then we're better able to talk about it. Having said that, Hedwig Richter's discussion about forms of early democracy in the *Kaiserreich* [the German Empire before 1918] was subject to similar criticisms, because there were political concerns about rehabilitating the *Kaiserreich* in some way. So possibly we might be sitting here in a hundred years' time and still be having this debate!

Eds: That we're maintaining the illusion of linear progress?

KH: Indeed, and of the bizarre split of modern German history into 'bad' before 1945 and then 'good' thereafter, but only in the West. The view that the GDR really needs to become, for better or worse, part of German history, destroys that 'two halves' view of this history. Germans from the former West also need to understand that if they want Germans in the former East to embrace West German history as their own – say, with the celebrations of the Basic Law [the *Grundgesetz*, the (West) German constitution] next year – to just pretend that it is everybody's history while what happened in the East is *not* everybody's history is a bizarre approach to take. So either we treat them as two separate strands of German history in the postwar era or we treat them – no matter where you are, as the lines blur further – both as *your* history, as a people, as a nation.

Eds: Thank you so very much indeed, both for your time and for sharing your thoughts and your work with us!

Self and Other: Becoming (in) the 'Second World'

Ágnes Györke

Affective Encounters: Central and Eastern Europe in Late-Twentieth-Century British Novels

Introduction: Encountering Central and Eastern Europe

'The past, it's full of too many things' – says Mr Brodsky, a washed-up conductor in Kazuo Ishiguro's *The Unconsoled* when trying to recall his confused memories in an unnamed Central European city.[1] Brodsky has mundane events in mind, such as the memory of a rude man he met years ago, yet his apparently trivial conclusion has a much larger relevance in the novel. The past is full of *too many things* that are irreconcilable and overwhelming: memories are not only confusing but also excessive and emotionally draining for Ishiguro's characters, who, due to this confusion, cannot make sense of the present either. As my chapter shows, this feeling of loss is a recurring motif in contemporary British novels about Central and Eastern Europe: although the distress Ishiguro's characters feel play out in different ways in Bruce Chatwin's and Tibor Fischer's writings, all novels explored here foreground confusion, excess, and absurdity as they map affective encounters with the 'Second World.'

Chatwin's *Utz* (1988), Fischer's *Under the Frog* (1992), and Ishiguro's *The Unconsoled* (1995) are not isolated examples of British writing on Central and Eastern Europe: they are part of a revival of interest in the region around and after the collapse of communism in 1989. Other examples include Ian McEwan's *Innocent* (1990), which is set in Berlin during the Cold War, and *Black Dogs* (1992), a more philosophically inclined exploration of the period. The fall of communism in the region was also a popular theme at this time: Julian Barnes's *The Porcupine* (1992), for instance, is set in a fictional post-communist country, which resembles Bulgaria, and Malcolm Bradbury's *Doctor Criminale* (1992) is a satire that takes the reader to post-communist Central and Eastern Europe in search of a mysterious philosopher. Ishiguro called this period the loss of provincialism in Britain when he discussed the wider context of the changes that unfolded in the 1980s:

---

1 Kazuo Ishiguro. *The Unconsoled*. New York: Knopf, 1995. 326.

In the early 1980s there was an explosion of tremendous interest in literature that suddenly appeared almost overnight. This occurred in foreign language literature with people like Garcia Marquez, Milan Kundera and Mario Vargas Llosa, who became very trendy people. At the same time there was a whole generation of younger British writers who often had racial backgrounds that were not the typical white Anglo-Saxon. Even some of the straight English writers were also using settings or themes that tended to be international or historical. So there definitely was this atmosphere where people were looking for this young, exotic – although exotic may be a somewhat unkind word – writer with an international flavor. I was very fortunate to have come along at exactly the right time. […] The British were suddenly congratulating themselves for having lost their provincialism at last. (Vorda and Herzinger, 'An Interview,' 134)[2]

The origin of the transformation Ishiguro comments on goes back to the post-Second World War period, when waves of immigrants from the Commonwealth arrived in Britain, and novels such as Doris Lessing's *The Grass is Singing* (1950), George Lamming's *In the Castle of My Skin* (1953), and Sam Selvon's *The Lonely Londoners* (1956) came out, introducing new themes and perspectives to fiction published in Britain. Nevertheless, Ishiguro is right in claiming that the transformation became fully visible in the early 1980s and Salman Rushdie's 1981 Booker Prize was a 'milestone'[3] in the process. The growing interest in the 'elsewhere' was due both to this larger trend developing since the post-war period, and, commensurately, to the collapse of communism, which added yet another dimension to it. Fischer's novel is, perhaps, the most profound expression of this turn towards Central and Eastern Europe, since both Ishiguro and Chatwin were already established writers by the time they started to write on the region: they published novels 'with an international flavour'[4] about a decade or so earlier (Chatwin wrote about South America and Australia, for instance, and Ishiguro's first two novels are set in Japan). *Under the Frog*, however, is Fischer's first published novel. The Booker nomination it received in 1993 shows that by the early 1990s the 'Second World' made it to the British publishing market as part of a larger interest in the 'elsewhere.'[5]

After the millennium, narratives of Central and Eastern Europe partly returned to old topics, such as the Cold War and post-communism, and partly introduced new ones, namely, the exploitation of Eastern European migrants in Britain. Rose Tremain's short story, for instance, 'The Beauty of the Dawn Shift'

---

2 Allan Vorda and Kim Herzinger. 'An Interview with Kazuo Ishiguro.' *Mississippi Review* 20.1/2 (1991): 134.
3 Vorda and Herzinger, 'An Interview,' 134.
4 Vorda and Herzinger, 'An Interview,' 134.
5 Fischer, however, received a large number of rejection letters before *Under the Frog* was accepted for publication (personal communication with Tibor Fischer). Most rejection letters contained belittling references to the topic of the novel and claimed that no one would be interested in the story of basketball players in post-war Hungary.

(2006) is set in Berlin after the fall of the wall; Tom McCarthy's *Men in Space* (2007) takes the reader to post-communist Prague; Simon Mawer's *The Glass Room* (2009) is set in Brno at the time of the Second World War. Ukrainian-British author Marina Lewyczka's *Two Caravans* (2007) depicts the everyday life of migrant labourers from Eastern Europe, China, Malaysia, and Africa, working in the British agricultural industry. Even Monica Ali, who focused on the Bangladeshi community in her first novel, *Brick Lane* (2003), puts a more diverse group of characters at the centre of *In the Kitchen* (2009), including Ukrainian and Moldovan migrants, some of whom were trafficked to work in Britain. Central and Eastern European themes, then, seem to persist in literary works published in Britain: new perspectives emerge as the sensation of the collapse of communism subsides, ensuring the region remains central in a number of twenty-first-century narratives.

The novels Chatwin, Fischer, and Ishiguro published around the collapse of communism present three different attitudes towards Central and Eastern Europe. Chatwin, a British travel writer, has visited Cold War Prague in the 1960s and wrote about the city just before the collapse of communism in 1989: his first-person narrator is fascinated by the nostalgic desire for grandiosity the title character displays, which is an escape for Utz under the absurd totalitarian regime. Fischer, a British writer of Hungarian origin, spent a few years in Budapest in the 1980s and wrote *Under the Frog* based on his father's account; his third-person narrator relies on the conventions of realism and black humour to portray Cold War Budapest, trying to take the reader as close to the world he describes as possible. Ishiguro's novel, the most imaginative narrative of the three, is based on no such experience; the writer has even claimed that *The Unconsoled* is not specifically about Central and Eastern Europe: 'you could almost set that thing down anywhere. It was by and large a landscape of imagination.'[6] Nevertheless, this profoundly ahistorical, first-person narrative evokes emotions that characterize perceptions of this region by depicting the unnamed Central European city its narrator visits as a confusing, Kafkaesque labyrinth.

The three novels this chapter explores, then, showcase the versatility of British writing on the region both in terms of themes, aesthetics, and narrative strategies: the attitudes displayed by the narrators reveal the desire to know more about the psychopathology of everyday life under communism (in *Utz*); the need to show ordinary heroic acts against totalitarianism to the wider world (in *Under the Frog*); and the assumption that this uncanny space reflects the innermost secrets of the 'Western Self' (in *The Unconsoled*). They also shed light on the peculiar impact Central and Eastern Europe had on the British popular imagination at the

---

6 Dylan Otto Krider. 'Rooted in a Small Place: An Interview with Kazuo Ishiguro.' *The Kenyon Review* 20.2 (Spring 1998): 151.

time when communism collapsed in the region. It is my contention that all novels discussed in this chapter construe this geopolitical space as a confusing, excessive, and absurd 'Other,' which is more threateningly familiar than the exoticised 'Other' in writings about the postcolonial world. Whereas the perception of the 'Third World' as a dangerous yet seductive 'Other' has been extensively explored by postcolonial critics,[7] the 'Second World' has not yet been theorised as the 'Other' of the West, despite the numerous claims that it has performed this role since the Enlightenment.[8] The 'Second World' is a blind spot, a gap, an uncanny space between 'the First' and 'the Third,' the known and the unknown: somewhat less seductive and dangerous than the 'postcolonial Other,' yet equally disturbing. Despite the versatile themes and aesthetic strategies of the three narratives, then, I argue that Chatwin's, Fischer's and Ishiguro's novels construe Eastern and Central Europe as a highly incongruous 'Other' on the periphery of the known world that needs to be confronted and rendered recognisable.

Prague in Chatwin's *Utz*

In the late 1980s Chatwin was already severely ill with AIDS when his wife, Elizabeth, suggested that he should write a novel based on the letters he sent to her from Prague more than 20 years ago.[9] The main character, Kaspar Utz, was inspired by Rudolph Just, a porcelain collector the author met at that time.[10] The novel is also based on a childhood experience: as a boy, little Bruce liked exploring his grandmother's curiosity cabinet, which was a family museum that contained many relics and narratives attached to these; as Chatwin's biographer, Nicholas Shakespeare puts it: 'In his last novel Bruce reaches back to his four-year-old self, to the young Utz visiting his grandmother's castle outside Prague and standing on tiptoe before her vitrin of antique porcelain and saying "I want

---

7 Octave Mannoni and Frantz Fanon explored the psychological projections that play a role in construing the native as 'Other' in the 1950s, and it was Edward Said's *Orientalism* (1978) that studied Western perceptions of the Eastern world in a systematic manner. (Octave Mannoni. *Prospero and Caliban: The Psychology of Colonization.* Transl. by Pamela Powesland. Ann Armor: University of Michigan Press, 1990; Frantz Fanon, *Black Skin, White Masks.* New York: Grove Press, 1966; Edward Said. *Orientalism.* London: Vintage, 1978).

8 Larry Wolff. *Inventing Eastern Europe: The Map of Civilization on the Mind of the Enlightenment.* Stanford: Stanford University Press, 1994. 7; see also Nataša Kovačević. *Narrating Post/Communism: Colonial Discourse and Europe's Borderline Civilization.* New York: Routledge, 2008. 3; Ágnes Györke and Imola Bülgözdi. 'Introduction: Central and Eastern Europe and the West: Affective Relations.' *Geographies of Affect in Contemporary Literature and Visual Culture Central Europe and the West.* Ed. Ágnes Györke and Imola Bülgözdi. Leiden: Brill, 2021. 7–9.

9 Nicholas Shakespeare. *Bruce Chatwin: A Biography.* New York: Doubleday, 2000. 498.

10 Shakespeare, *Bruce Chatwin*, 500.

him.'"[11] The cabinet is the very embodiment of excess: it contains a collection of random yet all the more meaningful objects displaced from their original contexts. According to Steven Mullaney, '[t]aken together, they compose a heteroclite order without hierarchy or degree, an order in which kings mingle with clowns.'[12] This is precisely what we see in Chatwin's novel as well: the English narrator tells the story of meeting Kaspar Utz, the collector of Meissen porcelain, who is said to be of noble origin, yet who is also an absurd figure: a restless, obsessive individual, mesmerised by his extravagant collection that he keeps in his humble flat on Široká street. *Utz*, therefore, is a narrative about excess: Chatwin himself described it as 'a tale of Marxist Czechoslovakia conceived in the spirit and style of the Rococo,'[13] suggesting that the juxtaposition of the excessive and the prosaic was a very conscious authorial decision based both on Chatwin's childhood memories and his trip to Czechoslovakia.

Utz begins with the detailed description of the title character's funeral, which already evokes the atmosphere of communism in a vivid manner.[14] The event takes place at 8 am since the authorities 'had decreed that all baptisms, weddings and funerals must be over by 8:30' to make sure that these 'retrograde Christian rituals' do not divert the People's attention.[15] A cleaning woman is working in the church, scrubbing the blazon of a prominent Bohemian family with soap, water, and brush; she is politely asked to allow the coffin to pass, then continues her job indifferently. The only mourners are Orlík, Utz's friend, and Martha, his housekeeper, later revealed to be his wife. This is a powerful vision of Utz's so-called 'greatness': the funeral is portrayed as an absurd event, reminiscent of Kafka's writings since it foregrounds the insignificance of human life and effort. It differs from other Kafkaesque accounts of Central and Eastern Europe, however, due to its focus on grandiosity: the novel juxtaposes the absurd discourse with the rhetoric of excess and nostalgia for the past. With the help of historical allusions and comparative references, the nihilism of the communist present is set alongside a grandiose, nostalgic, quasi-historical portrayal of Prague. The church in which the funeral is held, for instance, is highly ornamented, quite likely modelled on the baroque Church of St Ignatius, which, similar to the porcelain the main character collects, symbolizes the excess that is irreconcilable with the practices portrayed in the opening scene.[16] Furthermore,

---

11 Shakespeare, *Bruce Chatwin*, 38.
12 As qtd. in Shakespeare, *Bruce Chatwin*, 38.
13 As qtd. in Shakespeare, *Bruce Chatwin*, 500.
14 The episode is based on a wedding Chatwin attended in Prague (Shakespeare, *Bruce Chatwin*, 499–500).
15 Bruce Chatwin. *Utz*. London: Picador, 1989. 8.
16 On the significance of the baroque in literary representations of Central and Eastern Europe, see Ágnes Harasztos. *The Postmodern Baroque: Bruce Chatwin's* Utz *and British Fiction on*

Utz is called 'a Rudolf of our time' (*Utz* 16), referring to Rudolf II, the Renaissance emperor who collected exotica in an excessive way and kept his collection in Prague Castle. Not unlike Rudolf's collection, Utz's Meissen porcelain also evokes extravagance, luxury and, above all, excess, which is irreconcilable with the functionality the communist era imposed on the city and its inhabitants.

This incongruity lies at the heart of the narrator's affective encounter with Prague. The juxtaposition of apparently irreconcilable objects, historical periods, and emotions evokes a sense of hybridity, which is the trope of cultural encounter in the novel. This, however, is not the Bhabhaian concept of hybridity, which enables the colonized to create new transcultural conjoinings on the level of language and identity, for instance.[17] Rather, hybridity in Chatwin's novel exposes oddities yet does not point towards new alternatives and visions. The Meissen Harlequin in Utz's modest flat exemplifies this state of cultural hybridity clearly: similar to the main character himself, the collection is precious, ornate, and painfully out of place in communist Prague. The English narrator foregrounds these oddities yet offers no explanation, let alone solution, to the agonizing tension between them, which is the result of the turbulent history of the Central and Eastern European region. This feeling of loss and confusion at the sight of the 'Eastern European Other' is also the central theme of Ishiguro's *The Unconsoled*, discussed below.

Utz's Meissen collection evokes a sense of nostalgia for Mitteleuropa and Germanic cultures in general, which makes the present bearable for Utz. Trademarked as the first European porcelain, Meissen figurines stand for stylistic innovation, luxury, and cultural power; as Johannes Just puts it, 'the Meissen Manufactory reigned absolutely supreme' in the eighteenth century, 'and its unsurpassed artistic excellence represented the pinnacle of European porcelain art.'[18] Meissen was a Saxon town that became part of the GDR after 1949,[19] thus it is easy to see why the figurines became associated with a sense of greatness that disappeared by the time of the Cold War. The term Mitteleuropa

---

East-Central Europe at the Time of the 1989 Political Changes. Doctoral Dissertation. Budapest: ELTE, 2021.

17 Homi Bhabha argues that hybridity 'is the name for the strategic reversal of the process of domination through disavowal,' which enables the colonised to hold a crooked mirror to the coloniser (Homi K. Bhabha. *The Location of Culture*. 2nd edition. London: Routledge, 2004. 159).

18 Johannes Just. *Meissen Porcelain of the Art Nouveau Period*. Photographs Jürgen Karpinski. Transl. Edward Larkey. London: Orbis, 1985. 7.

19 The porcelain factory in Meissen was controlled both by the Nazi and the communist regimes; as Just points out, '[t]he years following the First World War were marked by efforts to have records of its accomplishments erased from history' (Just, *Meissen Porcelain*, 7).

echoes this greatness: coined by pre-First World War German thinkers,[20] it referred to a hypothetical German-led political and economic alliance of German, Hungarian and Slavic peoples extending from the Baltic Sea to the Mediterranean and the Black Sea, to be later exploited by the Nazis to justify their territorial aggression.[21] When Eastern Europe was construed as a geopolitical space behind the Iron Curtain politically and imaginatively, Mitteleuropa ceased to exist.[22] Likewise, Utz's imaginative Mitteleuropa, embodied by the Meissen Porcelain, is concealed in his shabby flat on Široká street, which was the main artery of the Jewish quarter at the time when Kafka was born. Nonetheless, it dominates the novel: the 'grand past' is perceived as a hidden yet persistent narrative still visible under the new stories inscribed on it in the twentieth century.

The concluding image of *Utz* returns to the idea that Mitteleuropa survives, which is one of the principal themes of the novel according to Chatwin as well.[23] However, the idea of survival is no longer expressed by the Meissen figurines hidden in Utz's flat: it acquires a less tangible yet more visible form. Before his death, Utz's collection disappears, and it never really becomes clear whether he himself destroyed it, the authorities confiscated it, or, perhaps, it was sold abroad. Trying to find out what happened, the narrator visits Martha, his widow, who lives in a small village called Kostelec close to the Austrian border. On his way to her house, he stumbles into a monument that might be read as a memento for Mitteleuropa: 'Beside the chapel there is the base of a monument which once would have borne the double K's – Kaiserlich und Königlich ['imperial and royal'] – of the Dual Habsburg Monarchy. It now supports a rusty, lopsided contraption commemorating a Soviet foray into space' (*Utz* 154). Therefore, the monument is a visible palimpsest of the past, the layers of which are profoundly irreconcilable: communist 'progress' is inscribed upon the 'grandness' of Mitteleuropa, and the result is an uncanny hybrid memento that exposes oddities yet offers no solution to the agonizing tension between the legacies of the historical periods it evokes.

The last sentence of the novel desperately reasserts the greatness of Mitteleuropa, and, at the same time, shows how out of place it is. Marta opens the door

---

20 Friedrich Naumann's book *Mitteleuropa* (1915) was translated into English as *Central Europe* and published in London (1916) and New York (1917).

21 Stefano Bottoni. *Long Awaited West: Eastern Europe since 1944*. Transl. Sean Lambert. Bloomington: Indiana University Press, 2017. 2.

22 The notion of Mitteleuropa, however, resurfaced again in the 1980s when the crisis of communism became apparent in the region and dissident public intellectuals made the claim that Central Europe was markedly different from the East and 'belonged to the Western sphere of civilization' (Bottoni, *Long Awaited West*, 5); see also Györke and Bülgözdi, 'Introduction,' 1–2.

23 Shakespeare points out that before the publication of *Utz*, Chatwin was upset by a proposed blurb and responded to it with a list of ideas that had not been put across, such as: 'One of the principal themes of the book is that Old Europe *survives*' (Shakespeare, *Bruce Chatwin*, 503).

of her tidy red-tiled house and greets the narrator as follows: 'Ja! Ich bin die Baronin von Utz' (*Utz* 154). Marta is described as 'an old peasant woman' (*Utz* 154), as if we met her for the first time, though she is a major character who was introduced at the very beginning of the narrative. The discrepancy between what she says and how she is perceived is immense, as if she were the living testimony to a grand, and by this time ridiculously outdated, Central European identity. Marta, who has never been a baroness yet allegorizes the 'greatness' of Mitteleuropa at this stage, presents a vision of Central and Eastern Europe as farce. This image is both absurd and nostalgic, suggesting that the conclusion of *Utz* evokes the two main discourses that construe Central and Eastern Europe in the novel: the Kafkaesque vision of communism and the nostalgic narrative of *mitteleuropäische* splendour. Through these discourses, the narrative exposes the irreconcilable tensions between Central European culture and communist functionality, past and present, grandeur and emptiness, yet, as I have argued, it does not offer a transformative vision. Seen from the outside, the region remains an absurd yet grandiose 'Other' in Chatwin's novel, imagined through binary opposites that do not point towards a third option.

Budapest in Fischer's *Under the Frog*

Under the Frog tells the story of post-WWII Hungary from the perspective of the allegorical 'little man' in a humorous and sarcastic way. The novel culminates in the portrayal of the 1956 revolution against Soviet oppression. The plot loosely follows the story of Fischer's parents, who were basketball players during the 1950s and emigrated to Britain in 1956. Therefore, although Fischer was born in England in 1959 and only learnt to speak Hungarian as an adult, his engagement with this region is based on communicative memory[24] and empirical experience. He first visited Budapest in 1982 and later worked there as a journalist between 1988 and 1990, living through the changes that took place at this time.[25] *Under the Frog*, in fact, might be read as an 'exilic' narrative that imagines Hungary from a

---

24 As opposed to cultural memory, communicative memory is non-institutional: it 'lives in everyday interaction and communication and, for this very reason, has only a limited time depth which normally reaches no farther back than eighty years, the time span of three interacting generations.' Jan Assmann. 'Communicative and Cultural Memory.' *Cultural Memory Studies: An International and Interdisciplinary Handbook*. Ed. Astrid Erll and Ansgar Nünning. Berlin and New York 2008. 110.

25 Gerd Bayer. '"I am very keen on tea and Shakespeare." An interview with Tibor Fischer.' *"Do you consider yourself a postmodern author?" Interviews with Contemporary English Writers*. Ed. Rudolf Freiburg and Jan Schnitker. Münster: LIT, 1999. 107–117. Fischer also visited Romania in 1989, just at the time of the Romanian Revolution, which inspired one of his short stories, 'Ice Tonight in the Hearts of Young Visitors.'

peripheral angle, not unlike other novels by writers of Hungarian origin, such as Agota Kristof's *The Notebook* (written in French) and Zsuzsa Bánk's *The Swimmer* (written in German), which also engage with Hungary during and after the Second World War.[26]

The dedication of *Under the Frog* reveals that Fischer's novel aims to showcase what happened behind the Iron Curtain after the Second World War to an English-speaking audience: 'For all those who fought. (Not just in '56. Not just in Hungary).' It addresses a translocal group of readers beyond the borders of Hungary and the region[27] by evoking shared emotions: courage, the need to fight against repression, the need to understand causes that point beyond their immediate geopolitical contexts. The revolution in Hungary is put in parenthesis, as if this larger context were more important than the very country where the novel is set. The translocal horizon evoked by the dedication, however, is in stark contrast with the places that appear in the novel, where Hungary is portrayed as a country cut off and isolated behind the Iron Curtain.

Whereas in *Utz* and in *The Unconsoled* the storyline is based on the idea that the narrator is a Western traveller who visits the region and describes what he sees there, in *Under the Frog*, there is no such mediator between the 'First' and the 'Second' world. In Fischer's novel, an apparently all-knowing, third person voice describes the everyday life of basketball players in the Hungarian capital, all of whom are young men. Their world is very boyish and masculine, reminiscent of Ferenc Molnár's *The Paul Street Boys* (1906), a very well-known Hungarian novel set in late nineteenth-century Budapest that explores male friendship, bullying, and competition. Fischer's protagonist, Gyuri is 14 years old in 1944, when the chronological narrative begins, similar to Molnár's boys, and he is 26 at the end of the novel, set in 1956 when the revolution breaks out. Women appear as sexual objects or idealised figures in *Under the Frog* (as Jadwiga, for instance, Gyuri's true love), who live in the young men's imagination. Events are mostly focalized through Gyuri's eyes, whose figure is modelled on Fischer's father; his thoughts are also reported directly by the third person narrator from time to time. For instance, we see what he thinks when the revolution is crushed: 'You don't get any braver you just get tired, bored with fear, *thought Gyuri* as he scrambled over the

---

26 For an analysis of these novels as 'exilic' literature see my article 'On the Periphery: Contemporary Exile Fiction and Hungary.' *The Journal of Postcolonial Writing* 57.3 (2021): 316–329. See also Ágnes Harasztos' reading of Fischer's novel as postmemory, which describes the relationship that the 'generation after' bears to the cultural trauma of their parents and grandparents: 'Photographic Origins of Postmemory in Tibor Fischer's *Under the Frog*.' *Neohelicon* 43 (2016): 185.

27 I understand translocality as a form of 'grounded transnationalism' that explores connections and the crossing of boundaries at various scales apart from the national. See Ayona Datta and Katherine Brickell (eds). *Translocal Geographies: Spaces, Places, Connections*. London: Routledge, 2011; Györke and Bülgözdi, 'Introduction,' 3–7.

wall to land in the Kerepesi Cemetery.'[28] This perspective takes the reader closer to the world described in *Under the Frog* than the traveller-narrators in Chatwin's and Ishiguro's novels, yet Fischer's narrator becomes somewhat didactic at times due to the semi-insider position from which he speaks.

In accordance with the themes introduced by his dedication, Fischer's narrator guides the reader towards the heart of traumatic events in communist Hungary. This is done by exploring hidden yet all the more significant places in Cold War Budapest and describing atrocities as directly as possible. One such notorious hidden place is the prison at Andrássy Street 60, which was the residence of the Arrow Cross Movement during the Second World War and the headquarters of the secret communist intelligence called 'State Protection Authority' (ÁVH) in the post-war period. Gyuri is taken to Andrássy 60 one night, although 'he had never felt important enough to be arrested' (*Frog* 124). The episode is described as follows:

> Gyuri was led underground and shown into a cell which had a feeble member of the bulb family lighting it [...]. On the wall, someone scraped 'I am a member of parliament': this statement didn't seem to be worth the trouble on its own – presumably it was an apotheosis, produced by the author's untimely removal from the cell. Underneath, in a different style, with a different sharpish instrument, someone had inscribed, 'I am a member of Újpest football club.' There was also in faded pencil (remarkable since Gyuri had had all his portable personal and impersonal items removed, as well as his belt and shoelaces) 'If you can read this, you are in trouble.'
> Well, thought Gyuri, here I am under the frog's arse. Under the coal-mining frog's arse indeed, at the very bottom of existence. (*Frog* 127–130)

This episode is set in August 1950, in the period when the control of everyday life became unbearable and suspicious people labelled as 'enemies of the system' were taken to prison for no apparent reason. The narrative attempts to describe the experience as directly as possible, exploring how it feels to be imprisoned, showing the inscriptions on the wall, taking the reader close to the heart of historical trauma. The title of the novel is evoked at the end of the episode: this hidden place 'under the frog's arse' (*Frog* 130) epitomizes the very bottom of existence in the narrative.[29] Encountering 'the Other' here means being led to secret spaces and seeing the world from a 'worm's-eye-view,' which literally translates as 'frog's perspective' ('békaperspektíva') in Hungarian. Nevertheless, due to the humorous tone of the narrator and his desire to describe communism as a farce, the narrative is not always realistic: both characters who are taken to

---

28 Tibor Fischer. *Under the Frog.* London: Penguin, 1992. 242–243 [emphasis added].
29 The English title is less explicit than the Hungarian translation, which is 'Under the Frog's Arse' (*A béka segge alatt*).

Andrássy 60 in the novel are released, which was seldom the case in communist Hungary.

The desire to expose the secret crimes of the age is juxtaposed with the desire to evoke its atmosphere, which is also expressed through the language of the novel. Fischer's text is interspersed with Hungarian words that resist translation, not unlike postcolonial novels that use foreign words and neologisms, such as Salman Rushdie's *Midnight's Children* (1981) and *Shame* (1983). In Fischer's novel, Gyuri and his friends 'Zrínyi out' of restaurants (18) whenever they run out without paying the bill, for instance. The narrator explains what this means explicitly, drawing a bathetic parallel between the heroism of a seventeenth-century Hungarian hero and the petty acts the basketball players perform under communism:

> They remembered that they had run out of a restaurant in the centre of town without paying the bill, *doing a Zrínyi*, as it was known in the Locomotive ranks, in memory of the great Hungarian general, Miklós Zrínyi, who had rushed out of his castle to do battle with a Turkish force that outnumbered him ten times (to be completely wiped out). They remembered they had *zrínyied out* of a restaurant, but having been so legless and brainless they couldn't remember which one [...] (*Frog* 18; emphases added).

Expressions such as 'doing a Zrínyi' and 'zrínyied out' are neologisms based on Hungarian history and English syntax; they show a narrator who is speaking from a semi-insider position, and they also create an ironical, playful tension between 'the great past' and the communist present. Other examples of Hungarian words include place names such as 'Hálás' (*Frog* 57–62, 64–65, 68, 71, 73, 76, 111), a Hungarian village, which literally means 'grateful,' and words associated with Hungarian culinary culture such as 'csárda' [tavern] (*Frog* 59–60, 62, 66, 72), 'kocsma' [pub] (*Frog* 90, 198), and 'pálinka' [brandy] (*Frog* 17, 63, 72, 91, 96, 117, 198). These words, similar to foreign expressions in postcolonial narratives, insist on the untranslatability of culture (pubs are indeed very different from Hungarian kocsmas), and they also help to situate the narrative even more emphatically in its Hungarian context. Nevertheless, due to the clear explanations the narrator gives (as in the case of Zrínyi) and to the clichéd implication of some expressions (the strong alcoholic drink called 'pálinka' is likely to be known by tourists who visit Hungary), these words and puns also serve the main aim of the novel, that is, they help introduce the region to the foreign reader by describing its atmosphere through images, sounds, and tastes, drawing them closer and closer to the heart of the 'Second World.'

Both *Utz* and *Under the Frog* evoke 'the glorious past' as an antithesis to life under communism. However, the strategies the two narrators use are rather different: whereas in *Utz* the prosaic communist present becomes bearable through escape into a bygone world exemplified by the Meissen collection, in

Fischer's novel characters try to survive the regime by mocking it through petty, irreverent games, which often counterpoise the greatness of Hungarian historical figures with the 'virtues' of their own anti-heroic and unambitious world. In other words, whereas Utz escapes into the past, Gyuri and his friends escape into ridicule, and ironically invoking 'the glorious past' is but one of their many tools. The example discussed above, 'doing a Zrínyi,' refers to the historical figure to describe a childish prank, and it also shows what kind of 'heroism' is possible under the communist regime. Such references to historical greatness are mainly used in Fischer's novel to foreground the anti-heroic, tedious life under communism, there is no desire in this narrative to escape into a bygone grand world.

The main character of *Under the Frog*, Gyuri, is also portrayed as an unambitious 'little man': his sole desire is to survive. Gyuri becomes involved in the revolution primarily for the sake of his beloved Jadwiga, a Polish girl who is a truly revolutionary spirit, inspired, perhaps, by the fifteen-year-old Erika Szeles, whose photo with a machine gun appeared in Western media in 1956 (see Figure 1: the image was also used as a cover photo on the Vintage edition of *Under the Frog* published in 2002).[30]

For instance, when Gyuri starts to feel ashamed for not participating in the fights, he walks into an apartment and fires a shot from a completely safe place: 'Gyuri, who still hadn't fired a shot, went into the old lady's flat, introduced himself to her husband, opened their window and fired off three shots in the general directions of the Radio. He closed the window and thanked the couple for their co-operation. He felt much, much better. He had taken part' (*Frog* 213). It is shame that makes Gyuri perform this act, not the desire to crush communist power; he would prefer to 'stick to his philosophy of staying in bed' (*Frog* 214) had he not been inspired by Jadwiga, who is much more courageous and ready to fight.

Nevertheless, once the revolution is in full swing, Gyuri starts to believe in it gradually, and a sense of seriousness enters the narrative. The event is portrayed as 'a bubble of decency' (*Frog* 230), which takes over Budapest for a short time: 'A bubble of decency had risen out of the earth's core and burst in Budapest. Peasants were driving in from the countryside with their carts to distribute food to whoever they came across, dishing out sacks of potatoes, apples, marrows, some late melons' (*Frog* 230). When a young boy calls his fellows to take up arms, contrary to what we have seen throughout the narrative, his plea is not treated as a joke: 'One enthusiastic youth, who couldn't have been more than fifteen, called them brothers and exhorted them to take up arms for the revolution. You could tell it was a revolution because this appeal didn't sound ridiculous' (*Frog* 213).

---

30 The photo was taken by the Danish photographer, Vagn Hansen, and it appeared on the cover of *Billed Bladet* on 13 November 1956. See also Harasztos, 'Photographic Origins,' 186–187.

Figure 1: Erika Szeles, Budapest, 1956. ©Vagn Hansen, courtesy of Henning Schultz.

Gyuri and his friends indeed become everyday heroes at this stage: Jadwiga, his lover, dies on the streets, and the portrayal of the revolution evokes the memory of Petőfi, a poet who had participated in the 1848 uprising against the Habsburgs: 'It would be funny, mused Gyuri, if a second revolution were to start here at the National Museum. It was here on these steps that Petőfi had read out one of his poems cutting the ribbon, as it were, to inaugurate the 1848 revolution' (*Frog* 211). However, Gyuri and his friends are never portrayed as venerated figures and historical icons; the narrative remains focused on the lives and the minds of ordinary men who become involved in larger-than-life events out of their control.

The perspective that unfolds in *Under the Frog* is typical of how Hungarian literary works and films engage with this period. In the 1980s, when the hard-line communist regime was already disintegrating, several films that portrayed 1956 were released, such as Péter Gothár's *Time Stands Still* (1982) and Péter Gárdos' *Whooping Cough* (1987). Similar to Fischer's novel, these films also explore the perspective of the helpless individual and the loss of hope due to the crushing of the revolution. The first novel allowed to be published that openly described 1956 is Ferenc Karinthy's *Autumn in Budapest* (1982), which portrays the revolution from a perspective akin to Gyuri's. Karinthy's novel also describes the mundane life of students, including their sexual adventures, focusing on how common people survive the totalitarian regime. The semi-insider narrative voice in *Under the Frog*, then, is reminiscent of Hungarian narratives that explore the period, yet the dedication, the use of Hungarian words and the explicit historical explanations invite English-speaking readers to enter the world of the 'Other' and experience this unfamiliar realm from an ironically distanced insider's perspective. The 'Second World' is, therefore, tamed and rendered recognisable through this particular narrative technique in Fischer's novel.

'The Elsewhere' in Ishiguro's *The Unconsoled*

The Unconsoled does not take its readers close to any identifiable Central and Eastern European place, yet Ishiguro's novel also reveals the impact this region had on the British popular imagination in the 1990s. In fact, *The Unconsoled* has more thematic affinities with Chatwin's *Utz* than appears at first sight. Many critics have claimed that the novel is a trauma narrative, primarily concerned with psychological issues,[31] which is supported by the author's interpretation of his own work as a 'landscape of imagination.'[32] However, *The Unconsoled* has already been read as a novel about Central Europe,[33] despite Ishiguro's claim that he is 'not interested in saying specific things about specific societies,'[34] and not only because of its setting but also the 'Central European character' of the narrative.[35] I would argue that Ishiguro's novel is a relevant example of British writing on the 'Second World' precisely because of its vagueness: *The Unconsoled* imagines Central Europe as a space where repressed psychological impulses come to light,

---

31 See Natalie Reitano. 'The Good Wound: Memory and Community in *The Unconsoled.*' *Texas Studies in Literature and Language* 49.4 (2007): 361–386; Matthew Mead. 'Caressing the Wound: Modalities of Trauma in Kazuo Ishiguro's *The Unconsoled.*' *Textual Practice* 28.3 (2014): 501–520; Cynthia Quarrie. 'Impossible Inheritance: Filiation and Patrimony in Kazuo Ishiguro's *The Unconsoled.*' *Critique* 55 (2014): 138–151; David Coughlan. 'The Drive to Read: Freud, Oedipus and Ishiguro's *The Unconsoled.*' *Parallax* 22.1 (2016): 96–114.

32 Krider, 'Rooted in a Small Place,' 151.

33 See Richard Robinson. 'Nowhere, in Particular: Kazuo Ishiguro's *The Unconsoled* and Central Europe.' *Critical Quarterly* 48.4 (2006): 107–130; and Melinda Dabis. 'Crisis of Crises: Reimagining Central Europe in Kazuo Ishiguro's *The Unconsoled.*' *English Studies*, 103.7 (2022): 1103–1115.

34 Vorda and Herzinger, 'An Interview,' 140.

35 Robinson, 'Nowhere, in Particular,' 111.

as if the region reflected the innermost secrets of a 'Western Self,' allegorized by the English narrator of the novel whose traumatic memories are projected onto the Central European landscape.

No famous locations or sights are mentioned in the novel that would help identify a particular setting. References are either fictive or bizarre. Our only certain knowledge is that the narrator is English: Mr Ryder, a famous concert pianist arrives from England, and he needs to perform a concert before travelling on to the next event in Helsinki. He is seen as a powerful and talented person, who is expected to revive the musical culture of the unnamed city. While it is clear where he comes from and where he is going, the present moment is vague and confusing, suggesting that this ambiguous, labyrinthine, Kafkaesque world is constituted by references to what it is *not*. Nevertheless, this world is also strangely familiar: the unnamed city turns out to be the place where Mr Ryder's family lives. The familiar and even the intimate are confronted in this alien environment; both people and objects that are unfamiliar at first sight turn out to be related to personal memories.

The Unconsoled has a Germanic atmosphere, although Ishiguro decided to use Germanic names rather late.[36] These are placed alongside Slavic names, suggesting that the novel is set somewhere in the borderlands between Germanic and Slavic regions. The host of Ryder is called Mr Hoffmann, his employee is Miss Stratmann, and street names are also Germanic, such as Herrengasse, for instance. Yet a gallery where Ryder gives a talk is called the Krawinsky Gallery, there is a piano teacher called Mrs Tilkowski, visiting performers are called Igor Kobyliansky and Jan Piotrowski. Perhaps we are in Prague or Brno, which were part of Austria-Hungary and witnessed the intermingling of Slavic and Germanic cultures, or in a Polish city such as Wrocław in Silesia, which was German before 1945. The admixture of Germanic and Slavic references might also suggest that we are in the GDR; however, the Slavic influence is not related to communist ideals in this novel, rather, it is integral to the identity of the city. Slavic names, in fact, are associated with artistic accomplishment and genuine talent in *The Unconsoled*: they are connected to the musical world of the unnamed city. The fact that it is impossible to identify a particular city suggests that the setting, if it represents anything at all, reveals how an outsider perceives the muddle that imperialism and communism created in Central and Eastern Europe due to partitions, annexations, and the constant redrawing of borders.

It is also uncertain when the novel is set. At one point the narrator goes to watch a film, *2001: A Space Odyssey*, which is one of the few allusions in *The Unconsoled* that is not fictitious. The film was released in 1968, thus the novel is supposed to be set between this date and 1995, during the Cold War or around the

---

36 Krider, 'Rooted in a Small Place,' 151.

time when communism collapsed. It has been read as an allegory of the collapse
of communism,[37] yet the intertextual reference to *A Space Odyssey* obscures this
since the film was released in the Eastern Bloc in the 1970s. I would argue that the
calamity the Central European city is undergoing is related to a more general
sense of identity crisis, not to the collapse of one specific system.

Another recurring reference point in the novel is the late nineteenth century,
which is often mentioned as a significant period in the city's history. This was the
heyday of the Austro-Hungarian and the German Empires, the time when Mitteleuropa still existed and dominated the region, which suggests that the
'greatness' the city is trying to revive might be connected to this imperial period.
There is a famous monument in the city of Max Sattler, an entirely fictitious
person, who played an important role in the life of the unnamed city in the
nineteenth century. He is implied to have been a divisive figure: as Ryder's guide
puts it, his memory "has gained a place in the *imaginations* of citizens" (Ishiguro
374) in the past century. Since the Central European region witnessed unprecedented urban growth in the late nineteenth century, the Sattler's monument, perhaps, also evokes this imperial period and its historical grandiosity.

Another late-nineteenth-century monument that appears in the novel is an
uncrossable wall Ryder stumbles into when he is trying to get to the concert hall.
A passer-by tells him why the wall is significant:

> To an outsider, particularly to one trying to get somewhere in a hurry, it must be an
> annoyance. I suppose it's what you call a folly. It was built by some eccentric person at
> the end of the last century. Of course, it's rather off, but it's been famous ever since. In
> the summer, this whole area where we're standing now, it gets completely full of tou-
> rists. Americans, Japanese, all taking photographs of it. (*Unconsoled* 388)

Both the Sattler Monument and the brick wall are mementos of late-nineteenth-
century creativity, which seems to be what the city has subsequently lost, and
which is not even intelligible in the present – especially not for an outsider such as
the narrator. The fact that the wall is also a 'tourist attraction,' of course, makes
this lack of understanding even more ironical. Apart from recalling lost 'greatness,' however, the wall also evokes the atmosphere of communism, alluding to
the Berlin Wall as an uncrossable border in a city. These confusing, dream-like
traces of something essential that has been lost haunt the narrative, suggesting
that the late nineteenth century was a period when more grandiose endeavours
could come to light than in the disoriented present moment.

The wall is not the only trope in the novel that evokes both nineteenth-century
grandeur and the atmosphere of communism. The very concert that Ryder came
to give is imagined along these lines. He is expected to revive the musical culture

---

37 Krider, 'Rooted in a Small Place,' 151.

of the city, as if he were a great authority whose originality could redress past mistakes. However, it turns out that before playing the piano, Ryder will have to answer questions about specific local issues on stage, although he knows nothing about these matters. To his utmost surprise, Ryder learns that questions will be projected on a huge scoreboard to 'help some of those present to remember the gravely important nature of the issues [he is] addressing' (*Unconsoled* 318). Again, the feeling of missing something utterly important dominates the episode, and the fact that Ryder is supposed to give specific answers makes the scene terrifying. Ishiguro's narrator seems to be enacting repressed traumatic experiences, which are projected onto the spaces and scenarios he encounters during his brief sojourn in Central Europe. Furthermore, the nightmarish scenario also recalls the show trials performed under communism: the oblivious Ryder is simultaneously put on a pedestal and in the dock since he knows nothing about the matters his interrogators expect him to address. The concert, then, originally associated with the revival of *mitteleuropäische* musical culture, turns into a Kafkaesque vision of an everyman helplessly subdued by powers outside his control, evoking both lost dignity and communist terror.

The contrast between historical grandiosity and the farcical present is akin to *Utz* exploring *mitteleuropäische* plenitude and communist nihilism, suggesting that the monstrous and unintelligible 'Other' Ryder encounters is indeed Central and Eastern Europe, hopelessly intermingled with his own phantasmagorias. In *The Unconsoled*, 'grandness' can turn into its exact opposite any time, mirroring how Ryder feels: he is both a nobody ignored and abused in the city and a grand authority everyone seeks to please. This mutability, however, does not sound unrealistic in the Central and Eastern European context at all, where grand metropolises indeed did turn into provincial cities behind the Iron Curtain over a few decades.

To conclude, I have discussed three late-twentieth-century British novels that portray affective encounters with Central and Eastern Europe. Although all the narratives imagine the region as a disorienting 'Other,' their aesthetic strategies are rather different. The first-person narrators of Chatwin and Ishiguro foreground the irreconcilable, unresolved tensions that characterize both the region and their own mental states, which are projected onto the world they describe in various degrees. In the more realistic world of *Utz*, the curiosity cabinet of Chatwin's grandmother is used to visualize *mitteleuropäische* culture, which is portrayed as the symbol of an excessive yet fragile splendour out of place in communist Prague. *The Unconsoled* depicts a similar contrast between late nineteenth-century creativity and the desolate present through public mementoes, which are not only traces of the unnamed city's lost grandeur but also tropes that express Ryder's inner thoughts. Fischer's third-person narrator, however, stays focused on the present of post-WWII Budapest and alludes to historical heroes only to highlight the anti-heroic nature of life under communism and everyday heroic acts performed in 1956. Whereas the narrators of *Utz* and *The Unconsoled* register obsession, fear, and shock as affective responses to the cultural and mental incongruities they perceive, Fischer's semi-insider narrator takes up the role of a chaperone and attempts to guide the reader to the heart of Cold War Budapest in a laid-back manner. In other words, whereas Chatwin's and Ishiguro's novels expose hopelessly irreconcilable views on the region, Fischer's narrative attempts to tame and explain this very irreconcilability. Despite their versatile narrative and aesthetic strategies, then, all three novels imagine Central and Eastern Europe as a highly incongruous 'Other' on the periphery of the known world, which needs to be confronted, assessed, and rendered recognisable so that its threatening familiarity could be dealt with.

References

Assmann, Jan. 'Communicative and Cultural Memory.' *Cultural Memory Studies: An International and Interdisciplinary Handbook.* Ed. Astrid Erll and Ansgar Nünning. Berlin and New York 2008. 109–118.

Bayer. Gerd. "'I am very keen on tea and Shakespeare." An interview with Tibor Fischer.' *"Do you consider yourself a postmodern author?" Interviews with Contemporary English Writers.* Ed. Rudolf Freiburg and Jan Schnitker. Münster: LIT, 1999. 107–117.

Bhabha, Homi K. *The Location of Culture.* 2nd edition. London: Routledge, 2004.

Bottoni, Stefano. *Long Awaited West: Eastern Europe since 1944.* Translated by Sean Lambert. Bloomington, IN: Indiana University Press, 2017.

Chatwin, Bruce. *Utz.* London: Picador, 1989.

Coughlan, David. 'The Drive to Read: Freud, Oedipus and Ishiguro's *The Unconsoled*,' *Parallax* 22.1 (2016): 96–114.

Dabis, Melinda. 'Crisis of Crises: Re-imagining Central Europe in Kazuo Ishiguro's *The Unconsoled*.' *English Studies* 103.7 (2022): 1103–1115.

Datta, Ayona and Katherine Brickell (eds). *Translocal Geographies: Spaces, Places, Connections.* London: Routledge, 2011.

Fanon, Frantz. *Black Skin, White Masks.* New York: Grove Press, 1966.

Fischer, Tibor. *Under the Frog.* London: Penguin, 1992.

Györke, Ágnes. 'On the Periphery: Contemporary Exile Fiction and Hungary.' *The Journal of Postcolonial Writing* 57.3 (2021): 316–329.

Györke, Ágnes and Imola Bülgözdi. 'Introduction: Central and Eastern Europe and the West: Affective Relations.' *Geographies of Affect in Contemporary Literature and Visual Culture Central Europe and the West.* Ed. Ágnes Györke and Imola Bülgözdi. Leiden: Brill, 2021. 1–17.

Harasztos, Ágnes. *The Postmodern Baroque: Bruce Chatwin's* Utz *and British Fiction on East-Central Europe at the Time of the 1989 Political Changes.* Doctoral Dissertation. Budapest: ELTE, 2021

–. 'Photographic Origins of Postmemory in Tibor Fischer's *Under the Frog.*' *Neohelicon* 43 (2016): 181–200.

Just, Johannes. *Meissen Porcelain of the Art Nouveau Period.* Photographs Jürgen Karpinski. Transl. Edward Larkey. London: Orbis, 1985.

Ishiguro, Kazuo. *The Unconsoled.* New York: Knopf, 1995.

Kovačević, Nataša. *Narrating Post/Communism: Colonial Discourse and Europe's Borderline Civilization.* New York: Routledge, 2008.

Krider, Dylan Otto. 'Rooted in a Small Place: An Interview with Kazuo Ishiguro.' *The Kenyon Review* 20.2 (Spring 1998): 146–154.

Mannoni, Octave. *Prospero and Caliban: The Psychology of Colonization.* Transl. by Pamela Powesland. Ann Armor: University of Michigan Press, 1990.

Mead, Matthew. 'Caressing the Wound: Modalities of Trauma in Kazuo Ishiguro's *The Unconsoled,*' *Textual Practice* 28.3 (2014): 501–520.

Quarrie, Cynthia. 'Impossible Inheritance: Filiation and Patrimony in Kazuo Ishiguro's *The Unconsoled.*' *Critique* 55 (2014): 138–151.

Reitano, Natalie. 'The Good Wound: Memory and Community in *The Unconsoled,*' *Texas Studies in Literature and Language* 49.4 (2007): 361–386.

Robinson, Ricard. 'Nowhere, in Particular: Kazuo Ishiguro's *The Unconsoled* and Central Europe.' *Critical Quarterly* 48.4 (2006): 107–130.

Said, Edward. *Orientalism.* London: Vintage, 1978.

Shakespeare, Nicholas. *Bruce Chatwin: A Biography.* New York: Doubleday, 2000.

Vorda, Allan and Kim Herzinger. 'An Interview with Kazuo Ishiguro.' *Mississippi Review* 20.1/2 (1991): 131–154.

Wolff, Larry. *Inventing Eastern Europe: The Map of Civilization on the Mind of the Enlightenment.* Stanford, Stanford University Press, 1994.

Melinda Dabis

Eastern European Orientalism and the Post-Socialist 'Other' in Kazuo Ishiguro's *The Unconsoled* (1995)

The turn of the late 1980s and early 1990s brought changes to the world order standing for almost half a century, and the Cold War division of Europe. As the Iron Curtain lifted or crumbled, border checkpoints were opened between countries, and grass grew over once heavily guarded border zones. With the return of the states from the grip of socialism to the West, the region became the focus of widespread attention. Politicians gave speeches with high hopes about the newly emerging Central Europe; treaties, agreements and joint ventures were created. The political and economic interest was accompanied by the attention to the cultural sphere, including literature and literary topographies. British writers explored Central European themes and settings: Bruce Chatwin dived into the life of a bizarre collector from Prague in *Utz* (1988), Julian Barnes set up the fictitious trial of a former Bulgarian dictator in *The Porcupine* (1992), Malcolm Bradbury ventured into the criminal underworld and the complexities of a fictionalized international crime scene in *Doctor Criminale* (1992), and Tibor Fischer evoked Hungary's 1956 revolution with fictionalized family anecdotes in *Under the Frog* (1992). After having established himself as a writer of historical fiction on the World War II period, Kazuo Ishiguro, weary of the 'Japanese author' label, portrayed a community unsettled by crisis in *The Unconsoled* (1995), whose unspecified Second World setting is unmistakeably a Central European city.

Ishiguro's protagonist Ryder is a world-famous British pianist, who has a knack of resolving critical situations with his insights about the community's life and problems. His arrival in the unnamed but undoubtedly Central European town conceptualizes East-West power relations when a master, an individual of superior knowledge and talent from the West, arrives in the East as a problem solver and saviour. The choice of the setting also fits into the emerging British literary interest in non-British subjects since the late 1970s, and more particularly in the Central European region from around the political changes in 1989. Harasztos[1] argues that the British East-Central European novel should be cate-

---

1 Ágnes Harasztos. *The Postmodern Baroque: Bruce Chatwin's Utz and British Fiction on East-*

gorized as a sub-genre, rooted in the tradition of the British travelogues, where these places function as 'quasi-utopian spaces'[2] for the literary imagination to act out wishes, utopias, but also nightmares and wanderings of the unconscious in this geographically real yet simultaneously imagined region of Eastern/Central Europe. These discursive and cultural explorations were border crossings, ventures into a new and exotic land. Ishiguro's visitor arriving from the West attempts to make sense and interpret the social and the geographical space, but collides with physical and cultural walls, losing himself more and more in the labyrinthine structures of an occasionally surreal urban landscape. The rational logics of space and time do not operate here, as Ryder attempts to find his way with increasing desperation.

The 1990s were the period that Tlostanova characterized as 'the historical juncture at which the postcolonial ghost emerges in the background of the postsocialist drama.'[3] According to Cold War terminology this region belonged to the Second World, but after the dissolution of the USSR, the classification seemed to have lost its substantive meaning. Western politicians and prominent figures (Henry Kissinger, even Queen Elizabeth II) welcomed the states back into the European family by calling them Central Europe, thus officially establishing the region. The countries were emerging from a colonial status under the Warsaw Treaty, but the decades of socialist past could not be left behind overnight. The euphoria about the opening borders and the rush towards the West and Western ideals and consumer products also led to an almost enthusiastic self-colonization, yielding to the soft power of the West, in particular, to the English-speaking sphere. The Western perspective, the literary portrayal of Central Europe as the 'other' can be therefore analysed in postcolonial frameworks.

Proceeding from the notion that Central Europe was a politically colonized region during the Cold War and has since engaged in cultural self-colonizing, I will examine Kazuo Ishiguro's *The Unconsoled* within the critical frame of Eastern European Orientalism to analyse the depiction and the self-representations of the novel's urban setting and its inhabitants. With a focus on the intricate dynamics governing their interactions, I will argue that Ishiguro's construction of a Central European town is aligned with the Western European perception of Eastern/Central Europe as the 'other.' It must be noted that an ambiguity is inherent already in the nomenclature, whether denoting the region as Central Europe or Eastern Europe. I shall employ the term Central Europe, while concurrently referencing scholarly discourse that occasionally designates

---

Central Europe at the Time of the 1989 Political Changes. PhD dissertation. Budapest: Eötvös Loránd University, 2021. 28–29.

2 Harasztos, *The Postmodern Baroque*, 28.

3 Madina Tlostanova. *Postcolonialism and Postsocialism in Fiction and Art: Resistance and Re-existence.* London: Palgrave Macmillan, 2017. 4.

the region as Eastern Europe. My terminological choice relies on reviewers and scholars writing about *The Unconsoled,* who locate the town featured in Ishiguro's novel in Central Europe (among others, Shaffer 1998; Tomkinson 2016; Robinson 2007[4]), as well as the prevailing political discourse of the 1990s calling the region Central Europe.

Central Europe, Orientalism and the 'other'

The terminological conundrum is partly explained by the fact that Central Europe is a construct; its location, nature, and characteristics are dependent on who describes it. Timothy Garton Ash famously claimed, 'Tell me your Central Europe, and I will tell you who you are.'[5] Historically the term was coined by German political thinkers in the nineteenth century, where *Mitteleuropa* was considered as a German sphere of interest, 'to safeguard it from Russian expansionism and British hegemonic ambitions.'[6] The idea was used by Hitler and Nazi ideology to justify the Third Reich's politics of expansion and occupation, which discredited the concept and it went dormant during the decades of socialism. This changed with the turbulent political events and the disintegration of the Eastern bloc in the late 1980s and early 1990s. International attention turned towards the region encompassing the states east of the Iron Curtain but the west of the (soon to be former) USSR. However, several ambiguities persisted regarding the constituents and characteristics of Central Europe. Earlier, in socialist times, Milan Kundera and other thinkers rejected Germany's involvement in the concept of *Mitteleuropa* as early as 1984, when he defined Central Europe and its historical identity as 'an uncertain zone of small nations between Russia and Germany.'[7] Identity has always been a complex matter, often difficult to comprehend for outsiders and possibly even ambiguous for people living within the region. According to an anecdote, Franz Kafka once met an officer of the Prussian army long before World War I. On inquiring about Kafka's nationality, Kafka gave him a lengthy explanation, but was unable to clarify the issue to the officer. Although he came from Prague, he was not a Czech; though he was Jewish,

4 Brian W. Shaffer. *Understanding Kazuo Ishiguro.* Columbia: University of South Carolina Press, 1998. Fiona Tomkinson. 'Ishiguro and Heidegger: The Worlds of Art.' *Kazuo Ishiguro in a Global Context.* Ed. Cynthia Wong and Hülya Yıldız. New York: Routledge, 2016. Richard Robinson. 'Nowhere, in Particular: Kazuo Ishiguro's *The Unconsoled* and Central Europe.' *Narratives of the European Border.* London: Palgrave Macmillan, 2007. 156–178.
5 Timothy Garton Ash. *History of the Present: Essays, Sketches, and Dispatches from Europe in the 1990s.* London: Allen Lane, 1999. 384.
6 Otilia Dhand. *The Idea of Central Europe.* London: I.B. Tauris, 2020. 5.
7 Milan Kundera. 'The Tragedy of Central Europe.' Transl. Edmund White. *The New York Review of Books* 31.7 (1984): 35.

he had broken away from the Jewish community; and though he wrote in German, he was most certainly not a German.[8] The region resists all the typical characterizations of religion, nationality, and language, as there are too many overlaps and exceptions. However, as intellectuals such as Milan Kundera, Václav Havel, and György Konrád suggest, the shared history and the elusive notion of culture can be considered a common denominator.[9] It is, therefore, in the arena of culture where a construction of identity should occur, allowing for the manifestation of a (Central) European identity.

Orientalism is a term introduced by Edward Said in 1978 to conceptualize colonialist discourses and cultural representations, denoting how Western perceptions and portrayals of the (Middle) East were shaped and manipulated by colonizing powers to assert dominance and justify their control.[10] He explored the Other as a colonialist concept, which involves the construction of cultural, social, or racial difference, resulting in the marginalization or exoticization of groups outside the power hierarchies. The discursively constructed perception of the colonized subject as the Other was, according to Said, instrumental in establishing a power hierarchy and asserting Western dominance. From the 1990s onwards, in the midst of the disintegration of the Eastern bloc and the emergence of new democracies, scholars began to apply Said's concept to certain Eastern European states and their relationship to the West.[11] Although these countries did not endure the forms of colonial marginalization, exploitation, and racial discrimination that was imposed on colonies in Asia or Africa and which inspired Said's propositions, scholars like Wolff, Tlostanova and Kovačević claimed that Western Europe has also long attempted to 'intellectually master Eastern Europe through description and classification, fixing it into lamentable cultural, political, and economic backwardness' or defining its peoples as 'noble savages.'[12] However, compared to other instances of colonial domination, the voluntary self-colonizing tendency of Central Europe is distinctive, a phenomenon that stretches back, in case of Hungary for instance, for a millennium.[13] According to Kovačević, 'Eastern European narratives' and their

---

8 Claudio Magris. 'Közép-Európa – egy fogalom igézete.' Transl. Miklós Mesterházy. *Közép-Európai olvasókönyv.* Ed. Péter Módos. Budapest: Osiris, 2005. 95.

9 Kundera, 'The Tragedy of Central Europe,' 33–38; Václav Havel. *The Anatomy of a Reticence: Eastern European Dissidents and the Peace Movement in the West.* Stockholm: Charta 77 Foundation, 1985; György Konrád. *Antipolitics: An Essay.* New York: Harcourt, Brace & Jovanovich, 1984.

10 Edward W. Said. *Orientalism.* London: Routledge and Kegan Paul, 1978.

11 Larry Wolff. *Inventing Eastern Europe.* Stanford: Stanford University Press, 1994; Maria Todorova. *Imagining the Balkans.* Oxford: Oxford University Press, 1997.

12 Nataša Kovačević. *Narrating Post/Communism Colonial Discourse and Europe's Borderline Civilization.* London: Routledge, 2008. 2.

13 Kovačević, *Narrating Post/Communism,* 4.

'preoccupation [...] with their various reflections in the Western mirror and concomitant self-stigmatizations or self-celebrations are perhaps the most elusive and least discussed avatars of what could be called [...] Eastern European Orientalism. [...] Eastern Europe's [...] acceptance of Western models has, overall, been far smoother, more voluntary, and more urgently executed than in other colonial locales.[14]

The voluntary self-colonization is accompanied and challenged by nationalistic tendencies. Quoting Derrida, Kovačević points out the crux of the matter, namely that 'opening [itself] onto that which is not, never was and never will be Europe' jeopardizes its own identification as European; but if it opens itself to another 'other,' then 'it can no longer even relate to itself as *its* other.'[15] Therein lies the dilemma that creates the paralyzing ontological insecurity for Central Europe: it appears preoccupied by the concern that a radical opening would render the entire concept meaningless. By accepting its own otherness, Central Europe would set itself apart from the idea of Europe; but rejecting it would challenge its essence and geopolitically unique situation of being relatively removed from centres of power. Non-belonging is a key characteristic of the region, being neither in the West, nor in the East, living in a status of in-betweenness, in ontological suspense and shape-shifting under the gaze of power. In the end, Central Europe is always emerging, always growing up, always defining itself in relation to a set of ideas called Europe, but not as Europe.

Self-colonization and nesting orientalisms

According to scholars like Wolff, the East is associated with the barbaric, the uncivilized, and a lack of culture, regardless of one's vantage point in Europe, which may also give a hint as to the sensitive issue of denoting oneself as Central European, not Eastern European. The pejorative connotations of the East are very much present, even though it is always a source of confusion. Apparently, Henry Kissinger began his speech in 1990 in Warsaw saying, 'I'm delighted to be here in Eastern, I mean Central Europe,' a slip of the tongue that kept occurring throughout his speech.[16] The concept of 'nesting orientalisms'[17] introduced by Milica Bakić-Hayden further complicates relations within the region, accounting

---

14 Kovačević, *Narrating Post/Communism*, 4.
15 Jacques Derrida. *The Other Heading: reflections on today's Europe.* Translated by P. A. Brault and M. B. Naas. Bloomington: Indiana University Press, 1992. 77.
16 Timothy Garton Ash. 'The Puzzle of Central Europe.' *The New York Review of Books.* 18 March 1999. <https://www.nybooks.com/articles/1999/03/18/the-puzzle-of-central-europe/> (accessed 15 Nov 2023).
17 Milica Bakić-Hayden. 'Nesting Orientalisms: The Case of Former Yugoslavia.' *Slavic Review* 54.4 (Winter 1995): 917–931.

for stratified social (cultural) hierarchies, where the urban intellectuals are gatekeepers to culture, and assume a superior position within society.

This internalization and replication of Orientalist tendencies can be traced in the inhabitants' discourse about the town's prevailing crisis in *The Unconsoled*. The crème de la crème of the town passes judgement on the value of actors in the cultural sphere. If they vote somebody out, they lose everything, like the musician Christoff, from social reputation to bare livelihood. Pedersen, a local city councillor, perceives that the city has arrived at a pivotal juncture, since the level of crisis has reached such an extent that even the 'ordinary citizen' begins to question the artistic merit of Christoff's musical performance. 'Ordinary people, decent citizens like Mr Kohler were now expressing such views. It was clear the pretence could no longer continue. It was time for us – all of us in positions of influence – to own up to our error, however far-reaching the implication.'[18] It is then the inner circle of people 'in positions of influence' around the Countess (the aristocracy features as a remnant of a bygone era under socialism, with their titles meaningless yet retaining some of the mystical glory and thus authority) who decide on the promotion of Brodsky and the invitation of Ryder. Both of them are foreign in the town; however, their circumstances differ significantly. Brodsky needs a complete makeover to conform to the town's standards and become presentable, whereas Ryder's mere three-day sojourn is perceived as adequate for the resolution of the prevailing crisis. This elite is the driving force behind the self-colonization, who identifies the existence of the crisis of values, and determines the means of resolving the situation. The power of cultural dynamics conceals a dimension of self-colonization in society, where 'orientalized subalterns' reproduce themselves as others within their own community, creating an 'internal societal orientalization.'[19]

Historically, the intellectuals of the evolving political landscape of Central Europe during and after the Cold War were spearheading the transformation and facilitating the broader discourse on the future, which aimed to reinstate the region as an integral part of the Western sphere 'that, kidnapped, displaced, and brainwashed, nevertheless insists on defending its identity.'[20] These intellectuals spoke multiple European languages, received a cosmopolitan European education, they read, quoted, and translated the likes of Shelley, Baudelaire, and Dante. Significantly, many of these intellectuals took on positions in political life and assumed roles even as political leaders in the emerging democracies of Central Europe, notably in countries like the Czech Republic (Václav Havel) or Hungary

---

18 Kazuo Ishiguro. *The Unconsoled*, London: Faber and Faber, 2005. 102.
19 Michał Buchowski. 'Social Thought & Commentary: The Specter of Orientalism in Europe: From Exotic Other to Stigmatized Brother.' *Anthropological Quarterly* 79 (2006): 466.
20 Kundera, 'The Tragedy of Central Europe,' 33.

(Árpád Göncz). As I have written elsewhere, culture was highly politicized; literature, music, theatre were a 'battleground of ideologies'[21] in the decades of socialism.

Such cultural infighting is both exemplified and ridiculed in the grave discussion about music among townspeople in Ishiguro's novel, and foregrounds the characters' preoccupation with the question of who has more authority to form opinions. Inviting Ryder is not their first attempt to solve the crisis; another candidate was Christoff, also an outsider who used to be cherished as the local truth-sayer, but who has lost credibility and reputation. The group of inhabitants fight among themselves, trying to defeat each other by discussing music and musical modalities.

> 'My own view is that Kazan never benefits from formalised restraints. Neither from the circular dynamic, nor even a double-bar structure. There are simply too many layers, too many emotions, especially in the later works.'
> I could feel, almost physically, the tide of respect sweeping towards me. The pudgy-faced man was looking at me with something close to awe. A woman in a scarlet anorak was muttering: 'That's it, that's it,' as though I had just articulated something she had been struggling to formulate for years. The man named Claude had risen to his feet and now took a few steps towards me, nodding vigorously. Dr Lubanski was also nodding, but slowly and with his eyes closed as if to say: 'Yes, yes, here at last is someone who really knows.' (*Unconsoled* 201)

After Ryder's *ex cathedra* proclamation, dethroning the previous 'laureate' musician, an almost irrational fury is unleashed on Christoff, evoking a torrent of emotions. In this town the matter of culture is not a polite conversation topic; instead, it embodies existential significance capable of making or breaking a person and unleashing utterly uncivilized forces. This sentiment could not be further away from stereotypically restrained British middle-class demeanour, but it fits the typical perception of the loud and intense emotions exhibited by the imagined colonized 'other.'

Coloniality of time and space

In post-socialist countries, both 'time' and 'space' have been subjected to a form of epistemological colonization, as Tlostanova suggested. Her concept of tempo-locality refers to intersections of temporal and spatial dimensions, where different historical eras and cultures interact. Within this framework, the past is characterized by what Tlostanova terms the 'coloniality of memory.'[22]

---

21 Dabis, 'Crisis of Crises,' 1112.
22 Tlostanova, *Postcolonialism and Postsocialism in Fiction and Art*, 157.

> Societies are offered certain sanctioned forms of constructed collective memory which does not conserve but rather erases the past still full of restless ghosts. In a way it becomes an unpredictable past that can be subsequently interpreted in any 'convenient' way.[23]

The Sattler monument in *The Unconsoled* is dedicated to the (fictional) Max Sattler who was an important citizen of the town about a century ago, and is a reminder of a piece of history that is still unresolved. Some unprocessed trauma divides the community, the past lurks in the background and frequently interrupts the present. This 'inability of the present to shake off the specters of the past which it continually proclaims to be dead'[24] impedes constructive discourse within the community, and any reference to it stirs up intense emotions. It is symbolic that it is the outsider Ryder who attempts to confront the inhabitants with the past by posing in front of the memorial, in order to prompt discussion and possibly force the community out of its deadlock. His endeavour, however, proves unsuccessful, the general attention is fixed only on his posing in front of the building, not so much on the monument itself, let alone its historical significance. At this point the self-colonizing notion, the invitation of the foreign master pianist who should redeem them all, swiftly turns into hostility and denies the outsider the understanding of the local complexities and the prerogative to offer counsel. Outbursts such as 'He'll take us too far. The Sattler monument, that's going too far' or 'We're better off the way we are!' (*Unconsoled* 370) illustrate the divisive nature of the Sattler monument: while some perceive it as a commemoration of an ambitious historical epoch, others view it as a distressing reminder, which underscores the lack of social consensus and the parallel values and interpretations within the community.

For the outsider, the ambiguity of the past and its memorial seems to be impossible to resolve. Ryder feels obliged to confess his failure to understand the complexity, 'I now saw the possibility that there was even more to the business of the Sattler monument than I had supposed' (*Unconsoled* 371). The presence of the past is impossible to penetrate for the visitor from the West; and much as with collective memory, the urban landscape presents insurmountable barriers.

The East has been depicted with attributes such as irrational, illogical, and mystical, and the old and new Central Europe is presented with similar Oriental signs, features that also describe Ishiguro's town visited by Ryder. The labyrinthine cityscape reflects the perceived political landscape of the post-socialist space: Robinson describes this as a 'materialisation of geopolitical stalemates

---

23 Tlostanova, *Postcolonialism and Postsocialism in Fiction and Art*, 157.
24 Kovačević, *Narrating Post/Communism*, 18.

which have led to surreal but nightmarishly concrete urban topographies.'[25] Perhaps the most tangible embodiment of the socialist legacy is the wall running through the middle of the city, blocking traffic. Ryder's exasperation is further intensified by a local woman's seemingly cynical ignorance about the monstrous barrier in the middle of the street. At this point it is impossible not to think of walls in the middle of European towns and cities, most notably the Berlin Wall, that demarcated post-World War II occupation zones and subsequently evolved into spheres of Soviet influence. The widespread popularity of espionage narratives set within the divided city of Berlin, by authors like John le Carré, David Downing and Philip Kerr, serve as evidence that English readers have been long familiar and captivated with the concept of the 'other' in the figure of intelligence operatives lurking in the intricate Central European urban texture.

The Western European visitor perspective evokes the tourist's gaze and its implications. Utilizing Foucault's 'medical gaze,'[26] Urry describes the tourist's gaze as visually and linguistically constructed, loaded with 'discursive determinations,'[27] and in this setting, the gaze is also instrumental in establishing power dynamics of culture and in exoticizing the post-socialist landscape as the 'other.' Ryder's stay at a distinguished hotel and his visits to prominent public venues should give him access but actually limit him to the 'presentable' parts of the city, where he would be received with high regard. However, Ryder's spatial agency diminishes immediately upon arrival: after long car rides away from the city, he is able to swiftly return to his hotel by strolling through poorly illuminated corridors. He opens ordinary doors which turn out to lead to hidden passages, cupboards and cubicles, all confined and uncomfortable places. Additionally, for most of the time the cityscape is strangely deserted, devoid of traffic or pedestrians. The narrator's desperate attempts to arrive at places echoes Ash's impressions of the Central European space as a 'garden maze, a maze in which mirrors conceal the hedges, giving the illusion of open space and free movement but also distorting wildly.'[28] As if following some elusive spectre, Ryder hurries through the winding streets and alleys, but unable to reach anything, whether it is his partner Sophie or the concert hall in which he is about to perform. The tourist (and the reader) cannot make sense of the maze-like place that seems to form organically, defying spatial dimensions, echoing Kundera's description of his-

---

25 Richard Robinson. *Narratives of the European Border*. London: Palgrave Macmillan, 2007. 165.
26 Michel Foucault. *The Birth of the Clinic: An Archaeology of Medical Perception*. Transl. A.M. Sheridan Smith. London: Pantheon Books, 1973.
27 John Urry and Jonas Larsen. *The Tourist Gaze 3.0*. London: Sage, 2011. 2.
28 Timothy Garton Ash. *The Uses of Adversity*. New York: Random House, 1989. 143.

torical Central Europe as a 'baroque' space, as opposed to the more rationally organized 'classical' France.[29]

Finally, the novel's use of German and Slavic words and names, and an occasional mention of the Hungarian café, underlines the region's linguistic and cultural mesh that is resistant to nationalistic characterization, as illustrated in the anecdote mentioned earlier about Kafka's attempt to define his identity. Incidentally, the German place names have a comforting familiarity for Britons raised on the traditions of the Grand Tour or nineteenth-century Continental tourism. *Bahnhofplatz, Steinberg Garden* and others create the familiar 'other' and evoke times when British aristocrats and wealthy upper-middle-class offspring toured Europe (or what they considered the civilised parts of Europe) as a rite of passage prior to assuming roles as subjects, intellectuals, and civil servants of the British Empire.

Conclusion

Ishiguro constructed his own version of Central Europe, creating an exotic milieu with the occasional familiar elements (an English expatriate character, a *Volksgarten* setting, etc.). This constructed space resists mapping, defying the logics of time and space. The place is inhabited by people steeped in a state of apprehension, paralyzed by an inferiority complex, desperate for progress but striving for redemption at the same time. Yet change is unwanted, the state of crisis is their modus operandi.[30]

When writing the novel, Ishiguro decided on the settings relatively late in the planning process, according to his notes.[31] There was a version when the narrator arrives in London, another one placing him 'in a 3rd world town – a bit like SE Asia, bit like Rio,'[32] locations distant and exotic to the British reader. It would seem that Ishiguro decided on the location in August 1991, but the political themes, the individual's political responsibility, and the cultural identity power struggle within communities had been part of his thinking since very early in the writing process. Even though only a single page is dedicated to the European setting in his notes, the political theme and the lack of control seem to be the perfect fit to this newly explored emerging region with its exotic post-socialist milieu as the unspecified setting of the novel. Later, Ishiguro rejected the pos-

---

29 Kundera, 'The Tragedy of Central Europe,' 35.
30 Dabis, 'Crisis of Crises,' 1109.
31 I am grateful for the research grant from ESSE that enabled me to conduct research in the Ishiguro Archive at the Harry Ransom Center, University of Texas at Austin, US in July 2022.
32 Kazuo Ishiguro. *The Unconsoled: Notes I.* Kazuo Ishiguro Papers, Harry Ransom Center, University of Texas at Austin, Folder 20.1, Novel 4 Structure.

sibility of having written a 'thinly veiled allegory about the collapse of communism,' claiming that the setting 'was by and large a landscape of imagination.'[33] Incidentally, however, *The Unconsoled* was written at a particular point in time, at a crossroads of global and European history, when British, and more generally Western, political and cultural interest was focused on the Central European region. By creating a city and community with features that can be ascribed to the region, his novel allows us to read its setting as a chronotrope of the Orientalized Eastern/Central Europe.

The Western traveller's journey to this Orientalized Eastern/Central Europe evokes long-established conventions of English literary interest, dating back centuries to the age of Enlightenment.[34] This enduring phenomenon highlights the inclination of the Western gaze to turn towards Eastern/Central Europe throughout various historical epochs. Tlostanova's juncture highlighted the end of the Cold War/Second World era and critically conceptualized the emerging new age. However, following the post-socialist awakening of the 1990s, the region slowly returned to a relative invisibility in the new millennium. Then a mere two decades passed and the Western gaze is yet again fixed upon the region, and the question where 'Europe' ends burns with new urgency – whether another post-socialist 'other' of the former Second World is deemed worthy to be part of the 'European family.' Consequently, the states of Central Europe are again grappling with the dilemma of othering: are they to define themselves once again as the 'other' to Europe, or does the 'other' lie even further East?

References

Ash, Timothy Garton. 'The Puzzle of Central Europe.' *The New York Review of Books.* 18 Mar 1999. <https://www.nybooks.com/articles/1999/03/18/the-puzzle-of-central-europe/> (accessed 15 Nov 2023).

–. *History of the Present: Essays, Sketches, and Dispatches from Europe in the 1990s.* London: Allen Lane, 1999.

Bakić-Hayden, Milica. 'Nesting Orientalisms: The Case of Former Yugoslavia.' *Slavic Review* 54.4 (Winter 1995): 917–931.

Buchowski, Michał. 'Social Thought & Commentary: The Specter of Orientalism in Europe: From Exotic Other to Stigmatized Brother.' *Anthropological Quarterly* 79.3 (2006): 463–482.

Dabis, Melinda. 'Crisis of Crises: Re-imagining Central Europe in Kazuo Ishiguro's *The Unconsoled.*' *English Studies* 103.7 (2022): 1103–1115.

---

33 Dylan Otto Krider. 'Rooted in a Small Space: An Interview with Kazuo Ishiguro.' *Kenyon Review* 20.2 (1998): 151.

34 See Wolff, *Inventing Eastern Europe.*

Derrida, Jacques. *The Other Heading: Reflections on Today's Europe.* Translated by P. A. Brault and M. B. Naas. Bloomington: Indiana University Press, 1992.

Dhand, Otilia. *The Idea of Central Europe.* London: I.B. Tauris, 2020.

Foucault, Michel. *The Birth of the Clinic: An Archaeology of Medical Perception.* Transl. A. M. Sheridan Smith. London: Pantheon Books, 1973.

Harasztos, Ágnes. *The Postmodern Baroque: Bruce Chatwin's Utz and British Fiction on East-Central Europe at the Time of the 1989 Political Changes.* PhD dissertation. Budapest: Eötvös Loránd University, 2021.

Havel, Václav. *The Anatomy of a Reticence: Eastern European Dissidents and the Peace Movement in the West.* Stockholm: Charta 77 Foundation, 1985.

Ishiguro, Kazuo. [1995] *The Unconsoled,* London: Faber and Faber, 2005.

–. *The Unconsoled: Notes I.* Kazuo Ishiguro Papers, Harry Ransom Center, University of Texas at Austin, Folder 20.1.

Konrád, György. *Antipolitics: An Essay.* New York: Harcourt, Brace & Jovanovich, 1984.

Kovačević, Nataša. *Narrating Post/Communism Colonial Discourse and Europe's Borderline Civilization.* London: Routledge, 2008.

Krider, Dylan Otto. 'Rooted in a Small Space: An Interview with Kazuo Ishiguro.' *Kenyon Review* 20.2 (1998): 146–154.

Kundera, Milan. 'The Tragedy of Central Europe.' Transl. Edmund White. *The New York Review of Books* 31.7 (1984): 33–38.

Magris, Claudio. 'Közép-Európa – egy fogalom igézete.' Transl. Mesterházy Miklós. *Közép-Európai olvasókönyv.* Ed. Péter Módos. Budapest: Osiris, 2005.

Robinson, Richard. *Narratives of the European Border.* London: Palgrave Macmillan, 2007.

Said, Edward W. *Orientalism.* London: Routledge and Kegan Paul, 1978.

Shaffer, Brian W. *Understanding Kazuo Ishiguro.* Columbia: University of South Carolina Press, 1998.

Tlostanova, Madina. *Postcolonialism and Postsocialism in Fiction and Art: Resistance and Re-existence.* London: Palgrave Macmillan, 2017.

Todorova, Maria. *Imagining the Balkans.* Oxford: Oxford University Press, 1997.

Tomkinson, Fiona. 'Ishiguro and Heidegger: The Worlds of Art.' *Kazuo Ishiguro in a Global Context.* Ed. Cynthia Wong and Hülya Yıldız. New York: Routledge, 2016. 59–68.

Urry, John and Jonas Larsen. *The Tourist Gaze 3.0.* London: Sage, 2011.

Wolff, Larry. *Inventing Eastern Europe.* Stanford: Stanford University Press, 1994.

Therese-Marie Meyer

Liminal Morality: Complicity in Patrick McGuinness's *The Last Hundred Days* (2011)

After the fall of the Berlin Wall in 1989, and its own subsequent, bloody revolution, Romania has occupied an interesting place in the British imaginary as a part of both Eastern and Western Europe,[1] especially since the country joined the EU in 2007. Nicolae Ceauşescu's nationalist Stalinism[2] and its repressive policies, including censorship, surveillance, and a cult of personality, have left a lasting mark on the country, and become a literary topos. British writers seeking to explore life under such oppressive conditions have portrayed the regime, while the country in turn has become an iconic symbol of totalitarianism, often short-circuiting the more complex historical realities on the ground. Patrick McGuinness's novel of the fall of Ceauşescu's regime, *The Last Hundred Days* (2011),[3] was praised by reviewers on publication, shortlisted for the Costa First Novel Award and longlisted for the Man Booker.[4] Yet in the long run, however

---

1 Cf. Adrian Otoiu. 'An Exercise in Fictional Liminality: The Postcolonial, the Postcommunist, and Romania's Threshold Generation.' *Comparative Studies of South Asia, Africa and the Middle East* 23.1&2 (2003): 87–105; Adrian Cioroianu. 'The Impossible Escape: Romanians and the Balkans.' *Balkan as Metaphor: Between Globalization and Fragmentation.* Ed. Dušan I. Bielić and Obrad Savić. Cambridge, Mass.: MIT Press, 2002. 209–233.

2 On the term 'nationalist Stalinism' see Keith Hitchins. *A Concise History of Romania.* Cambridge: Cambridge University Press 2014. 278.

3 Patrick McGuinness. *The Last Hundred Days.* London: Bloomsbury, 2011; hereafter cited in the text as *LHD*. While the protagonist's work as an English teacher at the University of Bucharest a few months prior to the revolution provided the framework, the epigraph clarifies that the characters are indeed 'composites, if not outright inventions. This includes the [anonymous] narrator' (*LHD* 3).

4 See e.g. Paul Bailey. 'Romanian Holiday: *The Last Hundred Days* by Patrick McGuinness.' *Literary Review* (September 2011). <https://literaryreview.co.uk/romanian-holiday> (date of access 16 August 2023); Stephen Finucan. '*The Last Hundred Days* by Patrick McGuinness: Review.' *Toronto Star* (21 July 2012). <https://www.thestar.com/entertainment/books/2012/0 7/21/the_last_hundred_days_by_patrick_mcguinness_review.html> (date of access 16 August 2023); Francine Prose,. 'Uncertain Times.' *The New York Times* (8 June 2012). <https:// www.nytimes.com/2012/06/10/books/review/the-last-hundred-days-by-patrick-mcguinness. html> (date of access 28 June 2023); James Purdon. '*The Last Hundred Days* by Patrick

undeservedly, it did not fare well with academic interests. By 2019, Oltean stated that the novel had been 'relatively ignored by criticism'[5] and this verdict still stands.

The novel's action in Bucharest during the last year of Ceauşescu's dictator-ship places a nameless, unmoored, expatriate protagonist-narrator, an Everyman figure, into a liminal city: the Romanian capital symbolizes a space where moral and interrelational boundaries are continuously contested. At its core, this is a philosophical and allegorical text, which considers its subjects' morality in the light of the transience of human existence. McGuinness uses the end of Ceau-şescu's rule to narrate a secular morality play about the human condition that is compromised, complicit, but at least involved. There are various contentions with this approach, not least that of a Western blindness to Central European realities which serve instead to provide scaffolding for Western imaginaries – but this will have to move momentarily to the end of my considerations.[6]

My first focus is to analyse how McGuinness develops his liminal morality. Moral complicity is at the heart of his novel. It applies to every character, espe-cially the protagonist's close confidant and mentor, Leo, the Vice figure. To this philosophical question of complicity, the novel adds a *Bildungsroman* angle, maturing the protagonist against the foil of two Romanian love interests.[7] His choice of the better woman of the two determines his departure from a path of corruption already taken. This path, the novel slowly reveals, is one well-trodden by his *alter ego*, Belanger. How this figure, absent for most of the text but constantly referenced, frames the protagonist's ethical choices is relevant to both plot and structure of McGuinness's novel. As is to be expected in an allegorical text, all are largely flat, exemplary characters who show almost no development, and often bear telling names. To these characters, caught in the many quandaries of ethical agency in a dictatorship in its death throes, the Romanian revolution of 1989 seems to promise liberation. Yet the novel rejects system change as a sol-ution to the moral dilemma of compromised choices, instead portraying the revolution itself as compromised.[8]

McGuinness – review.' *The Observer* (14 Aug 2011). <https://www.theguardian.com/books/2011/aug/14/last-hundred-days-patrick-mcguinness> (date of access 28 June 2023).

5 Roxana Oltean. 'Romance and Belligerence Behind the Iron Curtain: Cold War Gender Identities in Anglo-American Perspective.' *Synergy* 15.1 (2019): 8.

6 Cf. Maria Todorova. *Imagining the Balkans.* Oxford: Oxford University Press, 2009; Andrew Hammond. 'Through Savage Europe.' *Third Text* 21.2 (2007): 117–127.

7 Local women involved with outsider men are a trope of Cold War fiction cf. Oltean, 'Romance and Belligerence,' 14.

8 To achieve this closure, the author makes use of a conspiracy theory about the Romanian revolution that is still in circulation, though it has been refuted repeatedly by historians. More on this below.

To the protagonist, moral dissociation (as I term it), a focus on the separation of subject from action, is crucial. Yet the novel asserts that moral dissociation rejects commitment, and that it is only through the commitment to good that moral agency is possible, even if the outcome is unpredictable and not necessarily effective. Still, it also shows that one must practice moral dissociation to create bonds and, ultimately, a community. The closure then paradoxically hinges on the protagonist's decision to embrace both: moral dissociation *and* emotional engagement.

Since the novel remains little known today, a short synopsis is in order. Part I begins with the protagonist's arrival in Bucharest in mid-April 1989. He is unmoored by the death of his abusive father, whom he hated but who was a dominant figure in his life, 'a black sun around whom everything revolved' (*LHD* 44). With an unfinished bachelor's degree and no job interview, he has landed a job teaching English at the University of Bucharest, much to his own surprise. Leo presents him with a forged university degree immediately upon his arrival in Bucharest, adding to the surreal beginning of his narrative. Soon he is involved in Leo's racketeering, and an affair with Cilea, Deputy Minister Manea Constantin's daughter. Increasingly complicit, the protagonist thinks of expressing his disapproval of the totalitarian system by helping Trofim, a retired Stalinist, to write a second, secret version of his autobiography. This makes the protagonist feel 'proud, indispensable – in short [...] the way Trofim wanted [him] to feel' (*LHD* 57). Through Leo, he also meets a group of rebellious students, Petre, Vintul and a girl, and helps Leo take them to the southern border, where they attempt to swim across the Danube to Yugoslavia. Petre is subsequently found shot, the girl shows up in Belgrade as a trafficked prostitute, Vintul vanishes. Petre's death brings the protagonist into contact with Ottilia (Petre's sister), his second love interest. After his affair with Cilea falls apart, he eases into this new relationship. In exchange for information about Petre's death, the protagonist passes on information about the Danube border defences between Cilia's father and the British embassy. Thus begins the second part of the novel, which, at 80 days, is nominally closer to the 100 days of the title.

In October 1989, Trofim launches his autobiography, the censored version in Bucharest, the samizdat one in Paris, and only suffers house arrest in return because the international attention he garners saves him from ultimate reprisals. His support amongst cadres leads to the 'Letter of Five,' calling for reforms. (The novel uses here the historical 'Letter of Six' by Ceaușescu's internal party critics from March 1989.[9]) Serial disclosures show the students' escape attempt to have

---

9 For the 'Letter of Six' see Hitchins, *Concise History of Romania*, 289; also Nestor Ratesh. *Romania: The Entangled Revolution. The Washington Papers 152.* Washington: The Center for Strategic and International Studies, 1991. 11.

been compromised: Vintul turns up alive, member of the Securitate. Petre is exposed as a member of the Securitate, too, who fell victim to an internal feud between Cilea's father and his own superior officer – organized from Yugoslavia by Belanger (*LHD* 285–288). On a larger plane, the Romanian revolution takes off, yet Trofim and Constantin, Cilea's father, incrementally emerge as the master-minds behind it: It is a palace coup (*LHD* 339, 342–343, 362, 370).

The protagonist flies to Belgrade on the last plane to take foreigners out, just before Christmas 1989, watches the trial and execution of the Ceauşescu couple on television, and immediately returns to the seemingly liberated country to be with Ottilia. He knows the true state of affairs, however, and ironically the novel has him travelling on the same train as Belanger, who is returning to his old haunts. The novel ends with Leo, fully recovered and back to his racketeering, picking up the protagonist at the station, closing the frame between the first (innocent) and second (matured) arrival in Bucharest.

Much of the protagonist's character remains a cipher throughout the novel. If anything, he is notable for his passivity in the first part and his transition to a more active involvement in the second part of the text, in which he finds his place at Ottilia's side, as befits a *Bildungsroman*. From the beginning of the novel, the protagonist is aware of his unmoored, mediocre status and reflects on it re-peatedly: 'Not for me, for I was a passer-by; or, more exactly, a passer-through. Things happened around me, over me, even across me, but never to me. Even when I was there, in the thick of it, during those last hundred days.' (*LHD* 8)

While not quite true of the second part of the novel, in which he moves into erratic agency, it is a programmatic statement nonetheless. By the end of the novel, this characteristic of the protagonist – repeated in various versions throughout – has not changed: 'I wondered if there was a category for the Ba-nalescus of this world, floating in the interstices of history like specks of dust: a great, grey purgatory of mediocrity that amounted to more than the sum of its parts because it was where most of us finished up' (*LHD* 322). Evidently, the protagonist is Everyman and a stand-in for all readers ('most of us').

The Bucharest of Ceauşescu's nationalist Stalinism and systematisation[10] provides a liminal setting for this bland and shapeless character, 'a dystopian space of total devastation.'[11] Historically defined since the nineteenth century as

---

10 On the systematisation and its consequences for the cityscape of Bucharest, see Darrick Danta. 'Ceauşescu's Bucharest.' *Geographical Review* 83.2 (April 1993): 170–182; Hitchins, *Concise History of Romania*, 281; Sergei Melcher. 'Entstehungskontexte des Centru Civic: Auf dem Weg zum vertieften Verständnis des neuen Stadtzentrums der rumänischen Haupt-stadt.' *Kilometer Null: Politische Transformation und gesellschaftliche Entwicklungen in Rumänien seit 1989.* Ed. Thede Kahl and Larisa Schippel. Berlin: Verlag Frank und Timme, 2011. 121–142.

11 Oltean, 'Romance and Belligerence,' 12.

a city between Orient and Occident, though still part of neither, the 'Paris of the East' (*LHD* 15) here gains added layers of liminality. It is liminal in time, 'full of ghostly intersections of past and present' (*LHD* 50); it is liminal in space, revealing an occult, 'subterranean society [in which the] old Bucharest was being rebuilt and repeopled underground' (*LHD* 51) between old town and new town (*LHD* 12), the latter itself a 'rectilinear void' (*LHD* 64); and it is liminal in its life processes, which make it subject to constant brutalist de/construction (*LHD* 16, 24, 46, *passim*), culminating in the unfinished building site of the Palace of the People, 'an attack, a gaudy, brutal, humanity-denying mass of stone' (*LHD* 115). The city-as-moloch – 'both as location and as, in a sense, a character' of the novel (*LHD* author's note) – is dominated by human surveillance, with militia 'stationed every twenty yards [...] sinister and immaterial, restless shades' (*LHD* 26). It destroys the very life-essence of its other inhabitants, reducing them to mere shadowy tools of the system's surveillance. It thus symbolically embodies the liminal situation not only of the protagonist, but of modernity, totalitarian dictatorship, omnipresent surveillance, and so on: 'It was surreal, or would have been if it wasn't the only reality available' (*LHD* 8). This unreality of the real of the Second World remains the central feature of Bucharest. In the novel, urban environment and main character interact closely:

> I felt two things, two sensations that seemed at odds but which took me to extremes of myself: a sense of the world closing in, tightening up, an almost physical sensation of claustration; and something else: exhilaration, a feeling for the possible, something expanding around me as I looked out at that empty square. It was as if the agoraphobia the new city was designed to induce, and the political system it existed to make concrete, was translating itself inwards, becoming an intensive inner space. (*LHD* 22)

Lewis remarks that by such descriptions, 'McGuinness is fleshing out what Jeremy Bentham and Michel Foucault predicted about the internalization of surveillance.'[12] 'Everyman *in extremis*' is a phrase that suggests itself as a description of the protagonist. By the end of the novel, although he has moved from passivity to attempts at agency, there has been no change in this psychogeographic baseline: 'In spite of [Bucharest's] unreality, I had stopped being able to imagine my own life anywhere else either' (*LHD* 330).

As befits a morality play, the novel is about *psychomachia* – the battle for the soul of the protagonist – here in a secular version, as a battle for his integrity.[13]

---

12 Randolph Lewis. *Under Surveillance: Being Watched in Modern America*. Austin: University of Texas Press, 2017. 44.

13 On *psychomachia* as a feature of the morality play, see G. A. Lester. 'Introduction.' *Three Late Medieval Morality Plays: Mankind, Everyman, Mundus et Infans*. Ed. G. A. Lester. New Mermaids Anthologies. London: Bloomsbury, 2014. xv; cf. also Dorothy Wertz. 'Conflict Resolution in the Medieval Morality Plays.' *The Journal of Conflict Resolution* 13.4 (December 1969): 438–453.

Once again, the protagonist is aware of this, as he is also aware of the agents trying to encroach upon him for their own purposes: 'I lived in crowded isolation, moving from one to the other, keeping them separate but running them in parallel: Trofim's book, Cilea's bed, Leo's black market, Petre's concerts … Whatever was left over by the time I had subtracted them all from my life must, I supposed, have been myself' (*LHD* 143–144). The illusion of control, compartmentalising his self in the process, is maintained for some time, before disclosures reveal the extent of intrigues and counter-intrigues. 'I was complicit in it too and I even knew that. But now I felt both crowded out and alone, implicated and out on a limb, in a world whose terms where perpetually shifting, yet whose rules would never change' (*LHD* 205).

Part of the protagonist's maturing process is in coming to terms with complicity. Complicity, the novel insists, is everywhere, and never a matter of degree but posited as an absolute, thus universal. I use the term 'complicity' here in its philosophical, not legal, definition, and in the context of moral responsibility (further distinguished from causal responsibility[14]). As a concept, complicity focuses on forms of (in)action as opposed to the more passive 'implicated subject' after which Michael Rothberg's study is named.[15] In contrast to the 'implicated subject,' complicity does not consider social status; it does not demand agents 'occupy positions aligned with power and privilege,'[16] though it, too, operates from the balance between 'actions and inactions [that] help produce and reproduce the positions of victims and perpetrators.'[17] Gregory Mellema refers to the means by which one can become complicit back to the Scholastics, particularly Thomas Aquinas: 'by command, by counsel, by consent, by flattery, by receiving, by participation, by silence, by not preventing, and by not denouncing.'[18] The protagonist of McGuinness's novel becomes complicit in seven of these nine ways. He never commands. Neither does he ever employ flattery; he prefers sarcasm, confusing it with rebellion (e.g. *LHD* 181).[19] Excepting these two forms of complicity, however, there is is no way in which the protagonist does not

---

14 On causal responsibility vs. moral responsibility, see Matthew Talbert. 'Moral Responsibility.' *The Stanford Encyclopedia of Philosophy.* Ed. N Zalta and Uri Nodelman (Fall 2022). <https://plato.stanford.edu/archives/fall2022/entries/moral-responsibility/> (date of access 16 August 2023).

15 Cf. Michael Rothberg. *The Implicated Subject: Beyond Victims and Perpetrators.* Redwood City: Stanford University Press, 2019.

16 The protagonist's local privilege as Western is a tenuous one (see *LHD* 12).

17 Rothberg, *Implicated Subject*, 2.

18 Thomas Aquinas as qtd. in Gregory Mellema. *Complicity and Moral Accountability.* Notre Dame, Indiana: University of Notre Dame Press, 2017. 19.

19 To knowledgeable readers, the protagonist's insouciance or even openly sarcastic insolence towards Securitate interrogators or Deputy Minister Manea Constantin, with no consequences for himself whatsoever, is the least credible element of his narration. (see e.g. *LHD* 184–185, 253–254)

eventually participate in the totalitarian system around him. Following Christopher Kurtz, Mellema also cautions that the accountability of an individual in a system inherently reliant upon complicity is independent of that individual's importance or power in the system, and indeed of an individual's degree of internal assent: 'Claims of detachment cannot be separated from the reality of the actions one performs in [an] organization.'[20] Institutionalization as well as lesser organised forms of collectives are conducive though not necessary to such attempts at individual detachment from accountability in Kurtz's view: 'My point is not that this psychological distancing is peculiar to or inevitably accompanies collective activity, but only that collective activity often provides a framework hospitable to it.'[21]

This is particularly pertinent to the argument of moral dissociation. Complicity extends to every character. 'By the end of the novel, everybody seems to have played a double game, to have been a travesty.'[22] In fact, the novel insists, complicity in the Romanian dictatorship is global, it thus implicates everybody: 'The human tragedy of Romania was irrelevant. Ceaușescu had been imprisoning, starving, brutalising and lying to his people for the best part of two decades, mostly with the connivance of the West' (*LHD* 214).

This is the point at which the novel's morality play structure becomes most apparent. Had the story merely dealt with the liminal situations of a bygone Romanian era, the extent to which British readers would have been concerned – even by an Everyman narrator – would be contained. As it is, the novel instead makes a claim to universal complicity as the human condition. The character who best embodies this ubiquitous complicity is Leo, who also functions as the Vice figure of this morality play.[23]

> He was Bucharest's biggest black-marketeer, with a ramifying network of shady staff and shadier clients, dealing in booze, cigarettes, clothes, food, currency and antiques. He needed human cover, a straight man, and I was happy to comply. [...] Leo's contacts stretched across Bucharest. They connected it together in occult ways, subterranean branch lines which nobody saw but which mapped out a city of their own. (*LHD* 41)

Leo, jovial, ruthless, cynical, ever happy to lend a hand, becomes the protagonist's closest friend, also typical of the Vice. As a Vice figure, Leo is not quite of this world, and even Bucharest in all its extremity is only a backdrop to this preternatural figure: 'The place suits him, not because it resembles him but because

---

20 Mellema, *Complicity and Moral Accountability*, 35.
21 Christopher Kurtz. *Complicity: Ethics and Law for a Collective Age*. Cambridge: Cambridge University Press, 2000. 150.
22 Sorina Chiper. '*The Last Hundred Days:* The Death Thralls of Romanian Communist Dictatorship Through Foreign Eyes.' *Discourse as a Form of Multiculturalism in Literature and Communication*. Ed. Julian Boldea. Târgu Mureș: Arhipelag XXI Press, 2015. 397.
23 Leo, the lion, appears named in reference to 1 Peter 5:8–9, as the demonic devourer of souls.

he is so far in excess of it.' (*LHD* 21) His words are the final verdict on the post-revolutionary city and finish the novel: '"New brothel, same old whores – isn't that what you told us?" Leo waved it off. "Well, you know how it is ... after all, experience is what you want in a whore"' (*LHD* 377).

Two dichotomous representations of femininity (eros/agape) are tied to the protagonist. Cilea represents the corrupt and corrupted seductress: Sin, of old. Ottilia, on the other hand, is charitable Virtue. While Cilea[24] is part of the no-menklatura through her father, Deputy Minister Manea,[25] who ensures her privileged life, Ottilia is poor and struggling,[26] yet her name hints at her emotional riches.[27] While Cilea is a socialite,[28] who exudes sexual allure in every setting, Ottilia is a doctor who provides abortions and emergency care in a hospital (*LHD* 68). Much of her relationship with the protagonist is one of mutual care and healing. Cilea spies on the protagonist (*LHD* 181) and eventually replaces him with Belanger, her former lover (*LHD* 294–295). The protagonist experiences her sexual dominance as a form of emotional bereavement: 'As always, I felt the power of her sexuality and the loneliness that had haunted me whenever I was with her. My fullest moments with her had been felt as lack' (*LHD* 293). Ottilia, on the other hand, largely maintains her integrity even in the face of Leo's ongoing temptations. Like the protagonist, she voices an explicit awareness of the intrinsic corruption of a system that presupposes complicity (*LHD* 312). To the protagonist, her influence is a spring thaw:[29] 'I felt something breaking inside me. It was a far-off feeling, ice on a long-frozen lake starting to crack at some tiny bankside seam' (*LHD* 249–250).

Belanger, his *alter ego*, is the foil against which the protagonist must measure himself. His name[30] ironically indicates his constant precedence. His departure from Bucharest makes way for the protagonist's arrival,[31] the protagonist's job, his office (*LHD* 30), his furnished and decorated flat (which Everyman takes over without personalisation, see *LHD* 34), and his position as Cilea's lover (*LHD* 149).

---

24 Cilea, as a Romanian form of Celia, echoes Swift's streetwalker in 'The Progress of Beauty.' It is also a conventional name of nymphs in Restoration and Augustan poetry.

25 His name compounds the Romanian 'to shelter' [a mânea], with the Latin for 'steadfast,' defining his protection of his daughter.

26 All of Ottilia's possessions fit into one sports bag (*LHD* 215).

27 Ottilia means 'prosperous,' see Patrick Hanks and Flavia Hodges. *A Dictionary of First Names in English*. Oxford: Oxford University Press, 1991. Appendix 3 ('French Names'); the name additionally echoes Goethe's concept of elective affinities; in the eponymous novel, Ottilie is an introverted, emotionally rich character.

28 Cilea pays the hard wages of sin for her privileged sexual liberty when she is made available to political allies during state visits, e. g. by Milosevic (*LHD* 151–155).

29 See also Oltean, 'Romance and Belligerence,' 16.

30 Belanger is a variant of Beringer, one of the Paladins in the Charlemagne romances.

31 Finucan notes this similarity to Graham Greene's *The Third Man* (Finucan, 'Last Hundred Days: Review').

Closing the novel, as mentioned above, both men return to Bucharest on the same train from Belgrade. Like the narrator's, Belanger's character remains opaque throughout: 'They all mentioned his name, but no one ever said who he was' (*LHD* 213).

Much of the novel consists of revealing the extent of Belanger's actions in which he preceded the protagonist. He was the British embassy's first informant and go-between to the Securitate (*LHD* 195). He was Leo's first interest and pupil (*LHD* 278). He is the initially secret, eventually successful rival for Cilea's favours (*LHD* 210, 281, 294–296). He runs the human trafficking ring from Belgrade which kills Petre (*LHD* 279, 287). 'Belanger was everywhere, had preceded me everywhere. Even gone he was more here than I was' (*LHD* 279).

Obviously, the protagonist needs to discover his own agency and his own stance towards the corruption surrounding and involving him, to ensure his maturation. He can only do so once he has realised how much he has been living as Belanger did: 'I was living with his cast-offs, I had borrowed from his life to fund my own' (*LHD* 296). Turning away from a path of least resistance in a move of abjection also means that the protagonist next grows to openly hate Belanger, as he struggles to develop beyond the mould set by his predecessor: 'I hated Belanger, because of Leo, because of Cilea …' (*LHD* 296). Julia Kristeva's 'abjection' is particularly apt to describe this stage of the narrator's relationship to Belanger because, like her original definition, it places its individuals as 'neither subject nor object,' and emotionally oscillates between fascination and dread, creating 'a vortex of summons and repulsion.'[32]

One might expect the revolution to sweep away this system, but there is no redemption in this secular morality play: liberation is an illusion. By presenting Trofim and Constantin as the instigators of a palace coup masquerading as the revolution, the plot follows a conspiracy theory according to which Nicolae Ceauşescu and Ileana, his wife, were exterminated by forces within the Communist Party and/or the Securitate and/or the army. Initially, the situation was so unclear that it led to terms such as the 'Stolen Revolution.'[33] Subsequently, Florin Abraham[34] and Keith Hitchins[35] have tried to put this conspiracy theory to rest but it is still circulating on social media.

With the return of Belanger and his gangsters to Bucharest, corruption triumphs at the end of the novel, metamorphosed into the new system. No surprise

---

32 Julia Kristeva. *Powers of Horror: An Essay on Abjection.* Transl. Leon S. Roudiez. New York: Columbia University Press, 1982. 1.

33 Ratesh assesses this conspiracy theory in chapter 4 of his study; see Ratesh, *Romania*, 80–119.

34 Florin Abraham. *Romania since the Second World War: A Political, Social, and Economic History.* London: Bloomsbury, 2017. 114–115.

35 'The regime was not the victim of an organized coup.' Hitchins, *A Concise History of Romania*, 290.

then to see Leo back in his old glory, as well: The revolution is a farce. 'Otherwise, duplicity and foreign interests seem to continue their domination in Romania even after the televised execution of the Ceaușescus.'[36]

How, then, can the protagonist develop his morality in the midst of all this triumphant corruption, and step out of Belanger's shadow? Here, 'moral dissociation' between subject and action becomes imperative. The narrator maintains that such essential dissociation is owed to the situation of totalitarianism: 'The first thing I learned, and I learned it from Leo, was to separate people from what they did. People existed in a realm apart from their actions: this was the only way to maintain friendship in a police state' (*LHD* 23). The protagonist labels this tenet 'a species of reverse existentialism that would have given Sartre and his acolytes something to account for' (*LHD* 31). In fact, it dates back to Augustine of Hippo. The precept, better known as 'love the sinner but hate the sin,' was coined by Augustine in a letter: 'cum dilectione hominum et odio vitiorum' [by cherishing of the human (being) and by hatred of evil.][37]

However, like everything that comes from Leo, the separation of subject and action, while promising a pragmatic solution, has corrupting drawbacks. Moral dissociation leads to an isolation of the individual from his environment. By not judging the subjects he encounters and interacts with for their actions, the protagonist effectively refuses to engage with people and events around him. His isolation thus intensifies despite his increasing involvement with the more-than-active Leo. Kurtz notes 'that collective activity often provides a framework hospitable to [this psychological distancing],' which he labels 'an essentially *bureaucratic* frame of mind.'[38]

The protagonist's dilemma is conventionally resolved in the novel's romance plot, when he learns to fully engage with the 'other' through love. As he so fully depends on this loving interaction to ascertain individuation (while eros entails only further isolation), the Other, apposite of which he develops, strongly reminds of Levinas's use of the concept.[39] This beginning of the protagonist's maturity and his assumption of moral responsibility is linked to the moment when he realises that he has to distinguish himself from Belanger, briefly discussed above. However, his initial abjection of this *alter ego* without any change to his moral dissociation is quickly rebuked by Virtue, Ottilia, which leads to the

---

36 Chiper, 'The Last Hundred Days,' 398.
37 Augustine of Hippo, letter 211, as qtd in Susan Ratcliffe. *Oxford Essential Quotations: St Augustine of Hippo*. Oxford: Oxford University Press, 2017. [Online]. Available: https://www.oxfordreference.com/display/10.1093/acref/9780191843730.001.0001/q-oro-ed5-00000572?rskey=n3tlhG&result =1. Accessed 28 June 2023.
38 Kurtz, *Complicity*, 150 [emphasis in the original].
39 Emmanuel Levinas. *Time and The Other [and additional essays]*. Transl. Richard A. Cohen. Pittsburgh: Duchesne University Press, 1987; see esp. Chapter 'Eros,' 84–89.

anagnorisis of the protagonist: 'Maybe I *should* be compromised. Maybe that was my problem' (*LHD* 312; emphasis in the original). As Virtue, Ottilia immediately responds to his thoughts:

> 'Exactly that – to be compromised you need to have a stake in things, you need to have something to lose and something to gain. You have to be risking yourself, not all the time, but enough of the time to weigh things up, principle over self-preservation, the gains, the losses… You don't have that. You don't have any stake in any of this.' (*LHD* 312)

Virtue here points the protagonist to the path of engagement and their common future. The novel can end with his choice to return to Bucharest, Ottilia (and Leo!), actuating his decision for the good – in a surrounding dominated by ongoing corruption, yet paradoxically in full awareness for the need of ongoing moral dissociation.

There are, as I outlined above, several points of contention with this plot and its ethos. At its most basic, using Romania as sandbox setting to a secular allegory dominated by British characters using the country's upheavals for their diverse power struggles stands in the tradition of Kipling's literary (and political) imperialist trope of the Great Game.[40] Historical events in Romania during the 1980s become a backdrop to the hidden and allegorical rivalry of Leo and Belanger, the Revolution itself is a corrupted conspiracy. McGuinness's novel is in this respect no different from other imperialist imaginings of didactic utopias or dystopias in the 'Elsewhere.'[41] Yet a critically reflected engagement with the Romanian realities is necessarily lacking, due to the limitations of complexity imposed by the first-person narrator's maturing process – and his is the only perspective the novel allows its readers to share.

Martha Nussbaum has pointed out with reference to Henry James that 'the aesthetic is ethical and political'[42] – and so it proves in McGuinness's text. 'Ethical concerns are not a supplement because there is no narrative that is free of ethical issues, no reading, viewing, or listening to a narrative that does not require some ethical sensitivity and the exercise of moral discrimination on the part of reader,

---

40 On Kipling's seminal influence on the use of this term, see Seymour Becker, 'The "Great Game": The History of an Evocative Phrase.' *Asian Affairs* 43.1 (2012): 61–80.

41 'The Elsewhere is thus never a blank slate, and may be as discursively unfree as the metaphysical, political, and cultural conditions it seeks to redress. It is pre-occupied: its Crusoes will always come upon the footprints of other inhabitants.' Adam Zachary Newton. *The Elsewhere – On Belonging at a Near Distance.* Madison: University of Wisconsin Press, 2005. 17.

42 Martha Nussbaum. 'Exactly and Responsibly: A Defence of Ethical Criticism.' *Mapping the Ethical Turn: A Reader in Ethics, Culture, and Literary Theory.* Ed. Todd F. Davis and Kenneth Womack. Charlottesville: University Press of Virginia, 2001. 60.

viewer or listener.'[43] However, to declare commitment and involvement positive and even essential while maintaining the tenet of moral dissociation remains a paradoxical position. It is, to be sure, one that supports complicity as a general human condition. Moral dissociation also allows for forgiveness in the text, and for the formation of bonds beyond moral condemnation, such as the protagonist's lasting friendship with Leo.

This paradoxical stance, however, has also ethical problems. First and foremost, the novel never discusses what is a tolerable, minor transgression versus a serious sin within Romania's totalitarian past. Why Leo's extermination of Vintul, the Securitate member involved in Petre's murder (*LHD* 374–375), should be any different from Belanger's initial extermination of Petre, the double-dealing Securitate member, remains unclear. Leo is driven by revenge as well as the reassertion of his power, the identical motivation to Belanger's action.[44] Faced with Leo's announcement of the murder, the protagonist is neither surprised nor hesitant: 'In other words Manea had told Leo where to find Vintul and Leo had put the word out. There was always room in a revolution for the settling of old accounts – Manea's, Ottilia's, Leo's. Mine too now, it seemed' (*LHD* 375). The last sentence clarifies the extent of the protagonist's complicity as he makes this 'settling of old accounts' rhetorically his own. The protagonist's steadfast friendship with Leo indeed shows his moral dissociation: he continues to cherish Leo in full dissociation from (and so: complicity with) Leo's actions. His condoning response is chilling. There is not even interpersonal accountability for Leo, neither in this immediate situation nor afterwards.

A similar ethical problem arises in the protagonist's other choices of patron or friend. The protagonist admires Trofim, his grey eminence Stalinist father figure, whose old-world manners and sophistication are repeatedly emphasised. This admiration is unchanged once Trofim's long-term machinations for power are fully revealed. The protagonist notes his own former gullibility (*LHD* 57), but he still feels for Trofim 'what I imagined I would have felt for a father, had my father lived long enough to get old and had he been… well, like a father' (*LHD* 265). This is particularly curious. Although brutal and extensive, the small-town bullying and wife-beater cruelty, which the protagonist describes in his biological father, seem trivial in comparison to the scope of Trofim's intrigues. The protagonist however chooses the latter with no qualms or hesitation, admiringly praising Trofim as a successful 'puppet master running the show' (*LHD* 265). Similarly, he is fascinated by the Securist Petre, whose discourses on a form of socialist utopia

---

43 Jeremy Hawthorn and Jakob Lothe. 'Introduction: The Ethical (Re)Turn.' *Narrative Ethics.* Ed. Jeremy Hawthorn and Jakob Lothe. Leiden: Brill, 2013. 6.

44 The novel does not claim a vigilante motivation for Leo, or a gratification for the protagonist. It is an open revenge move by Leo which is condoned by the protagonist, tit for tat, 'settling of old accounts' (*LHD* 375).

(*LHD* 131–134) seem to the protagonist a form of commendable idealism, one 'adapted […] to make sense of all the constraint' (*LHD* 134).[45] Yet the protagonist fully rejects Manea, arguably also a reformer from within, and Trofim's collaborator. To cap this moral confusion, towards the ending he even admits to feeling envious at the full extent of Belanger's corruption. (first *LHD* 279; reinforced *LHD* 347)

It seems that McGuinness's protagonist does not understand that corruption is inherent in the system, and his individual agency is therefore inevitably complicit with this regime. Or does the text actually endorse Leo's ultimate cynicism? If this were the case, the novel's carefully constructed balance between dissociation and engagement would unravel with its closure.

Evidently, Patrick McGuinness's *The Last Hundred Days* offers a complex exploration of the human condition within the context of Ceauşescu's Romania, blending history, philosophy, and a *Bildungsroman* narrative into a moral allegory. It provides an inquiry into the complexities of ethical decision-making and the consequences of compromised actions. The notion of complicity permeates the lives of all characters even to the novel's closure. Furthermore, by intertwining the protagonist's moral development with his relationships (amorous as well as convivial) the novel asserts the importance of emotional bonds in the protagonist's ethical trajectory: morality entails emotional connections.

Though complicity is presented as a universal human condition, necessary ethical distinctions are lacking. The protagonist's enduring attachment to and condonement of morally questionable, criminal or corrupt figures (Leo, Trofim, Petre) exemplifies this. The novel's portrayal therefore suggests a failure to recognize that a system that is intrinsically corrupt cannot be divorced from individual agency. In the light of the (fallible) first-person narrator's Everyman status, this curious ending to the text may drive home ongoing temptations, coupled to apologetical biases and emotional entanglements, all of which mark human social interactions. The frame of the novel certainly suggests a focus on same-old 'new' beginnings, and serves as a timely reflection on the complexities of moral decision-making and the implications of complicity.

---

45 For Trofim's lengthy speech on the virtues of socialism which finds similar detailed attention, see *LHD* 240.

References

Abraham, Florin. *Romania since the Second World War: A Political, Social, and Economic History*. London: Bloomsbury, 2017.

Bailey, Paul. 'Romanian Holiday: *The Last Hundred Days* by Patrick McGuinness.' *Literary Review* (September 2011). <https://literaryreview.co.uk/romanian-holiday> (date of access 16 August 2023).

Becker, Seymour. 'The "Great Game": The History of an Evocative Phrase.' *Asian Affairs* 43.1 (2012): 61–80.

Chiper, Sorina. '*The Last Hundred Days*: The Death Thralls of Romanian Communist Dictatorship through Foreign Eyes.' *Discourse as a Form of Multiculturalism in Literature and Communication*. Ed. Julian Boldea. Târgu Mureş: Arhipelag XXI Press, 2015. 392–399.

Cioroianu, Adrian. 'The Impossible Escape: Romanians and the Balkans.' *Balkan as Metaphor: Between Globalization and Fragmentation*. Ed. Dušan I. Bielić and Obrad Savić. Cambridge, Mass.: MIT Press, 2002. 209–233.

Danta, Darrick. 'Ceausescu's Bucharest.' *Geographical Review* 83.2 (April 1993): 170–182.

Finucan, Stephen. '*The Last Hundred Days* by Patrick McGuinness: Review.' *Toronto Star* (21 July 2012). <https://www.thestar.com/entertainment/books/ 2012/07/21/the_last_hundred_days_by_patrick_mcguinness_review.html> (date of access 16 August 2023).

Hanks, Patrick and Flavia Hodges. *A Dictionary of First Names in English*. Oxford: Oxford University Press, 1991.

Hammond, Andrew. 'Through Savage Europe.' *Third Text* 21.2 (2007): 117–127.

Hawthorn, Jeremy and Jakob Lothe. 'Introduction: The Ethical (Re)Turn.' *Narrative Ethics*. Ed. Jeremy Hawthorn and Jakob Lothe. Leiden: Brill, 2013. 1–10.

Hitchins, Keith. *A Concise History of Romania*. Cambridge: Cambridge University Press, 2014.

Kristeva, Julia. *Powers of Horror: An Essay on Abjection*. Transl. Leon S. Roudiez. New York: Columbia University Press, 1982.

Kurtz, Christopher. *Complicity: Ethics and Law for a Collective Age*. Cambridge: Cambridge University Press, 2000.

Lester. G.A.. 'Introduction.' *Three Late Medieval Morality Plays: Mankind, Everyman, Mundus et Infans*. Ed. G. A. Lester. New Mermaids Anthologies. London: Bloomsbury, 2014. xi–xxxvii.

Levinas, Emmanuel. 'Eros.' *Time and The Other [and additional essays]*. Transl. Richard A. Cohen. Pittsburgh: Duchesne University Press, 1987. 84–89.

Lewis, Randolph. *Under Surveillance: Being Watched in Modern America*. Austin: University of Texas Press, 2017.

McGuinness, Patrick. *The Last Hundred Days*. London: Bloomsbury, 2011.

Melcher, Sergei. 'Entstehungskontexte des Centru Civic: Auf dem Weg zum vertieften Verständnis des neuen Stadtzentrums der rumänischen Hauptstadt.' *Kilometer Null: Politische Transformation und gesellschaftliche Entwicklungen in Rumänien seit 1989*. Ed. Thede Kahl and Larisa Schippel. Berlin: Verlag Frank und Timme, 2011. 121–142.

Mellema, Gregory. *Complicity and Moral Accountability*. Notre Dame, Indiana: University of Notre Dame Press, 2017.

Newton, Adam Zachary. *The Elsewhere – On Belonging at a Near Distance.* Madison: University of Wisconsin Press, 2005.

Nussbaum, Martha. 'Exactly and Responsibly: A Defence of Ethical Criticism.' *Mapping the Ethical Turn: A Reader in Ethics, Culture, and Literary Theory.* Ed. Todd F. Davis and Kenneth Womack. Charlottesville: University Press of Virginia, 2001. 60–79.

Oltean, Roxana. 'Romance and Belligerence Behind the Iron Curtain: Cold War Gender Identities in Anglo-American Perspective.' *Synergy* 15.1 (2019): 7–24.

Otoiu, Adrian. 'An Exercise in Fictional Liminality: The Postcolonial, the Postcommunist, and Romania's Threshold Generation.' *Comparative Studies of South Asia, Africa and the Middle East* 23.1&2 (2003): 87–105.

Prose, Francine. 'Uncertain Times.' *The New York Times* (8 June 2012). <https://www.nytimes.com/2012/06/10/books/review/the-last-hundred-days-by-patrick-mcguinness.html> (date of access 28 June 2023).

Purdon, James. '*The Last Hundred Days* by Patrick McGuinness – review.' *The Observer* (14 August 2011). <https://www.theguardian.com/books/2011/aug/14/last-hundred-days-patrick-mcguinness> (date of access 28 June 2023).

Ratcliffe, Susan. *Oxford Essential Quotations: St Augustine of Hippo.* Oxford: Oxford University Press, 2017. [Online]. Available: https://www.oxfordreference.com/display/10.1093/acref/9780191843730.001.0001/q-oro-ed5-00000572?rskey=n3tIhG&result=1. Accessed 28 June 2023.

Ratesh, Nestor. *Romania: The Entangled Revolution. The Washington Papers 152.* Washington: The Center for Strategic and International Studies, 1991.

Rothberg, Michael. *The Implicated Subject: Beyond Victims and Perpetrators.* Redwood City: Stanford University Press, 2019.

Talbert, Matthew. 'Moral Responsibility.' *The Stanford Encyclopedia of Philosophy.* Ed. N Zalta and Uri Nodelman (Fall 2022). <https://plato.stanford.edu/archives/fall2022/entries/moral-responsibility/> (date of access 16 Aug 2023).

Todorova, Maria. *Imagining the Balkans.* Oxford: Oxford University Press, 2009.

Wertz, Dorothy. 'Conflict Resolution in the Medieval Morality Plays.' *The Journal of Conflict Resolution* 13.4 (December 1969): 438–453.

Ágnes Harasztos

The 'Postmodern Baroque' as a Heterotopia for East-Central Europe in post-1989 British Fiction

Milan Kundera identified baroque visual arts and music as key features of seventeenth-century Central European culture. He claimed that baroque art was 'a
phenomenon that unified this vast region,' and believed that the early modern era
witnessed the birth of Central Europe, defined politically by the Habsburg empire, culturally by multinational communities, and in a religious sense by
Counter-Reformation Catholicism.[1] In his *Doctor Criminale* (1992), Malcolm
Bradbury echoed this attribution and described Hungary as a locus of the
postmodern where meanings are elusive, knowledge is ironic and intertextual,
and possibilities of the coherent self are tendentiously swept away by historical
cataclysms, with the 1989 revolutions as the latest example. Bruce Chatwin's *Utz*
(1989) epitomized socialist Prague in the person of an eccentric old art collector
who identifies with his rococo Meissen porcelains believing himself a glamorous
prince from the heyday of the baroque in Augustus the Strong's (1670–1733)
Saxony. Existing in a fold of historical identities which bind the region once to the
Western and, at other times, to the Eastern cultural sphere of Europe, the features
of the 'postmodern' and the 'baroque' are present in post-1989 British literary
discourses on East-Central Europe.

Postmodern cultural work is interpreted as a return of the 'baroque' by Gregg
Lambert in his 2004 book, which regards the 'baroque' as a 'recurrent sign of
history.'[2] Lambert develops the concept of the 'postmodern baroque' following
poststructuralist philosophy, especially the ideas of Gilles Deleuze, Walter Benjamin, Nadir Lahiji, Christine Buci-Glucksmann, and Julia Kristeva. This concept
of the 'baroque,' somewhat independently from its seventeenth-century appearance in art history, is a function reappearing in the course of the history of
Modernity as its subversion. This 'baroque' (hereafter employed without quotation marks) is a counter-modern vision which criticizes Enlightenment ra-

---

1 Milan Kundera. 'The Tragedy of Central Europe.' Transl. Edmund White. *The New York Review of Books* 31.7 (1984): 33–38.
2 Gregg Lambert. *The Return of the Baroque in Modern Culture*. London: Continuum, 2004. 11.

tionalism, its universal narratives, coherent subjectivity, and progressive perception of time similarly to postmodern ideas and thought which have subverted Modernity.

This chapter analyses three postmodern British novels, Chatwin's *Utz*, Tom McCarthy's *Men in Space* (2007), and Bradbury's *Doctor Criminale* in order to trace aspects of the 'postmodern baroque' in their literary representations of East-Central Europe. Their narrators and focalizers see Central European culture engaged in a continuous baroque reinterpretation of Modernity. Therefore, this discussion will first examine textual as well as thematic elements expressing this subversion in the novels in the paradigm of Deleuze's fold. Deleuze developed the notion of fold from Leibniz's philosophy of monadology. The fold is an abstract motion of physical and metaphorical space. Deleuze wrote about it in his book entitled *The Fold, Leibniz and the Baroque* (1993). In it, he describes the baroque where distinct qualities such as external and internal, cause and effect, or time and space do not exist in separate objective spheres, but rather turn into each other through the motion of the fold.[3] Secondly, 'postmodern baroque' art forms, following the philosophy of the fold, often subvert rational conceptions of time and space by staging them in loops where time is spatialized. East-Central Europe often appears as a locus for spatialized time in these novels. It is described as an isolated setting where time stops, turns back, or processes in circular loops instead of a linear line. This feature is especially characteristic in the portrayal of the special atmosphere of the 1989 political changes. Thirdly, as British novels about Central Europe reflect on its baroque Counter-Reformation heritage, aspects of baroque melancholy, originating in baroque Catholic art, are also mentioned. Historically, the spreading of baroque art in Central Europe can be linked to the Counter Reformation through a specific theology and philosophy. Baroque art was utilized in reconverting people after the Reformation by involving them in a seventeenth-century multimedia experience via highly decorated churches and artworks that foregrounded the expression of sentiments, devotion, and even suffering to a hitherto unimaginable extent. Baroque visual beauty was coupled with both the all-pervasive representation of God's power and absolutist temporal power. However, baroque beauty is associated with later historical and ideological developments as expressed by Walter Benjamin's thoughts about aestheticized force, its connection to institutionalized violence and inherent melancholy.[4] At last, this chapter examines the heterotopic gesture

---

3 Gilles Deleuze. *The Fold, Leibniz and the Baroque*. Transl. Tom Conley. London: Athlone Press, 1993. 8.
4 Walter Benjamin. [1963] *The Origin of German Tragic Drama*. Transl. John Osborne. London: Verso, 1998.

inherent in textual appearances of East-Central European self-colonization and self-perception as a simulacrum of the West.

East-Central Europe and the Baroque

The notion of East-Central Europe is a historically fluid one. Moreover, the term is ideologically loaded; therefore, it needs to be delineated. Larry Wolff, in his book entitled *Inventing Eastern Europe*,[5] claims that the East-West division of Europe dates back to the Enlightenment period. French and German travellers of the late eighteenth century described the East of Europe in terms diametrically opposing their own Western spheres. For them, the West was equal to civic boredom; whereas the European East was perceived as a sphere of authenticity, exoticism, and unfathomable irrationality.[6] As Wolff argues, Western travellers associated Eastern Europe with 'incomprehensible' languages, such as Hungarian or the Slavic tongues, which resulted in the image of nonsense gradually becoming an attribute of the region.[7]

In relation to the Eastern Europe Wolff researched in eighteenth- and nineteenth-century travelogues, East-Central Europe is situated between West and East and is defined by the historical predominance of the Habsburg Empire and Germany from the seventeenth century until 1945. This period strengthened the region's ties to the Western sphere of Europe. After WWII, East-Central Europe was incorporated into the Second World, its countries allied to the Soviet Union, that is, the Eastern Bloc. This Cold War antagonism paved the way to an inferior position inside the EU for the new member states (Czech Republic, Slovakia, Hungary, Poland etc.) admitted in 2004. These countries entered a European Union dominated by several larger and/or more prosperous countries of Western Europe, and the tendency to treat them as slightly less European still prevails even today. East-Central Europe has always been an in-between cultural territory. What Kundera claimed to be the tragedy of Central European countries was that they found themselves pushed from West to East[8] in the twentieth century, during the Cold War polarization of Europe. Wishing to be truthful to the varied cultural heritage of this area, the dual attributives of East and Central seem the most apt.

Historically and culturally, this territory experienced an intersection of dependencies both from East and from West. Being dominated, occupied, and ravaged by either Western or by Eastern empires is a joint traumatic experience

---

5 Larry Wolff. *Inventing Eastern Europe: The Map of Civilization on the Mind of the Enlightenment*. Stanford: Stanford University Press, 1994.
6 Wolff, *Inventing Eastern Europe*, 122.
7 Wolff, *Inventing Eastern Europe*, 106.
8 Kundera, 'The Tragedy of Central Europe,' 33.

that countries of East-Central Europe share. The history of subjugation by foreign powers started in the sixteenth century with the Ottomans and the Habsburgs, the irruption of the latter coinciding with the predominance of baroque art
and architecture. Baroque was the glamorous style of absolutist kings, an art
historical period expressing the gilded power of the state pushed to the extreme.
As Nadir Lahiji states, baroque art was 'the product of the Counter-Reformation
incarnated in the image of the absolutist big Other.'[9] The historical baroque can
thus be associated with the idea as well as the practice of domination. The
Habsburg Empire, which defined this area, was characterized by extensive use of
the baroque style in architecture, visual imagery, or other aesthetic expressions of
royal power. This imperial style left its mark on East-Central European cultures
not only with regard to the appearance of most of their Catholic churches and
urban areas. Habsburg and baroque heritage more broadly also had an effect on
East-Central European social systems. Examples include institutional practices, a
uniformly Prussian educational system, and highly bureaucratic administrative
traditions, all of which were the result of a sweepingly quick and mostly centrally
managed modernization that characterized the region in the second half of the
nineteenth century. The Central European tendency to accept repeated attempts
of centralization even when uncoerced by foreign armies can be attributed to this
baroque heritage.

The literary portrayal of shared political and cultural characteristics of East-
Central Europe will be investigated with the discursive concept of the post-
socialist Other, established by scholars like David Chioni Moore, Alexander
Kiossev, and Madina Tlostanova.[10] In describing intercultural encounters and
representations of Eastern and Central Europe, their studies made use of the
notion of the Other familiar from postcolonial studies, but adjusted to apply to
the postsocialist Other. Instead of the radical alterity of the Orient, Second World
countries represented a semi-alterity for British literary renderings. This special
relationship of the spected and the spectant cultures I wish to describe by the
notion of heterotopia developed by Michel Foucault. He argued that human
cultures often utilize symbolic spaces with physical dimensions, where they
project their otherness in order to be able to keep it inside as well as outside their
own selves. One example of such a gesture is the spatial metaphor of the mirror

---

9 Nadir Lahiji. *Adventures with the Theory of the Baroque and French Philosophy*. London:
   Bloomsbury Academic, 2016. 56.
10 David Chioni Moore. 'Is the Post- in Postcolonial the Post- in Post-Soviet? Toward a Global
   Postcolonial Critique.' *PMLA* 116:1 (2001): 111–128; Alexander Kiossev. [1995] 'Self-colonizing Metaphor.' *Atlas of Transformation* (2011). <http://monumenttotransformation.org
   /atlas-of-transformation/html/s/self-colonization/the-self-colonizing-metaphor-alexander-
   kiossev.html> (date of access 19 Sept 2023); Madina Tlostanova. *Postcolonialism and Postsocialism in Fiction and Art: Resistance and Re-existence*. London: Palgrave Macmillan, 2017.

where 'I see myself there, where I am not.'[11] I argue that the seemingly Other baroque East-Central Europe represented in British novels functions the same way posing as heterotopias for the British discursive self where it can project its outside.

A conspicuous aspect of this heterotopic projection is the alleged opposition of the Central European baroque to rationality, which is a typical feature of the 'postmodern' as well. By 'postmodern,' I point to cultural work which permeated all forms of art from the 1960s until the millennium. The postmodern is at once a late-capitalist condition, as theorized by Fredric Jameson, and an art historical period defining forms of artistic expression. The postmodern period, which, following Steven Connor, I treat as already over by the 2000s,[12] saw the super-session of fixed boundaries in modern scientific thinking with an interdiscipli-nary mindset, the mixing of genres in literature, and the questioning of hitherto unchallengeable concepts such as the 'coherent self.' Most importantly, it brought a multiculturalist and anti-elitist approach to culture and called atten-tion to the fragmentation of experiences, thus subverting grand narratives as Lyotard famously claimed. This postmodern cultural framework aptly describes East-Central Europe. The subversion of rationality and an experience of frag-mentation have been historical experiences of this region, whose political, ethnic, and religious boundaries have been subject to constant and often violent changes. British fictional discourses on East-Central Europe reflect this and can be described by the term 'postmodern baroque.' Apart from the novels' use of postmodern narrative techniques and imagery, the depicted East-Central Eu-ropean experience is also akin to these two cultural functions, together named the 'postmodern baroque.' As opposed to clarity and reason, East-Central Europe is often materialized – in words used by Lambert to describe the baroque – as the irrational and the 'cultural parody or pastiche of European forms of knowledge and culture.'[13] In what follows, I wish to highlight some literary critical examples from British novels on East-Central Europe showing the region in the function of a fictional heterotopia in its 'postmodern baroque' features.

---

11 Michel Foucault. [1967] 'Of Other Spaces, Heterotopias.' Transl. Jay Miskowiec. *Architecture /Mouvement/ Continuité* (1984): 3.

12 Steven Connor. 'Introduction.' *The Cambridge Companion to Postmodernism.* Ed. Steven Connor. Cambridge: Cambridge University Press, 2004. 15.

13 Lambert, *The Return of the Baroque,* 5.

The Fold

The first example attributes one 'postmodern baroque' function Gilles Deleuze describes, namely, the fold, as a typical Othering feature of the region. The concept of the fold 'allows us to extend the Baroque beyond its historical limits while giving it a precise condition. In other words, particular figures from various points in history are labelled 'Baroque' if and only if their work includes [re/un]folding in some way.'[14] A fold cannot be 'separate[d] into parts of parts, but rather divide[s] infinitely into smaller and smaller folds that always retain a certain cohesion.'[15] In this way, the Baroque

> can be defined by this severing of the facade from the inside, of the interior from the exterior, and the autonomy of the interior from the independence of the exterior, but in such conditions that each of the two terms thrusts the other forward. [...] If there is an inherently Baroque costume, it is broad, in distending waves, billowing and flaring, surrounding the body with its independent folds, ever-multiplying, never betraying those of the body beneath.[16]

As both the baroque and the postmodern are deeply rooted in the economic structures of (respectively early- and late-stage-) capitalism,[17] the fold also has a field of interpretation connected to the materialistic side of these linked cultural frameworks. What happens in the motion of the fold is essentially collection. In the example of the suntan, the hours can be collected resulting in a more intensive quality of skin colour. This collecting aspect of the fold is called homothesis which means a type of creation via collection, a postmodern instance of this gesture can be found in *bricolage* or *collage*. Contrary to the traditional notion of creation, homothetic creation does not operate by engendering new qualities or beings, but by gathering pieces and putting them together. Rococo statuettes are such objects in Bruce Chatwin's novel, *Utz*, which carry with themselves their corresponding cultures, worlds, or set of gestures. Each of them adheres to baroque aesthetics and philosophy, and carry the impression of being a set of varying parts themselves.

The Meissen porcelain figures of the novel are mostly actually existing pieces. One of them carries special importance in the story. This is the so-called Swan Service Tureen, the original of which was manufactured in the late 1730s. The artistic design of this piece is put together from distinct objects that would never

---

14 Alex Tissandier. *Affirming Divergence. Deleuze's Reading of Leibniz*. Edinburgh: Edinburgh University Press, 2018. 122.

15 Gilles Deleuze and Jonathan Strauss. 'The Fold.' *Yale French Studies* 80 (1991): 231.

16 Gilles Deleuze. *The Fold: Leibniz and the Baroque*. Transl. Tom Conley. London: Athlone Press, 1993. 121, 28.

17 Lambert, *The Return of the Baroque*, 42.

meet in nature, some of them being purely fictional. Among the ornamental reliefs of this giant bowl, there are swans, huge fish, mermaids, the obligatory cherubs and shells, all in an unnatural, disproportionate chaos. As the English narrator secretly thinks: 'but for the bravura of its execution, [it] would have been a monstrosity.'[18] This tureen seems to embody a monster created out of parts which in themselves are mostly natural and represent proportionate beauty. However, when put together, the overall effect can be repellent and chaotic. By transgressing the limit of separate qualities, it is the baroque fold which turns beauty into its very opposite and vice versa.

For the baroque, change in degree can be conceived as change in quality,[19] that is, change in ontological mode. The Swan Service Tureen, in its unnatural monstrosity, is folded out of objects taken from nature. By the very gesture of their being collected, 'the fishes, [...] the flowers, the shells, the swans, and a bug-eyed dolphin' (*Utz* 18) lose their original context and their original meaning. They are endowed with new meanings. In this particular case, this new meaning, the baroque idea that probably monstrosity would be included, i. e., folded, in natural objects themselves repels the English narrator. The idea that, via the fold, the beautiful can turn into the monstrous lingers over the narration as the Englishman's special East-Central European experience.

The English narrator of *Utz* describes the titular character in a very similar manner as if he was folded together from various identity parts.

> Politically, Utz was neutral. [...] He detested violence, yet welcomed the cataclysms that flung fresh works of art onto the market. [...] Utz listened politely while his cousin crowed over the victories in France [...] he felt, despite his better judgement, a surge of latent anglophilia. [...] during the reign of Reinhard Heydrich [...] he confounded his interrogators by pulling from its pocket his father's First War decoration. [...] His love of England vanished forever on hearing the B.B.C. announcer, 'There is no china in Dresden today.' [...] The rumours were true. He had collaborated. He had given information: a trickle of information as to the whereabouts of certain works of art...
> (*Utz* 6)

Utz is indeed presented as a collage of identities: a half German, half Jewish baron, presently a Czech. He is proud of his noble ancestors but lives in a bleak flat in Socialist Prague under a Czechoslovakian regime discriminative against former aristocracy. Consequently, he hates the totalitarian regimes that swept through his country in the twentieth century; nevertheless, he most probably had spied for all of them. His sympathies, as illustrated in this excerpt, to say the least, were very fluid. He seems to be the answer for the English narrator's adventure-seeking endeavours which fit into the tradition of eighteenth-century Western

---

18 Bruce Chatwin. *Utz*. London: Viking Adult, 1989. 18.
19 Deleuze, *The Fold*, 31.

European travelogues about the region. The narrator deliberately seeks this baroque unity folded out of Othernesses: 'I wanted to see the gloomy palace-fortress, the Hradschin, where this secretive bachelor [Habsburg Rudolf II] – who spoke Italian to his mistresses, Spanish to his God, German to his courtiers and Czech, seldom, to his rebellious peasants – would, for weeks on end, neglect the affairs of his Holy and Roman Empire and shut himself away with his astronomers' (*Utz* 6). After expressing his wish to see this baroque Habsburg who crystallized in his person the homothetic multiculturalism of East-Central Europe, a friend suggested to visit Utz, 'the Rudolf of our time' (*Utz* 4). 'Postmodern' and 'baroque' are linked here by similar gestures of the two historical times and a continuous resistance to Modern intention to think in distinct categories rather than blur. This colourful, polyglot, and multicultural unity of East-Central Europe folded out of fragments appears as a strange being seen through the narrative of the English visitor.

Spatialized Time

In fold, change, or difference, time can be seen as space. Time turns, or folds into a collection of moments via being objectified in photos or souvenirs. This process entails a spatialization of time since those objects which evoke memory, and finally the time passed, delineate a retrospectively meaningful space in the rectangular and geometrical conception of Modernity. By so doing, this 'postmodern baroque' gesture of the fold subverts the idea that time and space are distinct qualities. In the British novels about East-Central Europe discussed here, time and space flow into each other. This often takes the form of a specific *tempolocality*, a concept developed by Madina Tlostanova to denote multidimensional spatial and temporal equivalence in Eastern Europe.[20] Utz also spatializes time, especially the baroque time of Augustus the Strong, Elector of Saxony, by collecting Meissen porcelain statuettes from the Prince's court and furnishing his 1960s Prague flat with them. The Rococo figurines ornament his flat in the homothetic baroque way, giving rise to something else because they indulge the old bachelor in his fantasy of believing himself to be a different person existing in a different historical time: 'He came close to believing in his fantasy: that this *was* the "porcelain palace," and that he himself was Augustus reincarnate' (*Utz* 21). Notably, the text identifies Utz and Augustus, not content with a more reasonable gesture of stating the likeness of the two. They are folded into each other.

McCarthy's *Men in Space* also provides an example to the 'postmodern baroque' spatialization of time in an anecdote which illustrates the *zeitgeist* of the

---

20 Tlostanova, *Postcolonialism and Postsocialism*, 94.

immediate aftermath of 1989 in Prague when people quickly found themselves both literally and metaphorically hanging in mid-air. The following story is told in a pub in a circle of Czech and foreign guest students:

> 'A Soviet cosmonaut is stranded in his spaceship. [...] This guy went up as a Soviet, on a routine space mission, and then while he was up there the Soviet Union disintegrated. Now, no one wants to bring him down.'
> 'Why not?' asks Jan.
> 'The Russians say he's not their problem,' Hájek explains. 'He set off from the Ukraine, so they say he should go back there.'
> 'Fair enough,' says Jan.
> 'The Ukrainians don't think so,' Hájek tells him. 'They're saying, *Fuck off! This was a Soviet space project, and Soviet means Russian.*'
> 'This is true,' Jan concurs. 'What nationality is the cosmonaut?'
> 'That's the thing,' says Hájek. 'He's from Latvia or somewhere. So the Ukrainians and Russians are both turning to the Latvians saying, *You can foot the bill for all this.* Millions of dollars, you see.'
> [...]
> 'That story's old!' Sláva sneers across the room from his table. 'I heard it months ago.'
> 'Of course you did!' says Hájek. 'He's still up there. He's been there for months now!'
> 'What's he living on?' asks Jan.
> 'Supplies,' says Hájek. 'They have stuff, you know, all compressed, dehydrated ...'
> 'You got stuff?' Ivan asks him. A burnt-out flare lands on his shoulder; he brushes it to the floor. Hájek throws two small wraps onto the table.[21]

It is emblematic how, in the fashion of homothesis, traditional concepts of space and time are transformed in objects. The cosmonaut experiences time travelling precisely because of his life inside an object which directly derived from the past. This object made time spatial. In it, the person is Soviet, while the Soviet Union has already disintegrated, on Earth. Nobody claims citizenship to that country anymore, but this lost figure from the past in space. While the cosmonaut still lived in the socialist Second World, in a parallel time, his country already advanced to its future, which rendered him a homeless time traveller in a no-whereland. His spatial homelessness also opens up paradoxes in terms of a traditional conception of time. This novel especially draws on the picture of the newly liberated Eastern Bloc as floating in mid-air both physically and metaphorically.

A humorous third meaning is added, in the final sentence of the excerpt, to the literal and the metaphorical one. The conversation smoothly flows from the story to the speakers' reality via the topic of the cosmonaut's food supplies, which are described by the slang word 'stuff.' This carries the secondary meaning of some kind of party drugs, a suggestion strongly reinforced by the last sentences just

---

21 Tom McCarthy. [2007] *Men in Space.* London: Vintage, 2012. 42–43.

quoted, where the 'stuff' is presented in 'wraps,' that is, small folds of paper usually used for drugs. This parallel of eating, which the stranded astronaut and the students all did and the fact that the two are blurred in a postmodern way into each other binds the out-of-joint Soviet spaceman and the partying postsocialist students together in one common experience. Their situations, their hallucinatory unreality and desperate situations became entangled in a postmodern textual parallax, that is, parallel narrative structures. Identities, spaces and times are folded into each other, none being entirely fixed anymore.

Baroque Melancholy

Identity and a problematic relationship to oneself are fundamental elements of East-Central Europe and its neurotic subjecthood. This specific East-Central European neurosis can be identified as the 'baroque melancholy' or madness rooted in the rupture of Modernity, which, according to Foucault, violently tore away reason from other forms of knowledge.[22] Baroque madness or melancholy is a special state of self-pity and realization of the impossibility of communicating oneself because of the hopeless splintering of the signs within Modernity. Its baroque nature is also displayed in its controversial relationship to institutionalized power. Following Walter Benjamin's analysis of the German tragic drama, Christine Buci-Glucksmann argues that baroque melancholy stems from the need to endure of absolute power, it is a constant hopeless sadness in the face of total state control. She adds that, in baroque dramas, the most important function of the prince, who represents state control, is to avert the catastrophe to which the modern state is always heading. Thus, modern baroque reason is equivalent to existing in a state of constant fear towards a 'despotic worldly reality.'[23] In fact, she suggests that this reality is allegorically presented as deadly and violent in baroque tragic dramas,[24] but this artistic representation reveals a baroque way of thinking in which state power is inherently violent towards its subjects who display melancholy when confronted by the monolithic power of modern state. In Benjamin's understanding, baroque melancholy is heir to the Counter-Reformation aesthetic of the seventeenth-century baroque where beauty accompanied institutionalized violence. This aestheticized violence was a result of the gradually developing modern subjecthood which entails objectification of people.[25] This melancholy expressed by the baroque is a non-patho-

---

22 As qtd. in Lambert, *The Return of the Baroque*, 83.
23 Christine Buci-Glucksmann. *Baroque Reason: The Aesthetics of Modernity.* Transl. Patrick Camiller. London: Sage Publications, 1994. 69.
24 Buci-Glucksmann, *Baroque Reason*, 70.
25 Benjamin, *The Origin*, 222.

logical, but rather ontological melancholy. Analysing this melancholia in her book, *The Black Sun*, Julia Kristeva argues that it resides in the moment between two movements of the fold, that is, neither life, nor death, neither reality, nor hallucination, neither space, nor time.[26] In his *Book of Laughter and Forgetting*, Kundera refers to baroque melancholy using an untranslatable Czech word for sadness, 'lítost.' In his understanding, it is a complex feeling of inferiority complex enriched with anger directed against the more successful and a good deal of self-pity.[27] His interpretation was originally a poetic and individual suggestion, but since the publication of Kundera's novel, it has spread widely and appears not only in popular culture but also in scientific literature. Kyra Giorgi, for instance, centred her recent anthropological study around three national melancholic notions, one of which was Czech lítost.[28]

Lítost is primarily sadness at the breach of our desires and the real world. Incapacity to communicate, impotence and self-pity are key words here. In the character of Chatwin's eccentric and petty bourgeois Utz, we can identify this complex psychological and cultural state of mind. Utz makes a sarcastic remark on Czech national identity based on traumatic historical events that mirrors Baroque melancholy:

> It [Prague] was also a city of giants: giants in stone, in stucco or marble; naked giants; blackamoor giants; giants dressed as if for a hurricane, not one of them in repose, struggling with some unseen force, or heaving under the weight of architraves. 'The suffering giant,' he added without conviction, 'is the emblem of our persecuted people.' (*Utz* 13)

The paradox of the suffering giant aptly captures the nature of baroque melancholy. Giants are typically mythic figures representing greatness and power. However, they are not used here as such. These superhuman creatures are emblems for the failures and sufferings of the Czech nation which was unable to choose between representing its greatness and reminding people of their past traumas. They wanted to grab both the image of greatness and a desire to be pitied and thus ended up with neither. The sadness of it is precisely a moment in between the movements of the fold, as Kristeva described melancholy. Another complex metaphor that can be linked to the sadness of a Prague giant is the Golem myth which is also mentioned in the novel. It should also be noted how the

26 Julia Kristeva. *Black Sun, Depression and Melancholia*. Transl. Leon S. Roudinez. Columbia: Columbia University Press, 1989.
27 Milan Kundera. [1978] *A nevetés és felejtés könyve [Book of Laughter and Forgetting]*. Budapest: Európa, 2014. 152.
28 Kyra Giorgi. *Emotions, Language and Identity on the Margins of Europe*. New York: Palgrave Macmillan, 2014.

Golem is collaged together in a homothetic gesture of the fold existing, once again, in-between two statuses, that of the living and that of dead clay.

The baroque melancholy engendered by the rupture between reality and its folded image appears in Utz's fate. Towards the end of his life, Utz becomes bored with the fake aristocratic life into which he escaped from the bleak reality of Socialist totalitarian rule. However, much choice was not granted for him in this region and this historical era. In the 1960s, Utz takes yearly journeys to France where he keeps pondering over his chances of emigration, but refuses to act on it every single time:

> Not that he would be happy in Czechoslovakia. He would be harassed, menaced, in-sulted. He would have to grovel. He would have to agree with every word they said. He would mouth their meaningless, ungrammatical formulae. He would learn to 'live within the lie.' But Prague was a city that suited his melancholic temperament. A state of tranquil melancholy was all one could aspire to these days! (*Utz* 27)

The expression 'live within the lie' implies the mendacious discourse of the State Socialist ideology as well as his own ersatz baroque existence. According to Benjamin, the baroque saw the world as a theatre, a *theatrum mundi*. In this theatre, people moved as if puppets.[29] Utz's treatment of his own little Meissen shepherd boy and maiden girl sculptures can be seen as an allegory for creating a beautiful cage for subjects in the modern, capitalist world. Related from the British point of view, it suggests a lingering, persistent British longing for a world other than the capitalist where people are objectified immovable puppets.

At first, it seems that the 'Augustus reincarnate' fantasy has the potential to express at least some silent resistance to the socialist system. However, later the price of resistance also has to be paid in grovelling, primarily in front of his own courtly worldview akin to the worldview of a baroque absolute monarch. The novel shows the moment when the two possible worlds clash. The implied de-struction of the porcelain figures also appears as a possibility for an escape from grovelling in front of both: 'He had tried to preserve in microcosm the elegance of European court life. But the price was too high. He hated the grovelling and the compromise – and in the end the porcelains disgusted him' (*Utz* 52).

There is something inherently sad about being disgusted at the work of one's whole life and all its connotations that became one's life instead of changing that life. There is something inconsolably melancholic when a community bases its greatness on self-pity for all the historical struggles in which it had to participate instead of tackling the damaging social, economic or cultural results of those historical situations. This is a melancholy East-Central European neurosis re-

---

29 Benjamin, *The Origin*, 82.

siding in the limbo of indecision, in between suffering and violence, resistance and passivity.

Self-colonization and simulacrum as heterotopia

A passive and self-pitying tendency in the image of East-Central Europe is investigated here as the product of British literary discourse. However, the question of agency for such ideas on East-Central European cultures arises in many investigated texts. Bradbury's *Doctor Criminale* reflects upon the inferiority complex East-Central Europeans often display especially in the company of someone from western Europe. Francis, the English narrator who visits Budapest in the novel describes the town through the eyes of a Hungarian university instructor who calls attention to the whole city's inauthentic nature:

> 'Charming, yes,' said Hollo, lighting a cigarette, 'And now you see our trick. Here we have built a great European city, two in fact, one old and one new. Our only problem is our European cities are not in Europe at all. Budapest is Buenos Aires on the Danube, all a pretend.' 'How is it a pretend?' I asked. 'First, nearly all these buildings were not designed for here at all,' said Hollo, 'See there our lovely Parliament, down by the river, which hardly meets, by the way. The architect loved your House of Commons, so he made us one. The Chain Bridge, built by a Scotsman in a kilt. Eiffel from France made the railway station. Our boulevards are from Paris, our coffee houses from Vienna, our banks are English, the Hilton American. You see why they make films here, we are everything. And this old castle, Fisherman's Bastion, from which nobody has ever fished, by the way, was built as a fantasy at the turn of the century. So you see it is Disneyland, and we are Mickey Mouse.' (*Doctor Criminale* 99)

Budapest clearly appears here as a simulacrum of the West. It is not only a virtual and copied reality physically but also in the minds of the people. The Hungarian guide refers to the fact that these buildings were not designed here. His problem is not that they were not meant to stand in Budapest, but rather that 'the architect loved your House of Commons' so much that he simply copied it. According to Hollo, Budapest is a theatre setting behind which the inner meaning is not ours but that of the West. It is a deliberate word play that his name refers to the emptiness of such an identity: Hollo means 'raven' in Hungarian, which is a symbolic bird for death; it also evokes the sound of the English word 'hollow.'

This desire to recreate the West in Central European regions can be described by Alexander Kiossev's concept of self-colonization. Kiossev described Eastern European cultures as ones which display a self-imposed subjugation with relation to the Anglo-American cultural field. Even though Eastern European nations have not experienced colonization from any Western European state, their social imaginations still construct a self-image of 'cultures of absences' and 'cultures of backwardness' in relation to the West.[30] This self-colonization of East-Central Europe appears in the above excerpt, but with a diverse agency, since it is the English narrator-character who reports the self-colonization of the East-Central European Other.

This dialogue is narrated by an English narrator who is appalled by the Hungarian's self-perception of a lack of substance. The narrator is an English journalist, Francis, who desperately seeks meaning in Hungary and in the life and work of the great Hungarian scholar, Doctor Criminale. This fictional Hungarian philosopher gradually became equivalent to all the adventures, historical cataclysms, great thoughts the naïve young journalist wishes to find and decipher in East-Central Europe. However, in metafictional postmodern fashion, the novel does not provide answers to the questions it poses. Instead, it presents an interplay of literary discourses. The described Englishness, the autoimage of the British novel, is engaged in a postmodern identity play with the discursive heteroimage, that is, the representation of the Hungarians.

The effect of the heteroimage on the autoimage is textualized as an allegory of the hermeneutical process: Francis investigates and reads Criminale, and he writes himself in the course of this very process. The autodiegetic reader presumes and constructs the text, and the narrative constructs him as reader. In like manner, the interpreted story of Criminale and the interpreting story of Francis gradually become interchangeable: 'his story is also somehow mine.'[31] So, Francis, by the end of the book, although mimetically 'same' in his physical conditions, in his character or selfhood has transformed into someone else. As it is claimed by Mari-Ana Tupan, Francis, as an Oedipus educated in the spirit of French poststructuralism, steps into the place of Criminale, his symbolic father, and realizes their ontological sameness.[32] It is the 'postmodern baroque' subjectivization technique that can be discerned here. Francis's narrative identity is folded into the object of his gaze, and also into his act of searching for this object. The British narrator's identity is submerged in the East-Central European scene he finds so strange.

'Hungarian thinking' is a key metonymic stereotype of the novel, which primarily influences the Hungarian heteroimage. The recurrent prompt of Ildiko, that 'you should learn to be a bit more Hungarian' (*Doctor Criminale* 238), mostly encourages Francis to seek advantageous positions in corrupt and dishonest ways. 'Hungarian' also appears as a synonym of contrariness and complicatedness. Hungarian thinking occupies a critical point in Francis's development of

---

30 Kiossev, 'Self-Colonizing Metaphor.'
31 Malcolm Bradbury. [1992] *Doctor Criminale*. London: Picador, 2012. 340.
32 Mari-Ana Tupan. 'Malcolm Bradbury: The Quest for the Perilous East.' *When the World Turned Upside Down: Cultural Representations of Post-1989 Eastern Europe*. Ed. Kathleen Starck. Cambridge: Cambridge Scholars Publishing, 2009. 36–47.

personality. Ildiko empties Criminale's Swiss bank account in Lausanne and, attaching a farewell letter, she allocates a considerable amount of the money to Francis. At this point of the narrative, Francis begins to wonder what he should do with this ill-acquired money. Finally, he concludes that maybe this is the moment 'that I should really learn how to be Hungarian – keep silent, ask no more questions, take my winnings, disappear home' (*Doctor Criminale* 250). As he actually follows through with this plan, Francis's autoimage changes at this point, due to the impact of the heteroimage. What he so far has watched from the outside is now fulfilled from the inside. He succeeded in becoming 'a little bit Hungarian' (*Doctor Criminale* 259).

At the end of the novel, Francis ponders over his journey to East-Central Europe. He realizes that he learnt about postmodern relativism, scepticism and a certain sense of a 'historyless present' (*Doctor Criminale* 340) from the mysterious Hungarian scholar and the Hungarians: 'I wonder, if I was ever put to it, whether I or anyone like me could summon up greater moral powers than he did and didn't in his own particular day. [...] I would also assume nothing is true or certain. Life for me would therefore be a spectacle, a shopping mall, an endless media show' (*Doctor Criminale* 341). The English narrator refers to the Hungarian processing of the state socialist past and the moral issues it raises as an example which is solved in the 'Hungarian way' which, in the world of the text, evokes a devious, sceptic, even cynic way of overlooking moral responsibility. Hungary appears in this novel as an experimental, rather unrealistic place from where such lessons can be drawn for British society. Francis, coming from late Thatcherite Britain constantly puts postsocialist problematics beside British political and philosophical issues. By this, the novel represents Hungary as functioning fundamentally as a heterotopia, where Britain faces its issues in Hungary. The solutions that the fictional Hungarians provide aid the English journalist in finding his way in the new Europe.

Conclusion

The novels discussed here present East-Central Europe as a locus for irrationality, fragmentation, lack of clarity and modern distinction, all floating in mid-air, being insecure as well as unrealistically boasting and melancholic about its past. As a set of post-dependent cultures, this region displays a tendency for self-colonization. This feature of a self-imposed colonial gaze is strengthened by British literary discourse which presents East-Central Europe as undecipherable and incomprehensible, which are fundamentally negative terms. These characteristics evoke disgust and repulsion in the English narrators of the investigated novels, but also a desire to take part in this irrational world. English literary descriptions specify Central European qualities of irrationality describing them as both 'baroque' and 'postmodern.' My investigations aimed at creating a framework for such an English literary discourse by claiming that it presents East-Central Europe as a 'postmodern baroque' region.

Chatwin's *Utz* highlights the baroque fold in the form of the homothetic collection as an organizing principle for subjectivation of the Prague art collector. This motif makes East-Central Europe appear as a pile of fragmented identities, as an incoherent unity always in the process of becoming and being undone. Spatialized time, a postmodern perception of historical identity, appears in both *Utz* and McCarthy's *Men in Space*. This motif presents East-Central Europe engaged in circular loops of time. Baroque melancholy can be discerned in the analysed novels as well, a fundamentally pitiful aspect of the region which, having been subjected to domination and terror for a long time, reacts with collective and systemic neurosis deriving from the conflict between a grandiose self-image and a long-lasting self-pity. Finally, I analysed Bradbury's *Doctor Criminale* from the aspect of self-colonization and the Hungarian heteroimage presenting Hungary as a simulacrum of the West. Although the representation of East-Central Europe in these novels unanimously tends towards a postmodern baroque heteroimage, the English autoimage cannot detach itself from the described East-Central Europes either.

However repelled the Western narrator-characters are at the irrationality, the monstrosity, the amorality, or the self-colonizing self-pity of East-Central Europe, they are unanimously attracted to these areas. In the course of the novels they keep returning, investigating, and seeking encounters with the land and its people. *Utz*'s English narrator proudly distances himself from the monstrosity of the baroque porcelains, Francis is appalled at the devious and dishonest ways of Doctor Criminale, and the American teacher trainee can hardly connect to the postsocialist Prague students in McCarthy's novel. However, the novels also present a journey for these English-speaking narrators during which they return home wiser, richer and more understanding of their own culture. Contrary to its Otherness, postmodern baroque East-Central Europe is presented as a place for self-understanding, in this way, a heterotopia for the Western narrators. It is discursively formulated as the 'postmodern' and 'baroque' Other of the West and its coherent, progressive, and optimistic Modernity. Francis returns to Britain understanding the difficulty of applying strict morality retrospectively in eras following totalitarian rule. Moreover, he feels to be ontologically united with this inherently humane Hungarian figure who erred and moved on. McCarthy's shy American teacher returns home secretly pregnant with a murdered Czech artist's baby. *Utz*'s English narrator keeps watching the antique markets looking for Utz's Meissen porcelains which the protagonist probably destroyed in order to get rid of the fantasy world projected onto them. East-Central Europe is indeed presented as a heterotopia for these Western characters. Following Foucault's metaphor for the notion of heterotopia, their discursive East-Central Europes are mirrors for the West to face itself through its Other.

References

Benjamin, Walter. [1963] *The Origin of German Tragic Drama*. Transl. John Osborne. London: Verso, 1998.

Bradbury, Malcolm. [1992] *Doctor Criminale*. London: Picador, 2012.

Buci-Glucksmann, Christine. *Baroque Reason: The Aesthetics of Modernity*. Transl. Patrick Camiller. London: Sage Publications, 1994.

Chatwin, Bruce. *Utz*. London: Viking Adult, 1989.

Connor, Steven. 'Introduction.' *The Cambridge Companion to Postmodernism*. Ed. Steven Connor. Cambridge: Cambridge University Press, 2004. 1–19.

Deleuze, Gilles. *The Fold, Leibniz and the Baroque*. Transl. Tom Conley. London: Athlone Press, 1993.

Deleuze, Gilles and Jonathan Strauss. 'The Fold.' *Yale French Studies* 80 (1991): 227–247.

Foucault, Michel. [1967] 'Of Other Spaces, Heterotopias.' *Architecture /Mouvement/ Continuité*. Transl. Jay Miskowiec. (1984): 1–7.

Kiossev, Alexander. [1995] 'Self-colonizing Metaphor.' *Atlas of Transformation* (2011). <http://monumenttotransformation.org/atlas-of-transformation/html/s/self-colonizati on/the-self-colonizing-metaphor-alexander-kiossev.html> (date of access 19 Sept 2023).

Kristeva, Julia. *Black Sun, Depression and Melancholia*. Transl. Leon S. Roudinez. Columbia: Columbia University Press, 1989.

Kundera, Milan. 'The Tragedy of Central Europe.' Transl. Edmund White. *New York Review of Books* 31.7 (1984): 33–38.

Lahiji, Nadir. *Adventures with the Theory of the Baroque and French Philosophy*. London: Bloomsbury Academic, 2016.

Lambert, Gregg. *The Return of the Baroque in Modern Culture*. London: Continuum, 2004.

McCarthy, Tom. [2007] *Men in Space*. London: Vintage, 2012.

Moore, David Chioni. 'Is the Post- in Postcolonial the Post- in Post-Soviet? Toward a Global Postcolonial Critique.' *PMLA* 116:1 (2001): 111–128.

Tissandier, Alex. *Affirming Divergence. Deleuze's Reading of Leibniz*. Edinburgh: Edinburgh University Press, 2018.

Tlostanova, Madina. *Postcolonialism and Postsocialism in Fiction and Art: Resistance and Re-existence*. London: Palgrave Macmillan, 2017.

Tupan, Mari-Ana. 'Malcolm Bradbury: The Quest for the Perilous East.' *When the World Turned Upside Down: Cultural Representations of Post-1989 Eastern Europe*. Ed. Kathleen Starck. Cambridge: Cambridge Scholars Publishing, 2009. 36–47.

Wolff, Larry. *Inventing Eastern Europe: The Map of Civilization of the Mind of the Enlightenment*. Stanford: Stanford University Press, 1994.

Contributors

Katrin Berndt is Professor of English Literature and Culture at Martin-Luther-University Halle-Wittenberg (Germany). She works on contemporary historical writing, transcultural fiction, and the long eighteenth century. Her publications include the monographs *Female Identity in Contemporary Zimbabwean Fiction* (2005) and *Narrating Friendship and the British Novel, 1760–1830* (2017) as well as co-edited collections such as the *Handbook of the British Novel in the Long Eighteenth Century* (2022). She has established *Second World(s). Zweite Blicke auf die 'Zweite' Welt* as a main research area at Halle that also includes teaching, early career projects and events, interdisciplinary cooperation, and third mission activities.

Richard Brown, Reader in Modern Literature in the School of English at the University of Leeds (UK), is the author of many books, book chapters and articles on Modern Literature, especially the work of James Joyce, and on Contemporary English writers including J.G. Ballard. His published work on Ian McEwan includes the chapter 'Cold War Fictions' in *The Cambridge Companion to Ian McEwan* (2019).

Ulrich Busse is Professor of English Linguistics at the Martin-Luther-University Halle-Wittenberg (Germany). In synchronic linguistics his main research interests are (meta-) lexicography, lexicology, and languages in contact, in particular the impact of English on German and other European languages. He has published widely on Anglo-German language contact and its lexicographical description, including a book and a three-volume dictionary on the influence of English on present-day German.

Melinda Dabis is a senior lecturer at Pázmány Péter Catholic University (Hungary), active in the programmes English Literature and Culture, and Translation Studies. Her research interests focus on narratives, their forms and patterns in various fields: memory in contemporary writer Kazuo Ishiguro's fiction, post-colonial studies in the Second World, and the Arctic.

Ágnes Györke is associate professor at Károli Gáspár University's Department of Literary and Cultural Studies in English. Dr. Györke has been a visiting scholar at Indiana University, Bloomington, the University of Bristol, the University of Leeds, and a fellow at Central European University's Institute for Advanced Studies. Her recent publications include *Geographies of Affect in Contemporary Literature and Visually Culture* (Brill, 2021, co-edited with Imola Bülgözdi), 'On the Periphery: Contemporary Exile Fiction and Hungary' (*The Journal of Post-colonial Writing,* 2021), and *Urban Culture and the Modern City: Hungarian Case Studies* (Leuven University Press, 2024, co-edited with Tamás Juhász). She completed her habilitation at Eötvös Loránd University in 2024.

Ágnes Harasztos is assistant professor at Kodolányi János University Budapest. She holds a doctorate from the Eötvös Loránd University Budapest, acquired within the Modern English and American Literature and Culture Doctoral Pro-gramme. The title of her doctoral dissertation was 'The Postmodern Baroque: Bruce Chatwin's Utz and British Fiction on East-Central Europe at the Time of the 1989 Political Changes.' Her research explores the reflection of the 1989 Political Changes of East-Central Europe in postmodern British novels.

Katja Hoyer is a German-British historian, journalist, and the author of the widely acclaimed *Blood and Iron: The Rise and Fall of the German Empire, 1871–1918* (2021) and *Beyond the Wall: East Germany, 1949–1990* (2023). A visiting research fellow at King's College London and a fellow of the Royal Historical Society, she is a columnist for the *Berliner Zeitung* and host of the podcast The New Germany for the Körber Foundation. She was born in East Germany and is now based in the UK.

Robert Kusek is Jagiellonian University Professor in the Department of Com-parative Studies in Literature and Culture, Institute of English Studies at the Jagiellonian University, Kraków. His research interests include life writing gen-res, the contemporary novel in English, new nature writing, queer heritage, as well as a comparative approach to literary studies. He is the author of two mo-nographs, including *Through the Looking Glass: Writers' Memoirs at the Turn of the 21st Century* (Jagiellonian University Press, 2017), and several dozen articles published in books, academic journals, and magazines, as well as co-editor of fourteen volumes of articles, most notably *Travelling Texts: J.M. Coetzee and Other Writers* (Peter Lang, 2014). He was a researcher in a number of Polish and international projects, and is currently a principal investigator in the National

Science Centre-funded project entitled '(Un)accidental Tourists: Polish Literature and Visual Culture in South Africa in the 20th and 21st Centuries.'

Therese-Marie Meyer teaches English literature and culture at the Martin-Luther-University Halle-Wittenberg (Germany). She holds an M.A. in English, German and Comparative Literature Studies and a doctorate in English Literature. The author of *Where Fiction Ends* (2006), an analysis of Australian and Canadian literary scandals, and editor of an 1816 German translation of Matthew Flinders' journal of his circumnavigation of Australia (2014), her research interests include contemporary Anglophone literatures.

Paul D. Morris is Professor of English at the francophone Université de Saint-Boniface in Winnipeg (Canada), where he is also currently the Director of the university's *Maîtrise en Études canadiennes et interculturelles*. His varied research interests are focused in comparative literature and, more specifically, Canadian, American and Slavic literatures. Among his book publications have been *Vladimir Nabokov: Poetry and the Lyric Voice* (2010) and an edited collection *Le Canada: une culture de métissage / Transcultural Canada* (2019). His most recent book publication was the volume co-edited with Albert Braz, *National Literature in Multinational States* (2022).

Fiona Rintoul is a writer, journalist, and translator. While studying German at St Andrews University (UK) in the 1980s, she was an exchange student at Leipzig University. Her experience of living and studying behind the Iron Curtain was the start of a lifelong interest in the former East Germany that culminated in her novel *The Leipzig Affair* (2014), which was shortlisted in the Saltire awards and serialized on BBC R4's Book at Bedtime. A former *Times* columnist, she worked as a financial journalist before becoming an author.

Betiel Wasihun is a Literary Scholar and a Cultural Theorist, currently employed as a Lecturer at Arden University Berlin. She also teaches culture, literature and theory seminars at the Humboldt University and the University of Applied Sciences in Berlin. She was awarded a Marie Curie Senior Research Fellowship at the TU Berlin (2017–2020), and she was a Postdoctoral Research Fellow at the University of Birmingham (UK, 2021–2022), undertaking archival research at the Stasi Archive in Berlin for the project 'Knowing the Secret Police: Secrecy and Knowledge in East German society.' Before reallocating to Berlin, she was a Fellow of Lincoln College (2010–15) and a member of the Faculty of Medieval and Modern Languages at the University of Oxford (2010–17). She has published a monograph on Kafka, R. Walser and Beckett (2010), and co-edited and edited volumes on betrayal (2013) and surveillance narratives (2019). She has also written various articles on modern and contemporary literature and is currently engaged in writing her second monograph on surveillance and its cultural and literary manifestations.

Andrew Wells is Senior Lecturer in Early Modern History at the Historisches Seminar of the Christian-Albrechts-University of Kiel (Germany). His research centres on the cultural history of racial and political thought in the early modern British world. In addition to his published work in this field, he has written on twentieth- and twenty-first-century cultural history, especially on the representation of the *Titanic* disaster in Britain. He is currently preparing an article-length study of German representations of British slavery between the Kaiser-reich and GDR.

Index